Ocular Anatomy
and Physiology

Other books of interest

Orthoptic Assessment and Management
David Stidwill
0−632−02776−2

Eye Examination and Refraction
R.J. Allen, R. Fletcher and D.C. Still
0−632−02866−1

Glaucoma in Optometric Practice
F.G. Brown and R. Fletcher
0−632−02772−X

Diabetes and Primary Eye Care
A. Ariffin, R.D. Hill and O. Leigh
0−632−03142−5

Optometric Management of Visual Handicap
Helen Farrall
0−632−02774−6

Essential Contact Lens Practice
R. Fletcher, L. Lupelli and A. Rossi
0−632−03278−1

Clinical Optics
Second Edition
A.R. Elkington and H.J. Frank
0−632−03139−5

Ocular Anatomy and Physiology

Trygve Saude

Lecturer Kongsberg Inginør Høgskole

Translated by

R. Fletcher
MScTech, FBCO, FBOA, HD, FSMC (Hons), D.Orth, DCLP, FAAO
Emeritus Professor, City University, London
Docent II, Kongsberg Inginør Høgskole, Kongsberg, Norway

OXFORD

BLACKWELL SCIENTIFIC PUBLICATIONS

LONDON EDINBURGH BOSTON

MELBOURNE PARIS BERLIN VIENNA

© 1993 by Blackwell Scientific Publications

Blackwell Scientific Publications
Editorial Offices:
Osney Mead, Oxford OX2 0EL
25 John Street, London WC1N 2BL
23 Ainslie Place, Edinburgh EH3 6AJ
238 Main Street, Cambridge,
  Massachusetts 02142, USA
54 University Street, Carlton,
  Victoria 3053, Australia

Other Editorial Offices:
Librairie Arnette SA,
2, rue Casimir-Delavigne
75006 Paris
France

Blackwell Wissenschafts-Verlag GmbH
Meinekestrasse 4
D-1000 Berlin 15
Germany

Blackwell MZV
Feldgasse 13
A-1238 Wien
Austria

Norwegian edition published by Tell forlag a.s.,
  P.B. 62, 1390 Vollen, Norway under the title
  Øyets anatomi og fysiologi by Trygve Saude
  © 1992 Tell forlag, Norway

English translation published by
  Blackwell Scientific Publications 1993

Set by Setrite Typesetters Ltd
Printed and bound in Great Britain
at The Alden Press, Oxford

DISTRIBUTORS

Marston Book Services Ltd
PO Box 87
Oxford OX2 0DT
(*Orders*: Tel: 0865 791155
        Fax: 0865 791927
        Telex: 837515)

USA
Blackwell Scientific Publications, Inc.
238 Main Street
Cambridge, MA 02142
(*Orders*: Tel: 800 759-6102
            617 876-7000)

Canada
Times Mirror Professional Publishing, Ltd
5240 Finch Avenue East
Scarborough, Ontario M1S 5A2
(*Orders*: Tel: 800 268-4178
            416 298-1588)

Australia
Blackwell Scientific Publications Pty Ltd
54 University Street,
Carlton, Victoria 3053
(*Orders*: Tel: 03 347-5552)

British Library
Cataloguing in Publication Data

A catalogue record for this book is
available from the British Library

ISBN 0-632-03599-4

Library of Congress
Cataloging in Publication Data
Saude, Trygve.
    [Øyets anatomi og fysiologi. English]
    Ocular anatomy and physiology/Trygve
    Saude; translated by R. Fletcher.
    Includes bibliographical references
    and index.
    ISBN 0-632-03599-4
    1. Eye — Physiology. 2. Eye — Anatomy.
    I. Title.
    [DNLM: 1. Eye — anatomy & histology
    2. Eye — physiology. WW 101
    S255o]
    QP475.S2813 1993
    612.8'4 — dc20   92-48827
                                          CIP

Contents

Preface to the English Edition

The modern study of optometry includes knowledge of ocular anatomy and physiology at a reasonably high level and for which there are few suitable textbooks. Recent developments, such as contact lens practice and newer tonometers, have required some emphasis. Certainly, ocular structure and function are now taught in more detail than before in Optometry degree courses in Britain, in the USA and worldwide. This book provides optometry students with a suitable basic study text, presenting the necessary overall view, without needless references; an adequate bibliography gives most relevant sources. 'Visual' physiology, as distinct from 'ocular' physiology, is included only to support certain ocular features; in many courses there is a natural separation of topics and other books cover perceptual matters.

Professionals outside optometry will benefit from this text, such as student ophthalmologists, ophthalmic nurses, orthoptists and dispensing opticians, whilst medical students should appreciate the author's concise approach. Studied alongside more general accounts, including neurophysiology, cytology and histology, this book will make a good introduction to the eye and its function, in a clinical context.

Some Anglicised, latinate and sometimes Greek forms have been used for the translation, as most naturally used by the translator when teaching the subject. Thus certain older ways of naming structures after individuals have been replaced, whilst others persist, generally adapting to recent practice. Some licence has been used to avoid too stilted a translation.

This English edition has been made possible by the efficient co-operation between Hr T.C. Wagle of Tell Forlag (Norway) and Mr Richard Miles of Blackwell Scientific Publications. Very helpful suggestions were made by Hr Saude and Hr Bruenech.

R. Fletcher

Chapter 1
The Orbit

A DESCRIPTION OF THE ORBIT

The bony sockets of the eyes lie each side of the median plane between the face and the brain. Bones and cavities around the orbit include the following: the *anterior cranial fossa* (above), the *nasal cavities* (medially), spongy *ethmoidal air cells*, part of the upper jaw, the *maxillary sinus*, some of the central bones of the skull, the *mid cranial fossa* and part of the *zygoma*, with its depression.

Holding the eyeball, the orbital contents comprise muscles, nerves and vessels which serve the globe with an infilling of fatty tissues. There are also vessels and nerves supplying nearby regions.

Seven of the bones of the skull are involved.

- The maxilla (from the upper jaw).
- The palate bone (from the roof of the mouth).
- The frontal bone (of the forehead).
- The sphenoid (the great wing).
- The zygomatic bone (from the cheek).
- The ethmoid bone (spongy in structure).
- The lacrimal bone (for the tear duct).

The margins of the quadrilateral pyramid which forms the orbit lie forward and somewhat laterally, the point going back to the *optic canal*. This pyramid's sides are rounded, the widest part of the cavity being about 1.5 mm from the front. The medial walls of the two orbits are parallel to each other, whereas the two lateral walls make an angle of 90° (Fig. 1.1).

Adult orbital margins form a rounded rectangle, the average height being some 35 mm, while the width is about 40 mm (Fig. 1.2).

The roof of the orbit

This is approximately triangular, comprising the *frontal bone*'s orbital plate and the *smaller wing of the sphenoid bone*. The anterior part has the most concave form. The lacrimal gland fossa lies just behind the rim of the orbit. A small depression, the trochlear fossa for attachments of the cartilaginous pulley or *trochlea*, is found medially where a suture separates the frontal and lacrimal bones, about 4 mm back from the rim. The trochlea is a small fibrous pulley for the tendon of the superior oblique muscle. Small perforations for vessels and

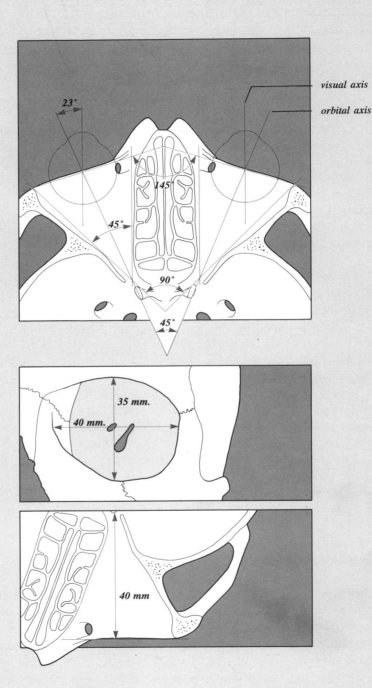

Fig. 1.1 The orbital angles. The medial wall of the orbit lies in the sagittal plane, at approximately 45° to the lateral wall. The average value of the angle between the orbital axis and the visual axis is about 23°.

Fig. 1.2 Average orbital dimensions.

nerves appear in the flat surface of the orbital vault. The structure of the roof is quite thin; in the elderly it may partially disintegrate, permitting communication between the orbit and the *dura mater* above (Fig. 1.3).

The medial wall

Lying in the sagittal plane, the medial wall is nearly rectangular and somewhat concave. It is comprized of the *maxilla*, the *lacrimal bone* and the *ethmoid bone* with a small section of sphenoid. Slightly behind the margin is the lacrimal sac fossa, a depression for the sac which is bounded by the anterior and posterior *lacrimal crests*. Superiorly the fossa has indistinct margins but lower down it carries the *nasolacrimal duct*. Extremely thin, this wall may manifest some large openings in old persons. Here there is risk of infection traversing the paper-thin barrier, producing orbital cellulitis (Fig. 1.4).

The orbital floor

Triangular, like the roof, it slopes downwards and laterally. Various bones combine, the *maxilla*, the *zygomatic* and the *orbital process of the palate bone*. Most of the floor is formed by the maxilla, the zygomatic bone providing the anteriolateral part, while the palatine contributes a small flat area behind the maxilla.

The *infraorbital sulcus* runs forwards across the floor then merges into a canal which ends in the *infraorbital foramen*; this emerges below the orbit on the cheek, carrying the infraorbital nerve and blood vessels. From the centre and forward aspect of the sulcus, alveolar canals descend carrying nerves and blood vessels to the upper jaw. The origin of the *inferior oblique muscle* is found just lateral to the naso lacrimal duct, at an uneven region of the floor. The *maxillary sinus*, a cavity in the upper mandible, lies beneath the base of the orbit, where the bony barrier is fragile. Hence a 'blow out' fracture can raise the orbital floor; again, it is possible for infection to move into the orbit (Fig. 1.5).

The lateral wall of the orbit

This is triangular, making an angle of about 45° with the sagittal plane. It is made up from the *zygomatic bone* and (posteriorly) by the *great wing of the sphenoid*. It is the most substantial of the orbital walls.

A shallow furrow extends laterally and forwards from the edge of the inferior orbital fissure, ending in the *zygomatic foramen*. Blood vessels and nerves of the same name go along this path. The zygomatic foramen partly extends into a canal, opening onto the cheek and elsewhere by the *temporal*

Fig. 1.3 Right orbit, front view.

optic canal

superior orbital fissure

sphenoid bone (great wing)

orbital tubercle

zygomatic foramen

zygomatic bone

inferior orbital fissure

infraorbital sulcus

supraorbital foramen (or notch)

posterior ethmoidal foramen

anterior ethmoidal foramen

frontal bone

nasal bone

lacrimal bone

lacrimal fossa (of sac)

ethmoid bone

maxilla

infraorbital foramen

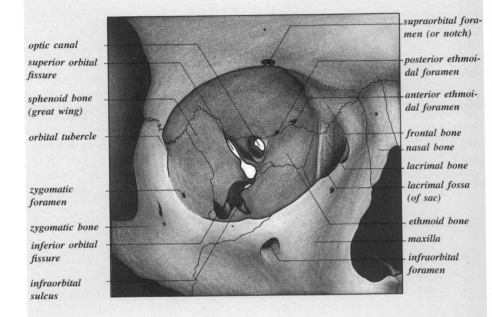

Fig. 1.4 The orbital medial wall.

frontal sinus

frontal bone

lacrimal bone

anterior lacrimal crest

posterior lacrimal crest

nasal bone

lacrimal fossa (of sac)

maxilla

infraorbital foramen

inferior nasal concha

anterior ethmoidal foramen

posterior ethmoidal foramen

optic canal

ethmoidal bone

palatine bone

foramen ovale

palatine bone

pterygoid process

hamulus (lacrimal bone)

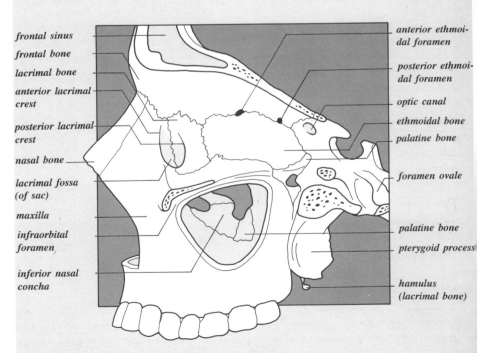

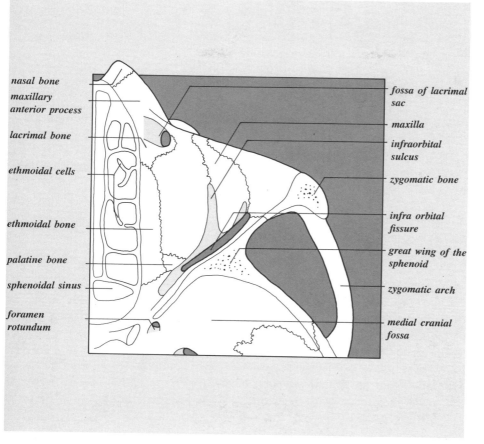

nasal bone	fossa of lacrimal sac
maxillary anterior process	
	maxilla
lacrimal bone	infraorbital sulcus
ethmoidal cells	zygomatic bone
	infra orbital fissure
ethmoidal bone	
palatine bone	great wing of the sphenoid
sphenoidal sinus	zygomatic arch
foramen rotundum	medial cranial fossa

Fig. 1.5 The orbital floor.

fossa. Division of the nerves can take place to reach two or more apertures in the bone.

The *orbital tubercle* is a small elevation on the orbital surface of the zygomatic bone. It is situated slightly inwards from the orbital rim, just under the suture which is the junction between the frontal and zygomatic bones. The following structures are attached to the tubercle:

- The check ligament from the lateral rectus muscle.
- The lateral palpebral ligament.
- The lateral horn of the aponeurosis of the levator muscle of the upper lid.

Apertures of the orbit

The *superior* (or *supra*) *orbital fissure*, the uppermost slit at the back of the orbit, is a large opening into the cranium. A series of nerves and vessels move into and out of the orbit through this opening.

- III cranial nerve, the oculomotor.
- IV cranial nerve, the trochlear.
- 1st division, V cranial nerve, the ophthalmic division of the trigeminal.
- Sympathetic nerves from the carotid plexus.
- Superior ophthalmic vein.
- Several minor nerves and blood vessels.

Many of these nerves divide up into orbital branches before their entry into the orbit (see Plate 1).

The inferior orbital fissure, lowest of the slits in the orbit, acts as a large gap between the orbit and the pterygopalatine fossa as well as the lower temporal fossa. Into the orbit via this fissure go these nerves and vessels:

- The infraorbital nerve.
- The zygomatic nerve.
- The infraorbital artery.
- Venous anastomoses between the orbit and the pterygoid plexus.

The anterior and posterior ethmoid foramina provide communication between the orbit and the ethmoidal sinuses, a two-way passage for vessels and nerves of the tissues.

The optic canal connects the interior of the cranium at the apex of the orbit. Its passage is laterally forwards, at an angle of some 36° to the sagittal plane. Separated from the sphenoidal sinus beneath by a sparse bony layer, the canal carries the optic nerve with its meningeal covering, plus the ophthalmic artery.

The orbital margins

This boundary separates the orbit from the surface of the face by the orbital aperture which, in adults, is a gently curved rectangle. Average orbital dimensions are approximately 35 mm high and 40 mm wide. An 'orbital index' is described by the formula:

$$\frac{\text{Orbital height} \times 100}{\text{Orbital width}}$$

Oriental races possess the largest orbital index, usually over 89, while some other racial values can be as low as 84. Caucasian values are inter-mediate. Children tend to have greater indices than adults and a gender difference exists, since the female index exceeds the male one.

The following bones make up the orbital margin:

- The frontal bone, above.
- The zygomatic bone, laterally.
- The maxilla, below and medially.

The periorbita

There is a covering of periosteum in the orbit which is continuous with that of the cranium. Posteriorly, at the *optic canal*, exists a direct association of fibres with the outer layer of the dura mater. Attachment to the bone is generally loose but more secure at these positions:

- At the orbital margin.
- Along sutures between bones.
- Where fissures and foramina occur.
- At the lacrimal gland fossa.

There is a complete lining of periosteum for the superior orbital fissure.

Müller's (orbital) muscle, a thin layer of smooth muscle fibres, lies in apposition to the periosteum in the vicinity of the inferior orbital fissure; the fibres impart a pink colour here. There is sympathetic innervation to this muscle but its function is unknown. Branches of the V cranial nerve in the region supply the orbital periosteum.

Age—related changes

Modifications of the orbit which accompany growth depend on development of the overlying skull and the facial bones below. The influences of neighbouring sinuses upon the orbit are also significant.

At birth the orbit is well defined and formed, affording good protection to the eye. By the age of seven there is greater rounding of the shape. The axis of a neonatal orbit points more laterally than in adults. A child's orbital axis is horizontal, depressing about 15° to 20° by adulthood. Orbital fissures are relatively large in children.

Note particularly the small separation between a child's orbits. It is for this reason that children may appear to have strabismus. As the frontal bone and the spongiform structures develop and produce extra interorbital separation, the eye region assumes a more normal appearance.

THE NASAL SINUSES

These 'accessory sinuses' are spaces within the maxilla and in the frontal, sphenoid and ethmoid bones. Their forms vary considerably in individuals and change with age. Mucous membranes form interior linings, the cavities being filled with air. Communications exist between some sinuses by means of rather narrow channels. Functionally, the sinuses assist voice resonance; they reduce the mass of the cranium by about 20% in humans (Fig. 1.6).

The *maxillary sinus* or the antrum of Highmore is the largest within the

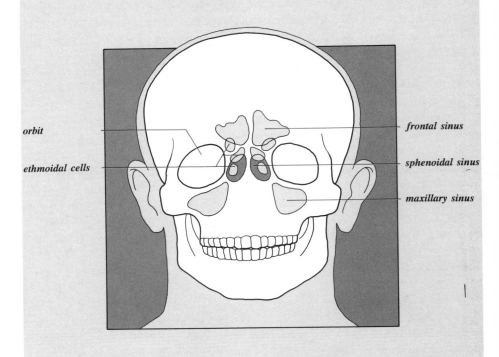

Fig. 1.6 Positions of the nasal sinuses in relation to the orbit.

orbit

ethmoidal cells

frontal sinus

sphenoidal sinus

maxillary sinus

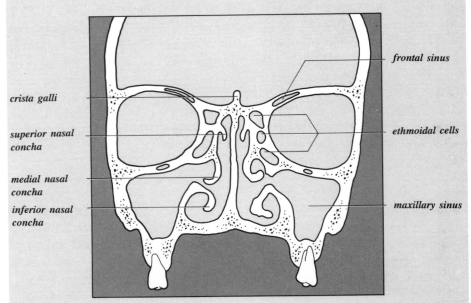

Fig. 1.7 Frontal section of nasal cavities showing ethmoidal cells and maxillary sinus.

crista galli

superior nasal concha

medial nasal concha

inferior nasal concha

frontal sinus

ethmoidal cells

maxillary sinus

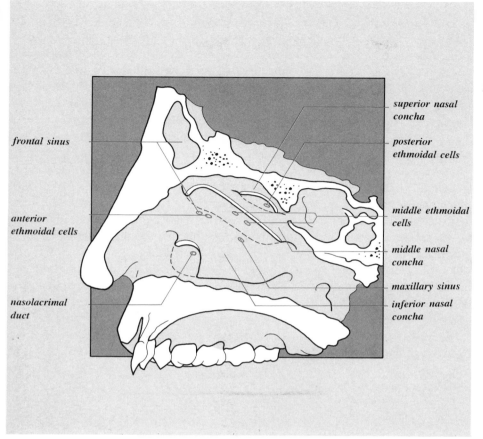

frontal sinus

anterior
ethmoidal cells

nasolacrimal
duct

superior nasal
concha

posterior
ethmoidal cells

middle ethmoidal
cells

middle nasal
concha

maxillary sinus

inferior nasal
concha

Fig. 1.8 Apertures communicating to nasal cavities (openings shown in red)

maxilla. Pyramidal in form, it comprises some of the lateral wall of the nose and points towards the zygoma. Its roof is the orbital surface formed by the maxilla, where the infraorbital nerves and vessels lie, while the floor comes close to the roots of the maxillary teeth. The front aspect of the sinus is in the facial plane. Also here is the infraorbital canal which transmits blood vessels and some of the nerves of the region. Posterior aspects of the sinus turn along the infratemporal fossa; the wall follows the back alveolar canal.

The medial wall is made up of several bones. The sinus communicates with the nasal cavity by a large passage, made smaller in the lower part where the *inferior nasal concha* lies. Covering the opening at the inferior and posterior aspects, is the palatine bone, with the ethmoidal bone making the gap smaller above. A relatively narrow opening, lined with mucous membrane, emerges into the nasal cavity below the medial turbinal structure of the nose into the *medial nasal meatus*. Since the opening from the sinus is situated high in its medial wall, inflammation of the nasal mucous membranes easily blocks it (Fig. 1.7).

The *frontal sinuses*, forming cavities within the forehead, are contained in the frontal bone and are separated from each other by a thin, bony septum. Each one has an approximately triangular form, terminating medially in the eyebrow region and stretching along the medial aspect of the orbital roof below and towards the back. There is a connection between the frontal sinus and the nasal structures via the *ethmoidal infundibulum*, opening into the medial meatus.

The *sphenoidal sinus* lies inside the body of the sphenoid bone and is variable in form and position. A thin bony plate divides it into two main chambers, the foremost tending to be within the nasal region while the posterior section extends some way back towards the sella turcica. The *cavernous sinus* shares a lateral wall with the sphenoidal sinus while above the latter, tenuously separated by thin layers of bone, are the hypophysis and the optic nerve, with the chiasma nearby. Communicating apertures run to emerge over the superior nasal concha.

The *ethmoidal cells* which form a spongy network, occupy a series of small cavities in the ethmoidal bone, also partly in the frontal bone. They lie between the orbits, medially and laterally in the nasal cavity, varying in number between three and eight, usually as anterior, middle and posterior groups of air cells. Paper-thin walls separate them from nearby structures which makes it easy for infection to spread around the region and into the orbit.

As with the openings from the frontal bone, the foremost group of these sinuses communicates with the nose through the medial meatus. Those most to the rear (reaching as far as the optic canal) open via the superior nasal meatus into the nose (see Fig. 1.8).

Chapter 2
The Outer Coats of the Eye

AN OVERALL VIEW OF THE EYEBALL

The *globe of the eye* is not completely spherical since the two main outer parts have different curvatures. The *cornea* protrudes at the front, occupying about $\frac{1}{6}$ of the whole surface; its radius of curvature is about 8 mm. The back part, the opaque *sclera* or sclerotic, occupies the remainder of the exterior and has a radius of about 12 mm.

The corneal apex forms the anterior pole. Diametrically opposite to this is the posterior pole, lying in a temporal position to the *optic nerve*, while the *optic axis* joins the two poles. Midway between the poles the equator of the eye forms a circle in the frontal plane. The *fovea centralis* lies slightly temporally to and rather below the posterior pole, so that the *visual axis* and the optic axis are not coincident.

The anterior−posterior diameter is approximately 24 mm, while the transverse dimension is about 23.5 mm. A flattening reduces the vertical diameter to some 23 mm.

The eye occupies a position within the orbit which is slightly forwards, towards the roof and to the temporal side. So a line joining the upper and lower orbital rims strikes the corneal apex, but a horizontal line from the lateral to the medial margins cuts the eye about a third of the way from the anterior pole. Thus, there is least protection from a blow coming from the temporal side (Fig. 2.1).

Three main regions of tissues give the eye its structure (see Plate 2):

- The fibrous coat: sclera, cornea and corneal limbus.
- The uvea or vascular coat: choroid, ciliary body and iris.
- The retina or neural coat.

Within lie the internal media: crystalline lens, vitreous and aqueous humour.

THE SCLERA

The fibrous sclera occupies the posterior $\frac{5}{6}$ of the outer coat of the eye. It is usually known as the 'white of the eye' seen from the front. In children, or in pathological states, the sclera is thin and looks bluish, since the underlying choroid is seen to some extent. Elderly people may have yellowing of the sclera from fatty deposits. The sclera is thickest (about 1 mm) behind, becoming thinner to the front and is particularly thin (0.3 mm) where the extraocular

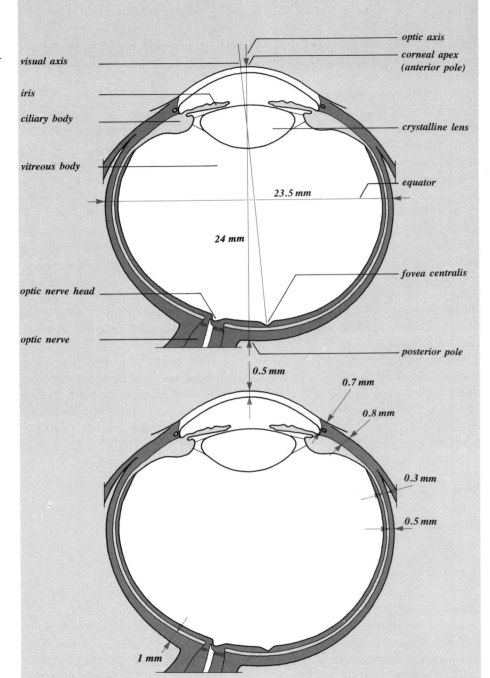

Fig. 2.1 Transverse section of the right eye.

Fig. 2.2 Thicknesses of the fibrous coat.

visual axis

iris

ciliary body

vitreous body

optic nerve head

optic nerve

optic axis

corneal apex (anterior pole)

crystalline lens

equator

23.5 mm

24 mm

fovea centralis

posterior pole

0.5 mm

0.7 mm

0.8 mm

0.3 mm

0.5 mm

1 mm

muscle tendons are inserted into the sclera. Here the tissues provide a strong anchorage. In old people, the insertions of the tendons may appear bluer because there is a localised weakening of the scleral network.

At the front there is a thickening where the sclera meets the cornea and the conjunctiva covers the eyeball. Externally, the sclera has an even and smooth surface, except where the extraocular muscles are inserted. Tenon's capsule (the bulbar fascia) envelops the sclera behind the limbus, attached by fine strands and fusing with the optic nerve sheath. The connective tissue network of the sclera forms a tough protection for the interior eye and, with the intraocular pressure, enables the eye to maintain a stable form. In addition, the tissues enable the extraocular muscles' tendons to be firmly fixed (Fig. 2.2).

The optic nerve, transmitting visual messages, lies about 3 mm to the medial side of the posterior pole. The 'entrance' (or exit) through the sclera is conical, its inner diameter being about 1.5 to 2 mm, compared to the external dimension 3.0 to 3.5 mm. A thin supporting network traverses the opening, the lamina cribrosa and on account of the relative weakness of the region at the 'papilla' it is possible for unduly high intraocular pressure to produce pathological excavation of the optic disc.

There are three groups of apertures in the sclera:
At the back, around the optic nerve, the posterior ciliary arteries (two long and 10–12 short) penetrate, together with the posterior ciliary nerves, of which there are two long and 6–10 short types.

Four *medial perforations* are found 3 to 4 mm behind the equator, one in each quadrant of the globe, transmitting the four *vorticose veins*. Anteriorly, between the limbus and the extraocular muscles' tendinous insertions, lie various small perforations carrying the anterior ciliary arteries and veins as well as '*aqueous veins*' from Schlemm's canal. Certain nerves also pass in or out here.

The scleral tissues

Histologically there are three types of tissue:

- Outermost, the *episcleral* layer.
- Centrally, the *stroma* or substantia propria.
- Innermost, the lamina fusca.

The bulk of the thickness of the sclera is stroma, made of collagenous fibres in bunches, distributed in patterns which vary in different regions. A distinct fan-like spread of fibres is typical in the posterior half of the globe, while in front of the equator most fibres have an equatorial course, enabling this region to give a firm hold for the external muscles. Such collagenous fibres are arranged in wavy directions; despite the absence of elastic tissue, this imparts definite elasticity to the sclera, most essential for the back part of the eye. High and sustained intraocular pressure diminishes this elasticity of the globe. At the region of the *corneal limbus*, stromal fibres merge directly with the cornea.

Innermost, the scleral layer called the *lamina fusca* comes directly into contact with the uvea, being just as much a part of the latter. Here one finds star-shaped pigment cells, similar to those of the uvea generally. They effectively prevent the unwelcome penetration of light into the eye. Blood vessels and nerves travel forwards within this layer. Superficially the sclera carries thin elastic *episcleral* connective tissue and the anterior, thicker, parts are richly supplied with blood vessels.

The scleral blood supply

This is derived from tiny branches of the posterior short and long ciliary arteries. Within the sclera itself, there are very small blood vessels and where the extraocular muscles attach there is a plentiful blood supply in the episcleral layer. The distribution in a linear network surrounds the limbus, where at a deeper layer, there are the limbal arcades. Supply here is from both long posterior and anterior ciliary arteries. When 'ciliary injection' (enlarged vessels) takes place, there is a deep, perilimbal, pinkish flush.

The nerve supply of the sclera

This is from the posterior ciliary nerves, the shorter ones supplying the back of the globe, while the two long nerves supply the front.

THE CORNEA

As a transparent $\frac{1}{6}$ of the eyeball, this admits light, although rather less than 1% of incident light is reflected. Truly an 'optical' medium, the cornea contributes about $\frac{2}{3}$ of the ocular power, rather more than 40 Dioptres. The refractive index is 1.376. In the older eye there are slight changes in form and power.

The cornea bulges out from the sclera, being apparently inserted into the latter like a watchglass. It is thinnest at the apex, at about 0.52 mm (0.46 to 0.67 mm) and thickest near the limbus, about 0.67 mm (0.65 to 1.1 mm). Hence the front curvature is different from that of the back surface. The average radius of the front surface is 7.8 mm (6.8 to 8.5 mm) with back radii ranging from 6 to 7 mm, with an average of 6.5 mm. At the external boundary, the cornea meets the sclera at a shallow groove, known as the *corneal sulcus* and approaching this the corneal periphery flattens. Opaque scleral tissue overlies the limbus, so the external corneal diameter is greater than the diameter of the visible iris. The latter is horizontally 12 mm (11 to 12.5 mm) but vertically 11 mm (10.5 to 11.5 mm). This tends to follow from the definitely elliptical outline of the cornea. It should be noted that the sclera extends forwards over the clear tissue round the limbus. The external diameter at the sulcus is between 13 and 15 mm.

It is not easy to determine and to describe the corneal contours. From data gathered in several ways, no mathematical model can be applied simply, but the 'corneal cap', the central zone, is some 4 to 5 mm in diameter, surrounded by a periphery about 3 to 4 mm wide (Fig. 2.3).

The *central zone* is usually described as having a spherical or toroidal form, often with an irregular margin, hence the terms 'circle' or 'ellipse' can hardly be applied to cross-sections. The apex is often displaced from the geometrical centre, but opinions as to the direction vary. While the radius is usually between 7.2 and 8.7 mm, there are individual variations, the vertical meridian tending to be steeper than the horizontal one. This *physiological astigmatism* is generally compensated for by an inverse toricity on the back of the cornea as well as by an 'against the rule' lenticular astigmatism.

The *peripheral zone* emerges rather imperceptibly as a substantial flattening of the curvature and together the two main zones make up the corneal topography, blending into the limbus. There are no significant gender differences.

Corneal tissues

Five well-differentiated regions are seen (see Fig. 2.4):

- The epithelium.
- Bowman's layer.
- The stroma or substantia propria.
- Descemet's membrane.
- The endothelium.

The *epithelium* is of the stratified pavement variety, five to six cells thick and fixed firmly to a basal membrane. The cells are continuous with the conjunctival epithelium, being about 70 μm thick. The basal membrane itself tends to be easily detached from Bowman's layer which lies beneath.

The *basal cells* form the deepest epithelial layer, attached well to the underlying basal membrane. They have cubical or cylindrical forms with varying heights, about 15 μm and rounded 'heads', being some 10 μm in diameter. Their metabolic rate is high, since it is chiefly this rank of cells which builds up and renews the epithelial layers. Fresh cells are produced by mitosis, migrating to more external layers and gradually changing form.

Above the basal cells the '*wing cells*' are more flattened, but polyhedral, about three layers thick. The nuclei become progressively oval but are retained and become parallel to the external surface. Evidently, there is some retention of metabolism at a reduced rate. The superficial layer of *squamous cells* contains very flat polygonal cells, providing the cornea with a smooth surface.

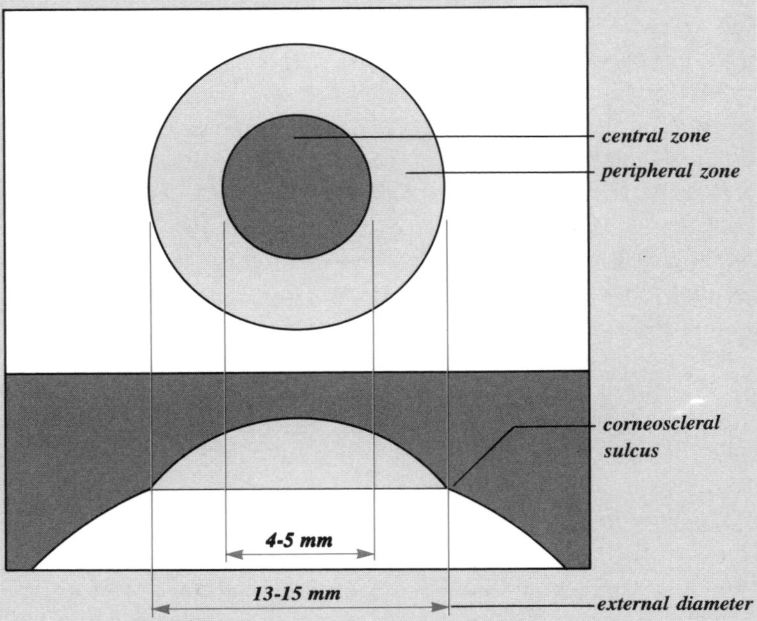

Fig. 2.3 Corneal zones. Front view and transverse section.

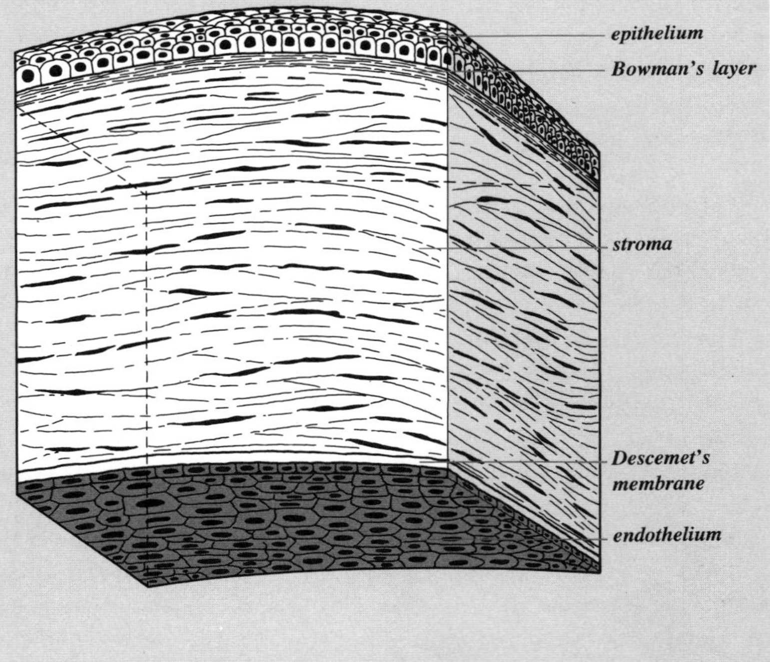

central zone

peripheral zone

corneoscleral sulcus

4-5 mm

13-15 mm

external diameter

Fig. 2.4 The corneal tissues.

epithelium

Bowman's layer

stroma

Descemet's membrane

endothelium

Nevertheless, these cells have microvilli and while opinions differ as to their functions, these tiny projections probably contribute to the stability of the tears film. It is likely that, with actin filaments, they assist movement and adhesion of the external epithelium layers.

The epithelium is renewed by reduplication of the basal cell layer, the 'turnover' time being about seven to eight days for the whole process of renewal, depending on metabolism. Minor corneal abrasions heal within a few hours. Repair takes place by surrounding cells migrating laterally, in a flattened form, sliding to cover over the denuded area. Severe injuries take longer to heal, depending on a build up of renewed cells from the lowest layer.

According to many experts, there is a very low metabolic activity in the central corneal zone, where epithelial replacement after bad damage depends upon radial cell migration from the limbal region and Vogt's palisades, the site of greatest mitotic activity.

In the event of complete removal of the corneal epithelium, some days elapse before recovery after which it is a matter of weeks before the full thickness is restored. Local anaesthetics can retard healing, since they slow down metabolic activity. The dye fluorescein stains the underlying Bowman's layer green after injury, showing where the epithelium has been lost (Figs 2.5 and 2.6).

Bowman's layer or the anterior limiting lamina, is about 12 μm in thickness, having a definite association with the basal lamina of the epithelium. The boundary merges gradually with the stroma. Bowman's layer is made of irregularly arrayed collagen fibrils, much more delicate than those in the stroma and is resistant to infection; damage can lead to residual opaque scars. The layer is perforated by unmyelinated nerve fibres arising from the stroma to supply the epithelium.

The *stroma* or substantia propria occupies almost 90% of the total corneal thickness, being about 0.5 mm across. As an avascular structure, it is built up from many regularly orientated lamellae, some 200 to 250 in all. These lamellae consist of collagen fibres which lie parallel to each other. They are often arranged in a definite pattern, sometimes with fibres in alternate layers being at right angles to one another. An extracellular mucopolysaccharide matrix between the lamellae binds them together. Frequently, neighbouring cells are joined by long projections. There have been observations of phagocytosis associated with these cells.

Mucopolysaccharides, which are highly hydrophilic, are found in the matrix of the corneal stroma to a greater extent than elsewhere in the eye. It is difficult for the stroma to regenerate and, following injury, disturbance of the arrangement of tissues is likely to result in opacities (Fig. 2.7).

Descemet's membrane, the posterior basal lamina, is a thin, elastic membrane which can be easily separated from the stroma. Its thickness is about 8–10 μm, increasing with age. It can reform, has good resistance against infective agents and acts as a basal membrane for the corneal endothelium, from which it is secreted.

Fig. 2.5 Sketch of the corneal epithelium.

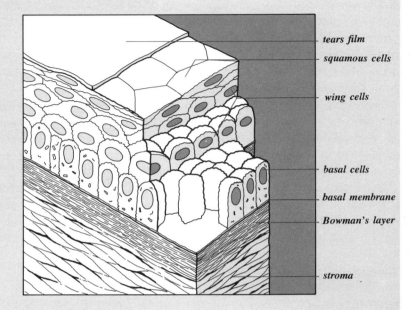

tears film
squamous cells
wing cells
basal cells
basal membrane
Bowman's layer
stroma

Fig. 2.6 The corneal epithelium. (*Microphoto: T. Saude.*)

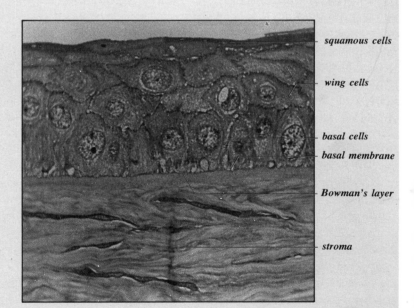

squamous cells
wing cells
basal cells
basal membrane
Bowman's layer
stroma

Descemet's membrane projects in fringes into the meshwork of the angle of the anterior chamber, the *'pectinate ligament'*, at the boundary of the anterior chamber.

The *endothelium* comprises a single layer of about 400 000 cells similar to epithelium, the number reducing with age. Intraocular surgery, or the use of contact lenses, sometimes causes a similar reduction (polymegathism). The ageing cells become larger, compensating for the scarcity. Indications of high metabolic activity come from the many intracellular organelles. Hexagonal in outline, the cells possess oval nuclei. Restricted or absent regenerative properties of the layer make it possible for injury to lead to blindness.

The cornea is avascular, deriving some nourishment (via the surrounding conjunctival vessels) from the ciliary arteries, which produce arcades at two levels at the limbus. The deeper scleral network of capillaries is from the anterior ciliary arteries, the more superficial vessels coming from the conjunctival arteries. Trauma or disruption of metabolism tends to cause corneal vascularization, with radial intrusion of new vessels into the corneal tissues. Following healing, these new vessels empty, becoming 'ghost' vessels which persist for a long time and may refill at the slightest provocation.

The nerve supply and sensitivity of the cornea

Sensory innervation comes from the *trigeminal nerve's* first division, the *ophthalmic nerve*, via the long ciliary nerves. The latter move forwards in the uvea and penetrate the sclera above the ciliary body to supply a limbal plexus. From here 70 to 80 nerves radiate into the cornea, losing their myelin sheaths at the limbus. On rare occasions, such bare fibres can be seen as grey threads within the cornea (Fig. 2.8).

The corneal nerves form plexuses at several levels in the anterior stroma, overlapping each other with probably about 70 to 80 fibres reaching $\frac{2}{3}$ of the cornea. Hence, even after surgery, such as for cataract, some corneal sensitivity persists.

Nerve fibres from stromal plexuses traverse Bowman's layer to form a subepithelial plexus from which branches move into the epithelium, reaching the squamous layer as bare nerve endings. The nerve supply is greatest centrally, diminishing towards the limbus.

The cornea is very sensitive, most near the apex and least in the limbal region. Ageing brings diminished sensitivity, a 70 year old having a third of that of a youth, its reduction being greatest during the sixth decade. Sensitivity does not differ between the sexes and the two eyes are normally similar. Blue eyes tend to be more sensitive than brown; and a temporal variation has been reported, lower sensitivity being found in the morning with an increase through the day. Hormonal variations, such as the menstrual cycle, can also change corneal sensitivity.

Following operations for cataract, normal sensitivity can be reduced to half

Fig. 2.7 Sketch of the
principal arrangements
of the collagenous
fibres in the corneal
stroma. The directions
of fibres in alternate
layers lie approximately
at right angles. Note
the end or side views of
the fibres and the
variation in thickness of
layers.

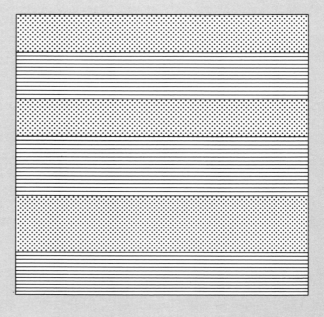

Fig. 2.8 Sketch to
show the entry of
corneal nerves. The
points represent nerve
endings, which are
densest centrally. The
insert shows a
transverse corneal
section near the limbus,
with different levels of
entry and the formation
of plexi in the anterior
corneal tissues.

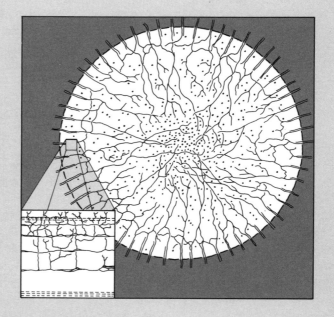

and may not be completely restored, although different tests tend to yield different results.

Hard contact lenses can diminish corneal sensitivity, starting from the initial hours' use; in some wearers this reduction may be down to $\frac{1}{3}$ of the normal, although there are individual variations in extent. The interference with sensitivity from soft contact lenses tends to be much less, or nil.

Corneal sensitivity is measured with an aesthesiometer, which uses a thin nylon filament in a holder to allow for changes in the filament length. Measurement takes place as the filament is pushed against the cornea and bent. Pressure is increased until the reaction of the patient is determined with a minimal filament length. Tables are used to relate the critical length to mg/mm pressure on the cornea, to measure the sensitivity.

It must be recognised that corneal sensitivity and its estimation with an aesthesiometer, will vary considerably with adaptation to contact lenses. Motivation is a potent factor influencing performance with contact lenses and sensitivity is another variable aspect. It is well to remember that use of an aesthesiometer presents a slight hazard of infection and trauma to the corneal tissues. Thus it is not usual to measure corneal sensitivity for routine contact lens fittings.

Corneal metabolism

Although every part of the cornea engages in some metabolic activity, there are significant variations. The epithelium and endothelium have relatively higher metabolic rates than the stroma. Such activity is essential to maintain temperature and renewal of cells and their contents, also to maintain transport processes in the cornea which need sustained metabolism.

Thus the corneal tissues require nourishment, particularly carbohydrates, aminoacids and oxygen as well as necessary minerals and vitamins.

Most body tissues derive their nutrients from a local blood supply. But the cornea is avascular, with the nearest vessels at the limbus; so it must draw nourishment from one of these encircling streams:

- The limbal arcades.
- The aqueous humour in the anterior chamber.
- The tears liquid.

The cornea derives its oxygen supply and food from the limbal capillaries, although transport of such supplies within the cornea depends on diffusion, almost exclusively from the restricted perilimbal regions. We are now considering really slow distribution of metabolites over comparatively long routes. Note that most of the cornea must be nourished via alternative routes.

Glucose is the most important energy-producing carbohydrate supplied to the cornea. It is initially broken down by what is termed *glycolysis* (Embden–Meyerhof route) and then reduced to carbon dioxide and water through the

Krebs cycle. Other catabolic processes are seldom involved in the cornea's energy production. Oxygen is required for some corneal metabolism but anaerobic glycolysis, leading to accumulation of lactate, is also involved. Energy produced is stored as ATP (adenosine triphosphate) of which 30 to 38 molecules can emerge from a single molecule of glucose.

Glycolysis is the usual term for a series of metabolic reactions which ensure that glucose is broken down to smaller molecules (pyruvate). Such metabolism can be both anaerobic and aerobic. The varied activities are identified with definite parts of cells, while glycolysis is not necessarily linked with particular organelles that are concerned with cellular cytoplasm.

Under aerobic conditions, the final result of glycolysis is pyruvate. By oxidation in mitochondria, through the Krebs cycle, carbon dioxide and water are produced. Under anaerobic conditions, lactate is produced instead of pyruvate; it then accumulates in the tissues.

Glycolysis produces a net yield of two molecules of ATP for each molecule of glucose which is metabolised. Further breakdown via the citric acid cycle, which depends on oxygen being present, results in 36 ATP molecules. In such a situation, anaerobic breakdown of nutrients is a highly inefficient means of providing the corneal cells with energy and results in an unfortunate build-up of lactate in the tissues.

Another significant situation affecting anaerobic energy production occurs when the cells take extra essential supplies to cope with their energy demand until their glycogen store is diminished.

Glucose occurs in very small concentrations in the tears liquid, at about 2.6 mg/100 ml. However, in the aqueous humour the concentration is more than tenfold. It is evident that corneal glucose supplies largely come from the aqueous.

Aminoacids are essential for corneal production of enzymes and for renewing tissues. It is believed that the tears liquid has a relatively high content of aminoacids, yet the cornea does not satisfy its needs from these, but gains its nourishment from the aqueous. We can make this assumption because the corneal epithelium is known to have very little permeability to both aminoacids and glucose.

Oxygen is necessary to support the high metabolic rate of the epithelium and endothelium, while the stroma has a relatively low metabolism. The film of tears covering the cornea has an oxygen 'tension' corresponding to the partial pressure of the atmosphere, i.e. 155 mm Hg, with an open palpebral aperture. The oxygen tension in the aqueous is about 55 mm Hg. In an 'open' and naked eye it follows that corneal tissues are supplied with oxygen from the tears; to a limited extent the endothelium and the posterior stroma have provision from the aqueous.

With closed lids the tears derive oxygen from the vessels of the tarsal conjunctiva; then the oxygen pressure in the tears is lower, at a similar level to that of the aqueous. In such a state, more of the corneal tissue depends on the aqueous for its supplies.

Inadequate supplies of oxygen within the cornea produce oedema (swelling from excess water), largely due to lower endothelial activity. Such reduced activity is not chiefly caused by the absence of oxygen supply for the endothelium; rather it is from a lowering of pH which handicaps metabolism. This fall in pH is the result of a build-up of lactate and carbonic acid within the cornea. Under these circumstances, it is also possible to see the limbal arcades dilated and greatly engorged and new blood vessels could intrude within the corneal tissues (neovascularization).

Corneal transparency

The cornea is very transparent and reflects less than 1% of incident light. It is made of various structures, involving different layers, so it is not easy to explain its transparency.

Up to now no cast-iron theory has emerged to explain the excellent light penetration through the epithelium and endothelium. But what happens in the stroma (representing about 90% of the corneal thickness) is of most interest. The account of the stromal anatomy mentioned how collagen fibres make up a series of regularly organised layers, orderly in thickness and form. A matrix substance binds the fibres and gives them a regular separation (see Fig. 2.9).

In 1957, Maurice put forward a theory to explain the transparency of the corneal stroma. This involved a lattice and suggested that the following conditions are needed for good stromal transparency:

- Constant thickness of the fibrils, arranged in parallel patterns.
- Constant separation between the fibrils.
- This separation must be less than the wavelength of light.

Goldmann subsequently modified this theory saying that a difference in refractive index will not be significant if this distance is less than 200 nm or half a wavelength.

Corneal transparency depends on the regular structure of the stroma. Healthy corneas naturally have a constant balance between solids and water, in the proportion 22% solids to 78% water. This is called normal *deturgescence*.

In addition, the cornea has a relatively high content of mucopolysaccharides in its matrix, 4.5% as compared to the sclera's mere 1.5%. This substance is highly hydrophilic, with a tendency to absorb liquid into the cornea, disturbing deturgescence. The barriers formed by the epithelial and endothelial layers resist this undesirable intrusion. Normally some force exists across the barrier, forming an essential 'pump' mechanism which always maintains proper deturgescence; currently this activity is considered to be mainly endothelial.

Any disturbance of endothelial metabolism, perhaps by deprivation of nutrients or oxygen, gives oedema and corneal swelling, reducing transparency, as the barrier fails; so does epithelial or endothelial damage. Intrusion of water

Fig. 2.9 Top: Normal
arrangement of corneal
stroma fibres with
constant separations.
Bottom: Cornea during
a spell of oedema with
transparency disturbed
by the derangement of
fibres caused by
waterlogging.

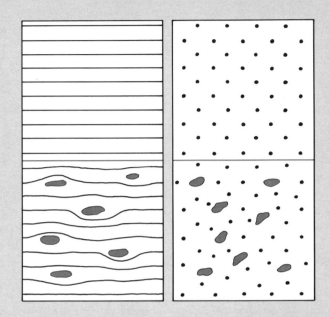

Fig. 2.10 Schlemm's
canal.

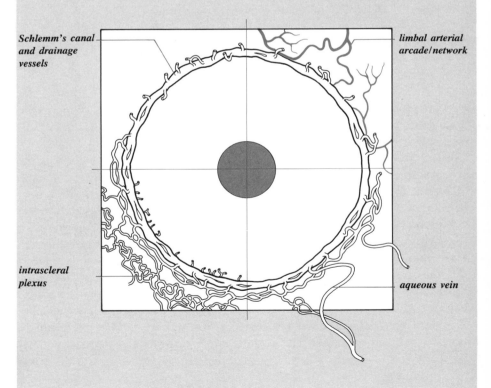

Schlemm's canal
and drainage
vessels

limbal arterial
arcade/network

intrascleral
plexus

aqueous vein

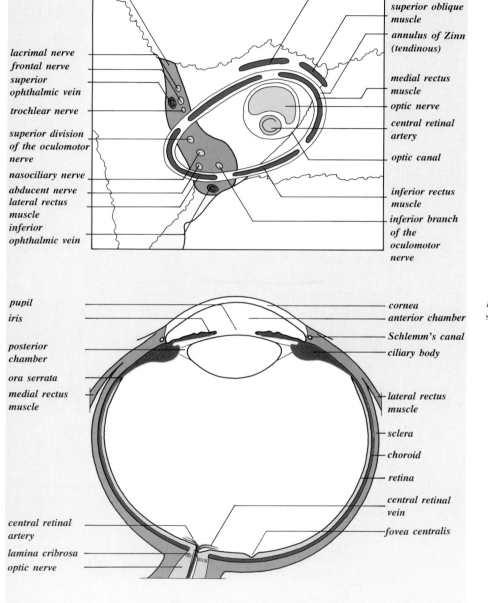

superior orbital
fissure

lacrimal nerve
frontal nerve
superior
ophthalmic vein

trochlear nerve

superior division
of the oculomotor
nerve

nasociliary nerve
abducent nerve
lateral rectus
muscle
inferior
ophthalmic vein

levator muscle

superior oblique
muscle

annulus of Zinn
(tendinous)

medial rectus
muscle

optic nerve

central retinal
artery

optic canal

inferior rectus
muscle

inferior branch
of the
oculomotor
nerve

Plate 1 The apex of
the orbit with nerves,
blood vessels and the
origins of some
extraocular muscles.

pupil
iris

posterior
chamber

ora serrata
medial rectus
muscle

central retinal
artery

lamina cribrosa
optic nerve

cornea
anterior chamber

Schlemm's canal
ciliary body

lateral rectus
muscle

sclera

choroid

retina

central retinal
vein

fovea centralis

Plate 2 Horizontal
section of the right eye.

Plate 3 The ciliary body and corneal limbus.

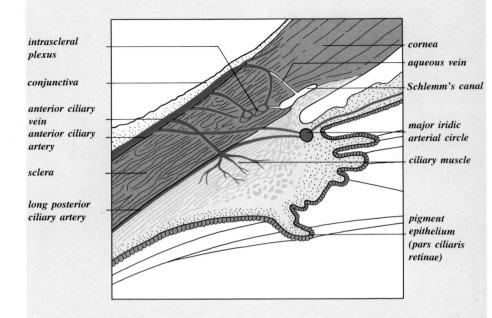

intrascleral plexus

conjunctiva

anterior ciliary vein

anterior ciliary artery

sclera

long posterior ciliary artery

cornea

aqueous vein

Schlemm's canal

major iridic arterial circle

ciliary muscle

pigment epithelium (pars ciliaris retinae)

Plate 4 The ciliary body. (*Photo: M. Helland.*)

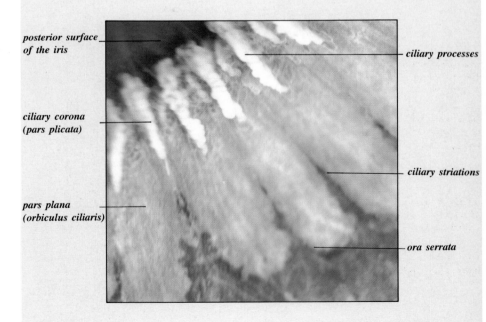

posterior surface of the iris

ciliary corona (pars plicata)

pars plana (orbiculus ciliaris)

ciliary processes

ciliary striations

ora serrata

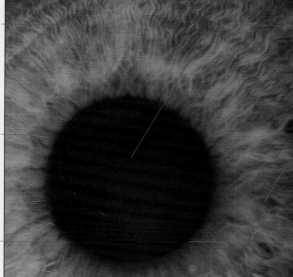

minor iridic circle

collarette (iris frill)

pupil margin

the pupil

crypts of Fuchs

pigment epithelium (pupillary ruff)

Plate 5 Front surface of the iris. (*Photo: M. Helland.*)

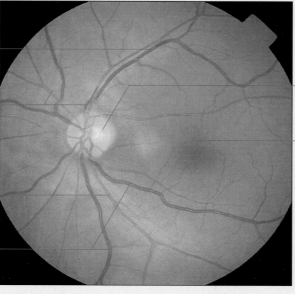

superior temporal branch of central retinal vein

superior branch of central retinal artery

inferior branch of central retinal artery

inferior branch of central retinal vein

optic disc or papilla

macula lutea

Plate 6 Fundus photograph of a left eye. (*Photo: M. Helland.*)

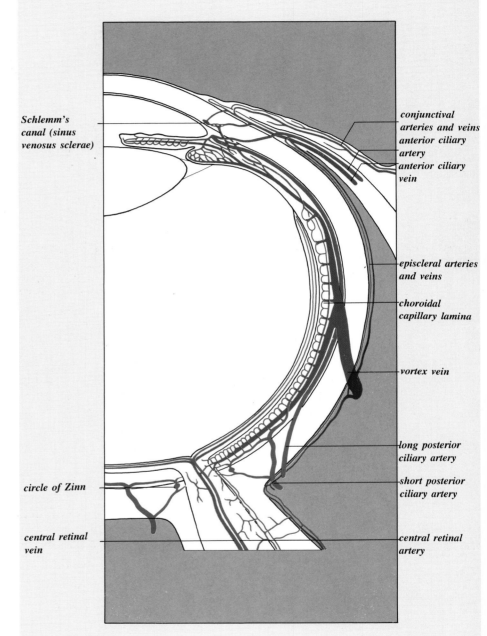

Plate 7 Blood vessels of the eye.

Schlemm's canal (sinus venosus sclerae)

conjunctival arteries and veins

anterior ciliary artery

anterior ciliary vein

episcleral arteries and veins

choroidal capillary lamina

vortex vein

long posterior ciliary artery

short posterior ciliary artery

circle of Zinn

central retinal vein

central retinal artery

eyebrow
(supercilium)

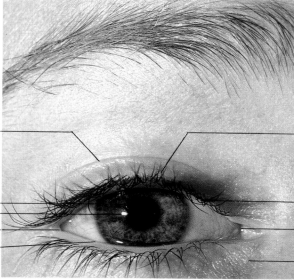

superior
palpebral furrow
or sulcus

superior or upper
lid

pupil
iris
lateral or outer
canthus
margin of eyelid

eyeball

inner or medial
canthus

inferior palpebral
furrow or sulcus

Plate 8 A right eye
and surroundings.
(*Photo: M. Helland.*)

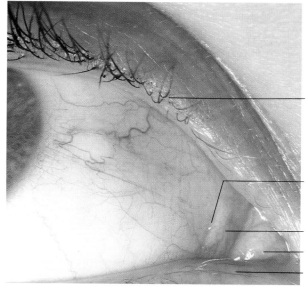

upper lid

plica semilunaris

lacrimal lake

caruncle

lower lid

Plate 9 The medial
canthus of a right eye.
(*Photo: M. Helland.*)

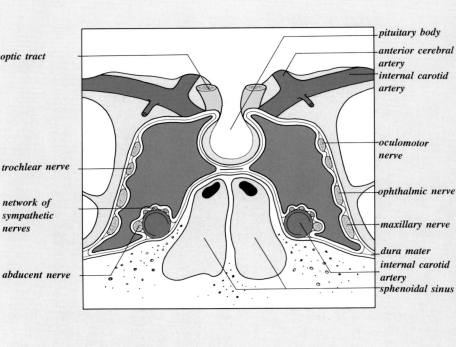

Plate 10 Blood vessels of the eyelids.

supraorbital vein
superior palpebral arcades
lacrimal artery
lateral palpebral artery
marginal arterial arcades
facial artery

supraorbital artery
frontal vein
supratrochlear artery
medial palpebral artery
facial vein
facial artery
infraorbital artery

Plate 11 Frontal section through the sphenoidal region and cavernous sinus.

optic tract
trochlear nerve
network of sympathetic nerves
abducent nerve

pituitary body
anterior cerebral artery
internal carotid artery
oculomotor nerve
ophthalmic nerve
maxillary nerve
dura mater
internal carotid artery
sphenoidal sinus

Plate 12 Coloboma in a right eye. (*Photo: B. Bjerke.*)

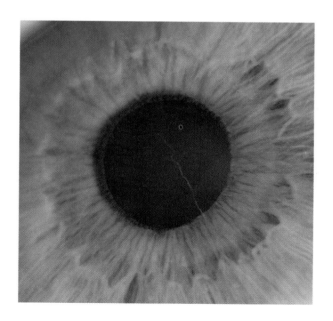

Plate 13 Pupillary membrane remnant in a 63 year old man. (*Photo: M. Helland.*)

Plate 14 Rear view of anterior part of eye. At the periphery, the ciliary body is seen with the ora serrata and ciliary processes. More centrally is the highly pigmented back surface of the iris, with the pupillary aperture. Refer also to *Plate 4*. (*Photo: M. Helland.*)

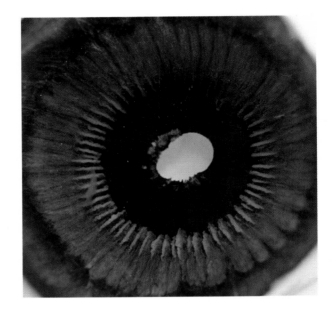

into the stroma upsets the arrangement of the collagen fibres, producing extra
the stroma upsets the arrangement of the collagen fibres, producing extra
scattering and absorption of light. Consequently the cornea appears slightly
'milky' with lower transmission of light.

THE LIMBUS

The corneo-scleral junction, the 'limbus' is a region between 1 mm and 2 mm
long between the sclera and the cornea. The important structures within this
boundary will be dealt with in detail later.

Here there is a lateral continuation of the various corneal tissues. The
epithelial layers of bulbar conjunctiva and cornea merge, covering and filling
(in humans) radial folds in the stroma known as Vogt's palisades, which
protrude slightly into the cornea. The increased epithelial basal cell thickness
between the ridges is important as a source of renewal for the corneal epithelium.

Bowman's layer makes interconnections with the connective tissue of the
conjunctiva and Tenon's capsule, while the fibres of the corneal stroma gradually
lose their well ordered arrangement in merging with the sclera.

Descemet's membrane has connections with the connective tissue cells of the
trabecular network, the spongiform mass of branching fibres at the filtration
angle. Open connections exist through this network between the canal and
anterior chamber. At the limbus, the endothelial layer of the cornea continues
laterally, to cover the trabecular fibres with a single layer of cells (see Fig. 4.4,
page 42 and Plate 3).

Schlemm's canal or the scleral 'venous' sinus encircles the limbal region
(Fig. 2.10). Generally oval in section, it is likely to divide into several canals
which interconnect. It lies within the scleral tissues, internally covered with a
solitary layer of endothelium; the latter prevents direct connection between the
anterior chamber and Schlemm's canal. To the lateral and dorsal aspect of the
canal, the scleral tissues form a triangular structure, its point towards the
cornea, the *scleral spur*. This is attached ventrally to the trabecular meshes and
dorsally to the ciliary muscle.

Schlemm's canal drains into the intrascleral plexus within the sclera, via 25 to
30 collector canals, then from here into the anterior ciliary veins. Some of
these outlets (the 'aqueous veins') penetrate the sclera more directly but also
empty into the anterior ciliary veins. Such aqueous veins are normally virtually
colourless, containing only aqueous.

Chapter 3
The Middle Coat of the Eye

THE UVEA

As the vascular layer of the eye, the uvea lies between the sclera and the retina and is comprised chiefly of blood vessels, comparable to the pia mater of the brain. The vessels are in a loose network of connective tissue, rich in pigment cells. The uvea resembles the walls of a camera as it prevents unwanted light penetrating into the optical system, the pigmented layer additionally reducing internal stray light and reflections. Another important function is to supply blood to the eye and to drain it out.

There are three parts of the uvea (Fig. 3.1):

- The choroid (vascular membrane).
- The ciliary body (with radiating striations).
- The iris (multicoloured membrane).

THE CHOROID

This mesh lying between the sclera and the retina stretches from the optic disc to the ora serrata. It is rich in blood vessels and clusters of dark brown pigment. At the posterior pole its thickness is about 0.2 mm, thinning to some 0.1 mm anteriorly. It is loosely attached to the sclera, except where it is traversed with vessels and nerves. The blood vessels of the choroid nourish the anterior parts of the uvea and the outer layers of the retina. Most of this blood is derived from the short and long posterior ciliary arteries but there are connections with the anterior ciliary arteries. Drainage of blood takes place via the four 'vortex' veins and the ciliary veins. The intraocular pressure (IOP) is normally between 10 and 22 mm Hg. Obviously, the intraocular vessels function only if the pressure within them is above the IOP and within these vessels pressure is higher than in most other parts of the body. Five distinct parts of the choroid can be distinguished (Figs 3.2 and 3.3):

- The suprachoroidea.
- Haller's layer.
- Sattler's layer.
- The choriocapillary layer.
- Bruch's membrane.

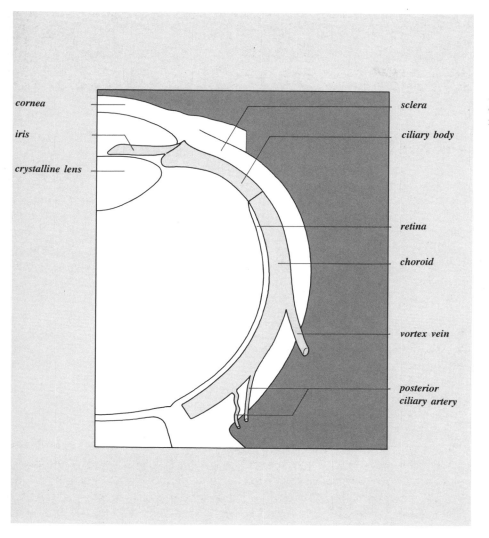

cornea

iris

crystalline lens

sclera

ciliary body

retina

choroid

vortex vein

posterior
ciliary artery

Fig. 3.1 Uveal
divisions and
relationships.

The *suprachoroidea* is contiguous with the lamina fusca of the sclera, being composed of collagenous and elastic fibres in a fine network. The fibres principally lie meridionally, containing a largely fluid-filled cavity. The long ciliary nerves and arteries move towards the anterior eye through this layer.

Haller's and *Sattler's layers* form the chief vascular layer of the choroid. Large size vessels (essentially veins) are in Haller's layer while Sattler's layer carries smaller vessels. Many anastomoses are to be found, the entire choroid being a plaitwork of vessels, between which are plenty of pigment cells.

The choriocapillary layer (choriocapillaris) is a very fine mesh of capillaries, chiefly concerned with nourishment of the outer layer of the retina. It is particularly dense behind the macula. Its capillary size is one of the largest in the body, supplied and drained by the choroidal vessel regions.

Fig. 3.2 Choroidal
tissues and divisions in
transverse section.

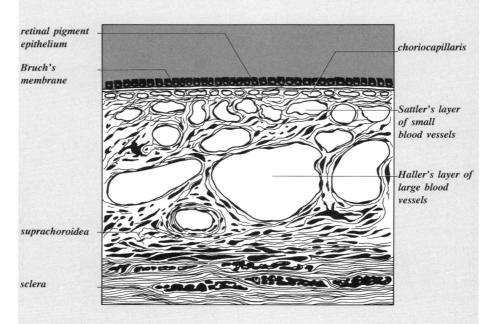

retinal pigment
epithelium

Bruch's
membrane

suprachoroidea

sclera

choriocapillaris

Sattler's layer
of small
blood vessels

Haller's layer of
large blood
vessels

Fig. 3.3 Unstained
section of choroidal
tissues. Light bands are
blood vessels. Dark
areas are pigmented
connective tissue.
(*Microphoto: T.
Saude.*)

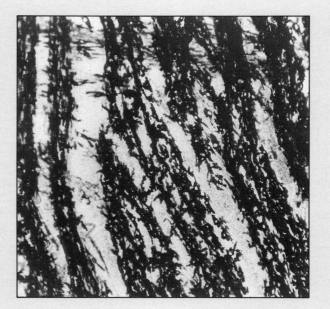

Bruch's membrane is a thin boundary layer between the choroid proper and the retina. Divisible into two layers, it has an outer elastic lamina contiguous with the choriocapillaris and an inner (cuticular) part which forms a basement membrane for the retinal pigment epithelium.

THE CILIARY BODY

This is an annular portion of the uvea, extending from the ora serrata to the root of the iris. In section it is triangular, the apex of the triangle extending to the region where the choroid merges with the ora serrata and the base at the root of the iris.

It can be considered as having two main parts. The posterior region, the *pars plana*, is about 4 mm wide. It is also called the *orbiculus ciliaris* and has a smooth, even, surface serrated with many delicate meridional stripes or 'striae ciliaris' (see Fig. 3.4 and Plate 4).

The anterior portion, the *ciliary corona* (pars plicata) is about 2 mm wide, being made up of between 70 and 80 radiating ridges, known as the *ciliary processes*. These ridges are 0.6 to 0.8 mm high, with unpigmented crests. The ciliary processes are highly vascular and contain small lymphatic spaces. It is here that the aqueous humour is produced. The ciliary body is structurally similar to the choroid although it lacks the choriocapillaris and the suprachoroidea is less developed. Structurally the ciliary body embraces:

- The ciliary epithelium.
- The stroma.
- The ciliary muscle.

The *ciliary epithelium* (pars ciliaris retinae) is composed of two layers of cubical cells, covering the inner aspect of the ciliary body. It is derived in the embryo from the double layer of cells of the secondary optic cup. Its inner or surface layer is unpigmented, being the continuation of the retinal nerve layer, and in a pigmented form it extends over the posterior surface of the iris. In this layer, cells contain organelles and resemble secretory cells elsewhere in the body. The pigmented outer layer is a forward projection of the retinal pigment epithelium and its cells also have many organelles. There are thus indications that both layers of cells are concerned with aqueous production.

The *stroma of the ciliary body* is a loose net, rich in pigment (melanin) and blood vessels. The ciliary muscle is interspersed with the stromal tissues. The profusion of blood vessels is derived from the ciliary arteries which also produce an arterial ring around the region at the root of the iris, the major (iridic) arterial circle.

The *ciliary muscle* arises from the front of the choroid at the ora serrata, running through the entire ciliary body. It is composed of smooth muscle and is traditionally considered in two arrangements of fibres.

Fig. 3.4 Ciliary body, transverse section.

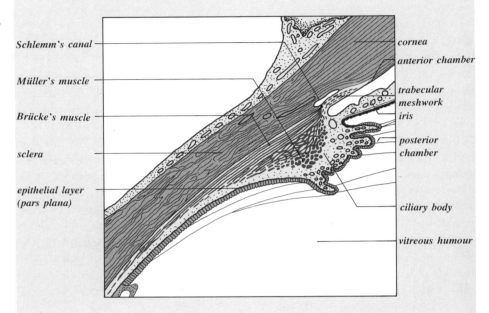

Schlemm's canal

Müller's muscle

Brücke's muscle

sclera

epithelial layer (pars plana)

cornea

anterior chamber

trabecular meshwork

iris

posterior chamber

ciliary body

vitreous humour

Fig. 3.5 The iris seen from the front.

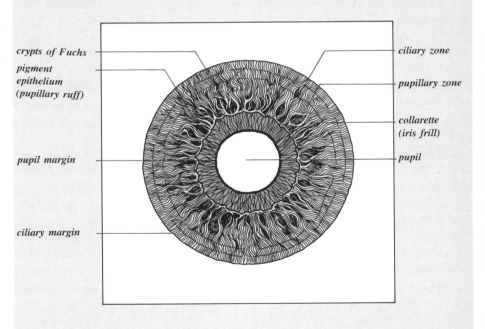

crypts of Fuchs

pigment epithelium (pupillary ruff)

pupil margin

ciliary margin

ciliary zone

pupillary zone

collarette (iris frill)

pupil

The *muscle of Bowman and Brücke* lies nearest to the sclera, running meridionally. The fibres originate at the *ora serrata* and *orbiculus ciliaris*, being inserted into the scleral spur. Since the muscle is associated with elastic tissue near the ora serrata, on contraction it causes a 0.5 mm forward movement of the ciliary body.

Müller's muscle lies internally to Brücke's muscle, its fibres tending to an equatorial course. Thus there is a continuous annulus of muscle surrounding and opposite the equator of the crystalline lens. On contraction of the muscle, the ciliary body draws nearer to the lens. *Radial muscle fibres* are situated between the above mentioned two parts of the ciliary muscle, there being some doubt as to their precise function.

Fincham (1937) considered it inadvisable to treat the ciliary muscle as if it had three distinct parts. He took it to be a network of interconnected fibres, with the chief variations of direction being meridional (outer) and circular (inner). 'Radial' fibres would then form an intermediate part of the network.

Hence the overall action of the ciliary muscle is such that contraction moves the ciliary body centripetally and forwards, which slackens the zonular suspensions of the lens and increases its sphericity.

THE IRIS

This is a thin disc in the frontal plane, the most forward part of the uvea, which lies in front of the lens. It is an annular, truncated cone about 12 mm in diameter, thickest about 2 mm from the edge of the pupil at the 'collarette', the thickness decreasing at the root.

The pupil is an aperture placed centrally or slightly nasally, whose diameter is under muscular control, usually between 2.5 and 4 mm. Mydriatic drugs dilate the diameter up to 8 mm. There appears to be no significant difference in pupil size between blue and brown eyes, nor between those of men and women, although opinions differ somewhat. There is, however, some variation with age: the pupil is relatively small in the newborn and becomes largest in early childhood, diminishing with subsequent ageing ('senile miosis'). Also, pupil reactions to light become slower with age.

A difference in the diameters in the two eyes is called *anisocoria*. Some 17% of people have a barely noticeable anisocoria (under 1 mm), while 4% have a pronounced difference in diameter size. The cause of the latter condition is a constant disturbance of nervous control and may point to a pathological condition.

The iris separates the liquid filled space behind the cornea into the anterior and posterior chambers, making an angle with the cornea known as the *filtration angle* or *angle of the anterior chamber*. The periphery of the iris, its *ciliary margin*, is joined onto the ciliary body by loose connections into the cornea through the 'pectinate ligament' (the term used in some species). The innermost border is the free pupil margin and the back surface rests on the front of the lens (Fig. 3.5).

The anterior surface of the iris has two zones or portions, the *pupillary zone* near the pupil and the *ciliary zone* which is the broader, outer part, stretching into the root of the iris. These zones meet as a delicate 'zig−zag' line, the *collarette* or iris frill. This is where the pupillary membrane starts in the embryo and here the iris is thickest. The edge of the pupil has a highly pigmented border, or 'ruff' coming forwards from the posterior epithelial layers which terminate here. Under magnification, the pupil is seen to have pronounced, radiating, wavy regions, giving a cogwheel appearance near the pupil. Around the collarette there are many deep open spaces in the surface tissues, the *crypts of Fuchs*, also found near the root of the iris (see Plate 5).

The iris tissues

The bulk of the iris is the stroma, made of loose connective tissue. Numerous blood vessels and nerves appear, with a radial arrangement, observed to become wavy when the pupil dilates. Pigment cells are contained in the stroma. Anterior to the compact stroma lies the *anterior layer* of finer connective tissue, more or less pigmented, while an incomplete *surface endothelium* extends over the front surface. It is questionable whether this is a true endothelium or a flattened type of connective tissue somewhat like that of the stroma. This layer is absent in Fuchs' crypts, where the aqueous comes into direct contact with the stromal blood vessels.

Neonatal eyes have relatively meagre pigmentation, so babies' eyes tend to be light blue. This arises from reflection and scattering of short wavelength light in the unpigmented iris, which preferentially absorbs longer wavelengths. As greater amounts of pigment appear, children's eyes become darker blue, grey or even brown depending on their future adult pigment density. In fact, eyes can start brown in highly pigmented families.

The rear surface of the iris has a covering of two layers of epithelium (both pigmented), the *pars iridica retinae* a continuation of the pars ciliaris retinae. The anterior cells have additional myofibril attachments penetrating into the *dilatator muscle* of the pupil. Note, again, the pigment ring at the pupil margin, where the epithelial layers end.

Contractile properties of the iris come from the presence of smooth muscle fibres. The *sphincter muscle* is about 1 mm in width, an annulus lying in the posterior part of the stroma, with fibres arranged in a circle round the pupil; muscular contraction produces miosis. This sphincter is under parasympathetic control from the III cranial nerve (Fig. 3.6).

The *dilatator muscle*, a layer attached by myofibrils, occupies the entire surface of the pars iridica retinae, forming the posterior boundary of the stroma. As mentioned above, projections from the front epithelial layer are involved. The dilatator muscle fibres run radially and it is regarded as an incompletely differentiated muscle, although it is really stronger than the sphincter muscle. It is under sympathetic nerve control and on contraction dilates the pupil (mydriasis).

The iris has many blood vessels. Arteries are derived from the *major arterial circle* in the front of the ciliary body, from which radiating vessels can be seen to run across the iris. There is an incomplete ring of arteries and corresponding veins near the collarette, the *minor iridic circle*. Veins run in the same way as the arterial pattern, while nerves accompany the vessels through the various iris structures.

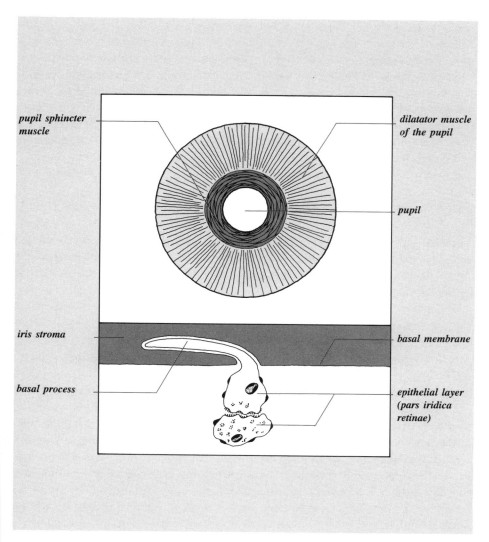

pupil sphincter muscle

dilatator muscle of the pupil

pupil

iris stroma

basal membrane

basal process

epithelial layer (pars iridica retinae)

Fig. 3.6 Above: Diagram of fibre distribution in the dilatator and sphincter muscles of the pupil. *Below*: Posterior epithelial layer of the iris, with basal processes which contain 'myofibrils' and which penetrate the dilatator.

THE PUPIL REACTIONS TO LIGHT

Light falling on an eye produces contraction or miosis of its pupil and there is a similar constriction in the other eye's pupil. The extent of the miosis depends on various factors, such as the retinal adaptation (to light), the intensity of the light, the intensity of the retinal illumination, emotional state, and so on. There are variations between subjects. If both eyes are simultaneously illuminated, there is some summation of response, so that the constriction can be greater than with monocular stimulation (see Fig. 3.7).

The nervous pathway for the light reflex starts at the retina, where the photoreceptors initiate the afferent stage, then goes up the visual paths via the optic nerve and chiasma to the optic tract. Here the light reflex route diverges towards the adjacent lateral geniculate body. The fibres travel downwards to end in the pretectal nucleus, by the superior colliculus. From here impulses reach both sides of the oculomotor (parasympathetic) cranial nerve, at the Edinger—Westphal nucleus, with a confluence of the crossed and uncrossed fibres, reminiscent of the chiasmal crossings. Hence, an anatomical explanation exists for the binocular miosis which comes from uniocular illumination.

From the oculomotor centre, efferent impulses travel to the orbit and a synapse in the ciliary ganglion. Postganglionic fibres enter the short posterior ciliary nerves, conveying impulses to the pupil sphincter. Examination of the light reflexes is an important method of establishing damage in either afferent or efferent nerve paths.

THE BLOOD SUPPLY OF THE UVEA

The rich vascular content of the uvea stems from the most important of the eye's arteries, the *ophthalmic artery* which is a branch of the *internal carotid artery*. Soon after entering the orbit, the ophthalmic artery divides into numerous vessels to supply the globe and orbital structures nearby.

The *short posterior ciliary arteries* consist of 10 to 20 branches which move through small holes in the sclera, making a ring around the optic nerve; they serve the choroid with blood. This ring is known as the *circle of Zinn*, from which the optic nerve exit (the papilla) and nearby retinal tissues are supplied.

The *long posterior ciliary arteries* are two vessels which penetrate the sclera on the temporal and medial sides of the short arteries. Moving forwards within the choroid, they produce branches ending in the ciliary body. Here, with the anterior ciliary arteries, they form the *major arterial circle* and supply the iris and ciliary body.

The *anterior ciliary arteries*, six or seven small vessels, arise from the arteries to the (extraocular) rectus muscles and from the *lacrimal artery*. They move through the sclera to the major arterial circle but before this, send tiny branches forwards to the limbus and the deep limbal arcades. They anastomose with the conjunctival vessels.

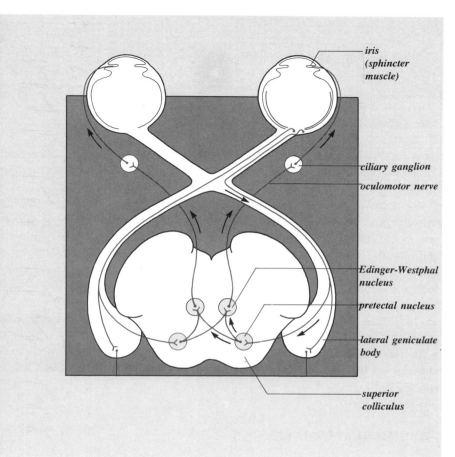

Fig. 3.7 The pupillary light reflexes.

iris
(sphincter
muscle)

ciliary ganglion

oculomotor nerve

Edinger-Westphal
nucleus

pretectal nucleus

lateral geniculate
body

superior
colliculus

The uveal veins generally follow the arteries, draining the choroid by means of four vortex veins which leave the eye just behind the equator, each draining one quadrant. Ciliary veins drain the front part of the eye, including much of the emerging aqueous humour (see Plate 7).

THE MIDDLE COAT OF THE EYE **35**

Chapter 4
The Internal Ocular Media

THE ANTERIOR AND POSTERIOR CHAMBERS

The space in front of the crystalline lens and the vitreous body is occupied by *aqueous humour*, the region behind the back of the cornea being divided by the iris.

The *anterior chamber*, or foremost part, has the cornea as its anterior boundary and 1 to 2 mm of sclera peripherally, at the filtration angle, with its rear being the iris and the front surface of the lens. Thus it is the shape of a half moon. There is a distance of about 3.5 mm between the front of the cornea and the front of the lens, a distance which decreases some 0.2 to 0.3 mm on accommodation. The diameter is about 12 to 14 mm. The space has an incomplete lining of endothelium.

The *posterior chamber*, which is the space at the rear of the iris, in section is almost triangular, with its apex towards the pupil and its base at the ciliary body. It is bounded by the lens periphery and the anterior vitreous and occupies an annulus around the lens equator. It is divided many times by the zonular system.

THE CRYSTALLINE LENS

This is a transparent, biconvex body situated between the vitreous and the back of the iris. Between its anterior and posterior poles is the lens substance. The circumference which lies in the frontal plane is called its equator.

The *equatorial diameter* in childhood is 5 to 6 mm; by the age of 20 this has increased to between 9 mm and 10 mm, but its growth diminishes with increasing age.

The *axial thickness* depends on the state of accommodation. At birth it is 3.5 to 4 mm, unaccommodated, while the increase in thickness through life can reach a figure of up to 4.75 or 5 mm. The radius of the posterior surface is about 6 mm, shorter than the 10 mm radius of the front surface. On accommodation the radius of the anterior surface decreases to about that of the back of the lens. At birth, amplitude of accommodation can be 15 to 16 Dioptres (D), reducing to 7 to 8 D by the age of 25. By the age of 50 to 60 years the figure is virtually zero.

The *ciliary processes* surround the equator of the lens with a space of about 0.5 mm, it being here that there is an attachment to the *ciliary body* by means of the zonular fibres.

Human lenses possess a relatively soft cortex around a central, somewhat

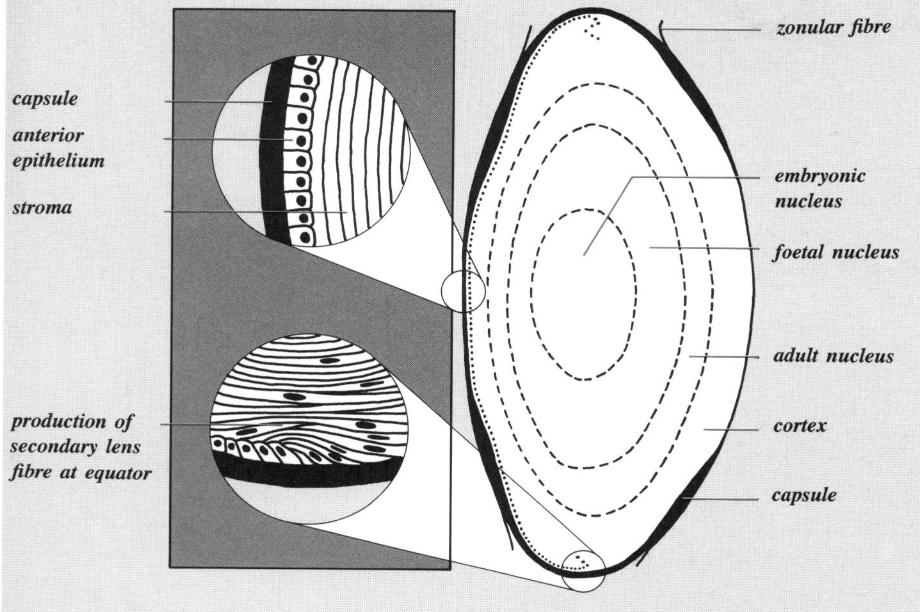

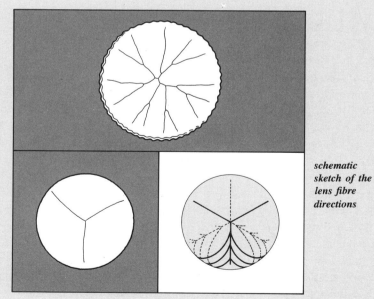

capsule

anterior
epithelium

stroma

production of
secondary lens
fibre at equator

zonular fibre

embryonic
nucleus

foetal nucleus

adult nucleus

cortex

capsule

Fig. 4.1 Right:
Transverse section of
the lens, with
exaggeration of the
capsular thickness to
emphasize variations.
Left: Details seen at
anterior pole and at
equator.

Fig. 4.2 Lens sutures.

the lens in a
mature person

the foetal lens

schematic
sketch of the
lens fibre
directions

harder nucleus. At about 30 to 35 years of age, the nucleus develops and at its centre shows a light yellow—brown colour. With increasing age the nucleus becomes larger, virtually comprising the entire lens by the age of 70. In addition, the lens progressively flattens its curvature and by a combination of factors accommodation fails.

The layers of the lens have different refractive indices, increasing progressively towards the nucleus. The cortex has an index of 1.38 as compared to 1.41 in the nucleus.

The lens fibres

Several layers are involved in the construction of the lens (Fig. 4.1).

- The capsule.
- The epithelial layer.
- The stroma, composed of fibres.

The *lens capsule* is an elastic basal membrane enveloping the lens. The thickness is not uniform, being greatest near the front and back regions of the equator where the zonular system is attached; here the thickness is about 20 μm. The thickness increases with age.

The capsule acts as a basal membrane for the lens epithelium, from which it is derived. Flattened lens fibres grow backwards from this epithelial layer.

Compression of the lens substance results from the elastic nature of the capsule, so that when the ciliary muscle contracts and relaxes tension on the zonule, there is a tendency to accommodation, increasing the power of the lens.

The *lens epithelium* is situated below the capsule, only anteriorly. However, the back epithelium of the (embryonic) lens vesicle produces the initial fibres filling the back part of the lens. The solitary anterior layer between capsule and stroma is made up of cubical epithelial cells. And while it has little mitotic activity centrally, this increases peripherally to a maximum at the equator. Here a lengthening of cells takes place, eventually forming fibres of which progressive layers are laid down, onion-like, to cover existing fibres. The cell nuclei remain in the equatorial region.

Lens fibres therefore appear initially as *primary fibres* or stretched posterior epithelial cells. These are later covered by *secondary lens fibres* which come from the anterior epithelium at the equator. Secondary fibres extend, so that one part moves backwards while the apex grows towards the anterior pole of the lens. Initially, the nuclei of these cells are intact, but later they fragment and vanish. Simultaneously most of their organelles disappear.

Throughout life, more lens fibres are produced in this way, the activity decreasing with age. Older fibres are compressed as they are overlaid, forming a stable 'adult nucleus'.

In section, the lens fibres are hexagonal, measuring some 10 mm long, and are arranged meridionally from front to back in a U-shaped manner. Since each fibre is not long enough to reach between poles, those ending at the back pole only extend to a position just beyond the equator. Fibres ending near the back region of the equator can reach the anterior pole however.

Thus *lens sutures* are formed and looking with the slit lamp at the lens from the front or back, one can readily trace stellar configurations. The eyes of newborn babies exhibit an erect Y anteriorly, with an inverted Y behind. With age the 'lens star' becomes more complex (Fig. 4.2).

Completely avascular from early in embryonic life, the lens is nourished and oxygenated by diffusion from the aqueous. Katabolites leave by the same route. Metabolism within the lens builds up cells and fibres, contributing to internal transport of substances. The crystalline lens has continuous need of energy from ATP for such purposes. Demands of the epithelial layer account for the bulk of the metabolic activity. The aqueous is relatively rich in glucose (the most important food required) and supplies this, as well as oxygen. ATP is formed essentially by glycolysis, just 3 to 4% of glucose being broken down further through the Krebs cycle. Most of this energy production happens to be anaerobic, which results in a build up of lactate in the lens. Lactate then diffuses out into the aqueous, explaining why the latter has such a high concentration.

The reason for the relatively high anaerobic production of energy in the lens is still not clear. However, assuming that the lens tissues tend to exist at 'subsistence level' one can see how even slight disturbances can cause trouble.

Age-related changes in the lens produce a hardening of the lens substance, lower transmission rates and a consequent reduction of vision. Older eyes absorb relatively more blue, short wavelength, light. This has an important bearing on the choice of the colour of illumination for the elderly. When the opacity and reduction of sight is significant, the term *cataract* is used. Senile cataract may be either *nuclear* or *cortical*. In the former type the oldest lens fibres of the nucleus become opaque, while in cortical cataract the cortical fibres may swell or opacify.

Types of cataract other than 'senile' exist, with distinctive features. Metabolic disturbances of the lens may produce cataract, e.g. in diabetes. Cataract may also occur as a result of chemical side effects from medicines or poisons. There may be damage to the lens as a result of ionizing radiation, while ultra-violet effects can appear in later years. The effects of low doses of energy on the lens are not considered significant at present, although we have known for many years that 'glass blowers'' cataract results from infra-red damage, usually after long periods of exposure. Congenital types of cataract can be the result of disturbances of lens growth before birth; an all too frequent cause is maternal rubella at a critical stage of pregnancy.

Finally, one must consider the damaging influence of dehydration, perhaps from diarrhoea or heat effect, on the lens. This may account for the prevalence of cataract in foreign lands with poor hygiene.

THE VITREOUS BODY

This is a transparent gel which occupies the innermost part of the eye between the lens and the retina. Its anterior boundary extends to the lens and the posterior chamber. In front it is hollowed into the *hyaloid fossa* (fossa patellaris) for the posterior lens surface.

The vitreous has attachments to the underlying tissues at the ora serrata and at the optic disc, being very loosely in apposition to the remainder of the retina. At the annular rim of the patellar fossa, the vitreous has some attachment, more pronounced in the young, but weakening with age.

Using special methods of illumination, a narrow canal can be observed, 1 or 2 mm wide, running from the optic disc to the back pole of the lens. This is the *hyaloid canal* which, before birth, carries the hyaloid artery. This artery degenererates and should disappear completely some six weeks before birth, when the canal is filled with liquid. Sometimes, remnants of the artery can be observed ophthalmoscopically near the posterior pole of the lens or at the optic disc.

The vitreous is a colourless, transparent gel with a high water content. It resembles the aqueous in chemical composition, with a proteinous material making up a small part. Collagenous fibres appear as a loose network which, with mucopolysaccharides, forms the structure of the gel. A condensation at the outer boundary of the vitreous forms a type of membrane. This condensation is particularly noticeable in the patellar fossa, where it amounts to a genuine membrane at the back surface of the lens, known as the *hyaloid membrane*.

There is a small space between the hyaloid membrane and the back of the lens, called the *retrolental space*, which may contain some blood or exudate in some ocular pathological conditions.

Cells are found only in the outer layers of the vitreous, principally near the ora serrata; these are *hyalocytes*, from the primary vitreous, possibly helpful to vitreoretinal adhesion.

From about the age of 40, alterations in the vitreous gel content begin. The gelatinous consistency in the rear part tends towards greater liquidity. By old age this process has reached the front of the vitreous. Thus, as the space tends to be filled with less viscous fluid, the boundary of the vitreous and the internal limiting membrane of the retina have decreased mutual adhesion. In an acute loosening, flashes of light or unusual movements may be seen. In cases of trauma, prolapse of the vitreous is possible, the more definite regions of attachment to the retina being disrupted. This can lead to damage to retinal tissues and their possible detachment near the positions of vitreous adhesion.

THE AQUEOUS HUMOUR

This is normally a clear and colourless liquid occupying the anterior and posterior chambers. It is important in ocular metabolism and significant in certain diseases. Primarily it nourishes internal avascular structures, bringing nutrients and oxygen to the lens and part of the cornea, and removing their wastes. The aqueous contributes to the shape of the eye, governing its IOP, which itself assists in retaining the retina in place.

In internal ocular inflammatory conditions, the aqueous carries away excess protein, blood and other products. Disturbance of the circulation of the aqueous can be connected with abnormally high IOP.

The composition of the aqueous

In relation to blood plasma, the aqueous contains little colloid (protein), suggesting that it is a combined product of filtration and secretion. It enters the eye across the 'blood—aqueous barrier' in a manner similar to the kidney processes.

Aqueous contains various electrolytes, glucose, HCO_3, ascorbic acid, etc. Important components are also sodium and chloride. In addition, ocular internal avascular tissues receive oxygen and aminoacids via the aqueous, whilst CO_2 and lactate are removed. Diffusion takes place between the aqueous and nearby structures. Note particularly the two-way access between the frontal tissues of the iris and the aqueous (Fig. 4.3).

Analysis of aqueous from different parts of the eye is difficult in practice. Hence much data on the subject comes from animals which impedes our understanding of the composition and movement of aqueous in man. However, we do know, from various sources, that several substances found in aqueous differ in concentrations from those found in plasma.

Aqueous production

Opinions have changed on this subject over the last century. Secretion by the ciliary processes was favoured initially, then about 50 years ago ultrafiltration and dialysis became a more acceptable theory. Today, it is the general view that secretion by the ciliary epithelium, along with filtration and diffusion, combine to produce aqueous. The osmotic pressure difference between plasma and aqueous gives a bias for the movement of water and solutes to the posterior chamber, combined with active secretion by the unpigmented ciliary epithelium.

In glaucoma, various drugs are used to reduce aqueous production, such as the beta—adrenergic antagonist (blocker) 'Timolol', or 'Diamox' (acetazolamide) which inhibits carbonic anhydrase action.

Surgery or trauma which punctures the globe reduces IOP and disturbs the blood—aqueous balance. Dilatation of blood vessels results, with abnormal amounts of protein in the aqueous. Using the slit lamp, this presence of excess colloid can be seen because of scattered light. This is also an early sign of ocular inflammation such as cyclitis.

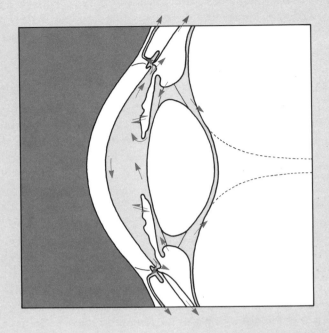

Fig. 4.3 Movements of aqueous in the eye.

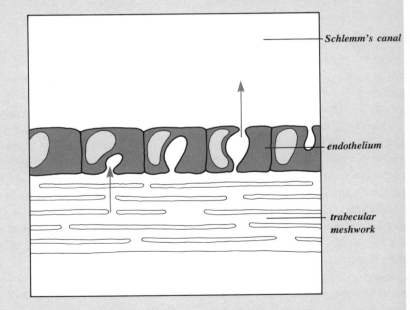

Fig. 4.4 Outline of the movement of vacuoles through the endothelial covering of Schlemm's canal.

— Schlemm's canal

— endothelium

— trabecular meshwork

Aqueous flow through the eye

It is clinically important to understand the method of entry and exit of aqueous, and particularly its drainage. Alternative exit routes are the 'episcleral' or uveoscleral path, to the optic disc via the vitreous with some liquid uptake by the cornea. Two-way diffusion with the blood vessels of the iris has some role in drainage. Aqueous removes wastes from within the eye, including large molecular structures. Debris flows towards Schlemm's canal, down which proteins and loose blood cells are carried. As age progresses, drainage can be obstructed resulting in a rise in IOP.

The volume of aqueous production can be studied with radioactive materials and the movement of fluorescent dye. Thus it is known that about 1.5% of the contents of the anterior chamber is renewed each minute. The half-life of anterior chamber aqueous is some 45 minutes, corresponding to a daily production of about 2.8 ml.

A thermal circulation exists within the aqueous since the cornea is several degrees colder than the inner eye, so cooled aqueous sinks. If there is a high colloid level in the aqueous, as in pathological states, one notices deposits of proteins on the inferior back surface of the cornea. These precipitates are seen as small grey flecks, with the larger ones being lowest. They are often distributed in a triangle, base down. Pigment cells also circulate within the aqueous and by collecting at the drainage angle can be associated with pigmentary glaucoma. The vertical collections of debris on the back of the cornea are called Krukenberg's spindle.

The trabecular drainage mechanism

Aqueous is produced fairly constantly. To maintain IOP at a constant level, the drainage mechanism must regulate the flow via the *trabecular* tissues into *Schlemm's canal* and hence to the venous outlets.

The trabecular meshes lie at the angle of the anterior chamber near the limbus, a three-dimensional network of laminated connective tissue which extends from Descemet's membrane and connects with the ciliary muscle through the scleral spur. The fibres have endothelial covering and comprise a labyrinth through which aqueous reaches Schlemm's canal (see Plate 3).

Schlemm's canal (the sinus venosus sclerae) is a circular, irregular canal within the scleral tissues, internally clad with endothelium. Running round the limbus, while dividing into two or three branches which reunite, it drains into a series of 'aqueous veins' and then into the anterior ciliary veins. There are connections between the canal and the *intrascleral plexus*, into which some of the aqueous escapes (see Fig. 2.10).

Much is known about drainage into Schlemm's canal but the passage of the aqueous through an endothelial barrier of the trabecular meshwork into the canal is complicated. However, it has been discovered that small molecules can move between cells, water and other minute molecules. Electron microscopy shows that vacuoles in the endothelial cells pass from the trabecular tissues through the cells, to empty themselves into the canal. The main function of these vacuoles is to act as a transport mechanism and move large molecules through the barrier (Fig. 4.4).

The IOP is in the region of 15 mm Hg, while in the orbital tissues the pressure is lower, perhaps nearer to zero. Ocular tissues are impervious to liquid, so a special exit is needed. The layer of endothelium at the filtration angle is incomplete, so the tissues of the ciliary body can be reached easily from the anterior chamber. This allows aqueous to pass to the suprachoroidal space and thence to vessels through the sclera and into the orbit.

The so called '*uveoscleral route*', according to many researchers, accounts for 10 to 15% of the aqueous escape. Other exit routes for liquid enable it to reach the optic nerve and retinal vessels via the vitreous. It is estimated that there is relatively little transport via the retina, since the nerve layers contain much fatty tissue. Also, some liquid is taken up from the aqueous into the cornea.

Mechanical and neural regulation

As stated earlier, some trabecular fibres are attached to the scleral spur which has connections with Bruch's part of the ciliary muscle. Contraction of this muscle thus applies traction on the trabecular tissues and encourages drainage through the latter. It is reasonable to suggest that accommodation is involved in the drainage mechanism.

Various drugs can affect the IOP because of their influences on the autonomic nervous system. Sympathetic stimulation appreciably reduces the tension. Langham and Rosenthal (1966) showed in animals how strong sympathetic vasoconstriction in the uvea lowers IOP. Other experiments indicate some sympathetic influence on the drainage mechanism.

Parasympathetic stimulation leads to extra aqueous production through added uveal blood supply. Ruskell (1971) found that parasympathetic branches of the facial nerve go through the *pterygopalatine ganglion* to the eye, innervating choroidal vessel networks and probably other ocular vessels. Vasodilatation follows stimulation of these nerves, increases aqueous production and raises IOP. Ruskell also demonstrated a permanent fall in IOP if the pterygopalatine ganglion is destroyed.

Electrophysiological measurements show that afferent impulses influence the IOP. This suggests that baroreceptors with low thresholds produce changes in the IOP. Such receptors may exist in the uvea and the trabecular tissues. There have been no actual demonstrations of the IOP being controlled by afferent control.

THE INTRAOCULAR PRESSURE (IOP)

The average 'tension' within the eye is 15.50 mm Hg, as measured with the Goldmann applanation tonometer. Authorities state that within a normal population one can find values ranging between 10.50 and 20.50 mm Hg. There is no normal distribution curve as there is tendency towards the higher pressures. No absolute upper limit can be given for normality, since a grey area exists between 20 and 30 mm Hg, within which some people's eyes remain healthy and perfectly functioning. Others within this group can, in time, reveal early signs of glaucoma.

IOP may rapidly alter on account of external influences. Direct pressure on the eye, perhaps by tightly closed lids or by a finger (even by contraction of the recti) can dramatically raise pressure. A variation in IOP of 1 to 2 mm Hg results from the arterial pulse within the eye, while body position also has an influence. Changing from sitting to supine positions raises the tension between 2 and 3 mm Hg. Note that a subject's bodily tension may affect IOP because even restraining respiration can produce abnormally high readings (Fig. 4.5).

There is a diurnal variation in IOP of up to 5 mm Hg, ranging from a high level, usually in the morning, to an evening fall. This variation tends to be more marked in glaucomatous eyes, where an abnormally high tension may be found in the morning, despite more normal values later on. Tension is usually equal in the two eyes, while a difference of more than 3 mm Hg to 5 mm Hg suggests a pathological ocular state. The IOP changes constantly, so a single measurement is not likely to represent the long term situation.

Measurement of the IOP

Using a 'manometer' for this would necessitate penetrating the eye with a cannula and this is impossible in practice. Thus several types of instruments called *tonometers* have been developed, using different principles. The 'tension' which is assessed depends partly on the pressure within the eye and partly on the resistance of its outer coats.

The Schiøtz tonometer

This was introduced in 1905 and various modifications have emerged since. It is the most widely used tonometer, worldwide, on account of its simple construction and its practical accuracy. Its use involves measuring the indentation of the cornea (or sclera) using a known weight. A central moving plunger, loaded with different small weights, moves within a footplate which rests on the eye. A mass of 5.5 g is generally used, alternatives being 7.5, 10 or 15 g. The plunger indents the cornea until the ocular resistance stops it. A reading is then taken where a pointer registers against the instrument's scale. This is converted into mm Hg, using tables (Fig. 4.6).

Applanation tonometry

Many tonometers use the principle of applanation (Imbert and Fick's law). Here pressure against the cornea flattens a standard area or the extent of flattening is measured. This account will be restricted to two basic methods. Goldmann's tonometer measures the pressure needed to applanate an area of cornea 3.06 mm in diameter. The tonometer probe is a 7 mm plastics cylinder, attached to a spring-loaded arm, which pushes the probe forwards, using a scale. The technique involves a yellow−green fluorescein staining of the tears.

When the cornea has been flattened, the tears are expressed from beneath the end of the probe, which is surrounded by an annular meniscus of tears. Accurate estimates are aided by two prisms within the cylinder, so that the fluorescent ring is seen as two semicircles, one above the other. When the probe applanates the circle 3.06 mm in diameter, these semicircles form an uninterrupted letter S and the IOP is read directly in mm Hg (Fig. 4.7).

Types of 'non-contact' tonometers have recently appeared. Their main advantage is absence of direct contact with the cornea, so anaesthetic drops and sterilising of the instrument are avoided. A pulse of air directed at the corneal apex produces a flat area. An oblique beam of infra-red radiation is reflected when the cornea is applanated, onto a sensor. The time taken between the air pulse and peak reflection is used to assess the IOP, using a direct digital scale.

This outlines only one type of non-contact device, but other variations exist and the reader should refer to individual descriptions (Fig. 4.8).

ACCOMMODATION

The adjustment of the focus of an emmetropic eye from distance vision to near vision requires an increase in dioptric power. The mechanism of accommodation is involved in this change.

Accommodation is brought about in different ways in different animals. Certain fish retract their lenses, while frogs and snakes move their lenses forwards to focus on near objects.

Human accommodation has been studied for centuries and about 150 years ago Helmholtz wrote about the mechanism with such accuracy that his approach is still respected today. He proposed these three elements:

- The ciliary muscle.
- The lens capsule.
- The zonular system.

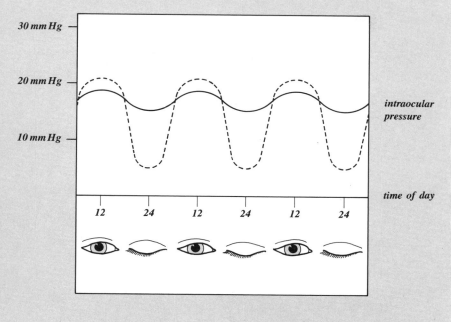

30 mm Hg

20 mm Hg

10 mm Hg

intraocular pressure

time of day

12   24   12   24   12   24

Fig. 4.5 Diurnal variation of IOP. The dotted line shows the variation of aqueous production. (*After Erickson, 1958.*)

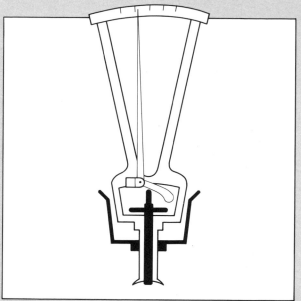

Fig. 4.6 Schiøtz tonometer.

Fig. 4.7 Goldmann tonometer.

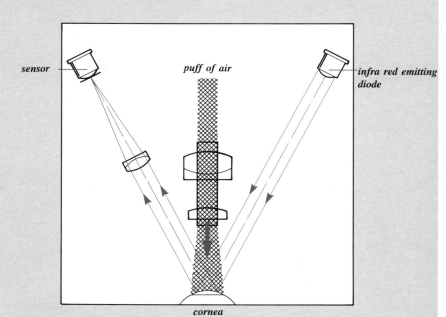

Fig. 4.8 Diagram showing principle of 'non-contact' tonometer.

sensor

puff of air

infra red emitting diode

cornea

The *ciliary muscle* was mentioned earlier, so it suffices to stress here that when this muscle contracts there is a forward and centripetal movement of the annular ciliary body, some 0.5 mm towards the equator of the lens.

The *capsule of the lens* as described above, is an elastic covering around the substance of the lens. This elasticity exerts an internal pressure which tends to change the form of the anterior lens surface, decreasing its central radius of curvature and increasing its dioptric power. Such an increase is opposed by the centrifugal tension of the zonular fibres. The alteration of the front surface of the lens is accompanied by a forward movement of about 0.25 mm, while its radius approximates more to that of the back of the lens. Most authorities accept that the central part of the anterior lens surface becomes more steeply curved than its periphery.

The *zonular fibres* supporting the lens extend from the ciliary body to the equatorial region of the lens. These collagenous fibres are about 10 nm in diameter and are arranged in an annulus forming at the back the boundary between the vitreous and the posterior chamber. The precise arrangement of the fibres is controversial and there are individual variations. Tradition suggests that there are four different types (Fig. 4.9):

- *The orbiculo-posterior capsular fibres* are at the back, arising from the ora serrata region and moving forwards to the posterior equator of the lens.
- *The orbiculo-anterior capsular fibres* originate from in front of the ora serrata and travel anteriorly to their attachment just in front of the equator.
- *Cilio-equatorial fibres* are hardly present in childhood. They emerge from spaces between the ciliary processes and fasten themselves at the equator.

Rohen and Rentsch (1969) described another arrangement of the zonular system, as shown in Fig. 4.10.

There is elastic tissue in the region of the iris root and near the ora serrata. Such tissue pulls on the zonule, holding it taut, so that the zonular tension itself on the lens equator counteracts capsular elasticity. Thus relaxation of accommodation restores the eye to focus on distant objects.

Contraction of the ciliary muscle, as mentioned above, moves the ciliary body inwards and forwards. This slackens the zonular tension and the effect on the capsule weakens. Consequently, the curvature of the lens increases with its power, effecting accommodation.

The amplitude of accommodation is the extent to which focusing for near objects can be accomplished. This lessens with age. At the age of 10 it is some 14 Dioptres (D), reducing to about 6 D by the age of 40 and usually being less than 1 D by the age of 60.

Various other changes take place in the eye, with accommodation. Convergence of the two eyes takes place, ensuring fusion of the two retinal images and contraction of both the pupils. Miosis restricts light paths through the lens to the central region, improving near vision and the depth of the eye's field.

The triad of accommodation, convergence and miosis is controlled by the

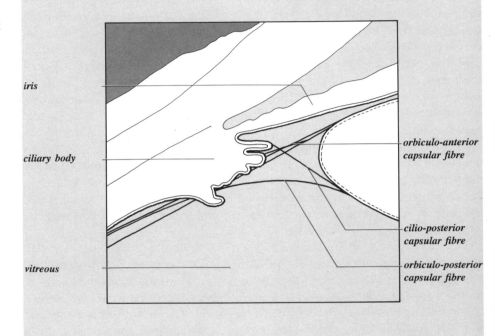

Fig. 4.9 The classical view of the zonular suspensions. Connections between ciliary processes and the equator are omitted.

iris

ciliary body

vitreous

orbiculo-anterior capsular fibre

cilio-posterior capsular fibre

orbiculo-posterior capsular fibre

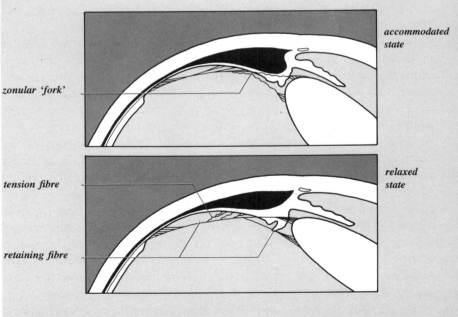

Fig. 4.10 Arrangement of zonular fibres according to Rohen and Rentsch.

zonular 'fork'

tension fibre

retaining fibre

accommodated state

relaxed state

third cranial nerve, impulses being carried along separate paths. Central co-ordination takes place at a higher level in the central nervous system. The interdependence of these three functions is debatable and research continues.

It is known, however, that accommodation and convergence are linked by a common neural control, which usually operates both simultaneously. Diplopia tends to be a stronger stimulus (to convergence) than retinal blur (to accommodation), this being the chief feature which brings about the 'near-response'. Young subjects are thus provided with well focused retinal images of near objects, while convergence-induced accommodation lessens with age.

It appears that miosis is rather less dependent on convergence but more tied to accommodation. If accommodation fails in presbyopia, miosis tends to respond to the stimulus.

Loss of accommodation can be attributed to:

- Changes in the lens substance.
- Altered elasticity of the lens capsule.
- Changes in the ciliary muscle/body.

There are changes in the lens substance, due to the ageing nucleus becoming harder as growth proceeds, at the expense of the cortex. This takes place particularly after the age of 40. These changes and loss of the ageing capsule's elasticity, are recognized as essential causes of presbyopia. However, weakening of the ciliary muscle is considered to be a less likely cause of accommodation loss (Fig. 4.11).

The mechanism of accommodation uses parasympathetic innervation via cranial nerve III, from the Edinger–Westphal nucleus in the mid-brain. It is thought that an 'accommodation centre' exists near or in Brodmann's area 22 in the cerebral cortex, stimulation here producing the near reflex of accommodation, convergence and miosis.

There is some controversy over how accommodation is stimulated. Its link with convergence is mentioned above. In addition, it is thought that probably impulses are retinally initiated. There are several theories: blur of the retinal image is the most likely, whilst interpretation of chromatic aberration is a possibility. Evidently, no single element is responsible for the stimulus, rather a series of visual phenomena.

Recent research has confirmed that in the dark or in a featureless field of view, the eye tends to adopt a 'dark focus' state of accommodation, related to 'night myopia'. This amounts to up to 1.25 D, with individual variations. It is caused by a certain autonomic activity. Positive accommodation (for nearer objects) is regarded as a parasympathetic innervative activity, while 'negative accommodation' (for relaxation of power) is under sympathetic control.

Consequently, accommodation seems to enjoy a delicate balance between the two autonomic systems. Ciliary muscle control by parasympathetic innervation is well accepted but sympathetic involvement is less certain. One theory suggests that while Müller's (circular) muscle has parasympathetic innervation,

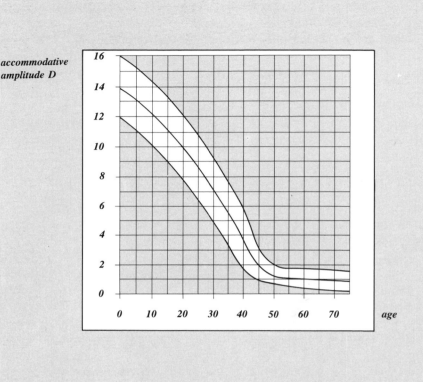

Fig. 4.11 Ocular accommodative amplitude in Dioptres, and age variations.

Brücke's (meridional) fibres are controlled by the sympathetic nerves. If this is so, a suitable autonomic imbalance could explain, for example, how myopia is produced by certain stressful situations.

Even a rapid glance at a near object can produce the 'near reflex', comprising accommodation, convergence of the two eyes and miosis. However, the degree of miosis can depend on lighting conditions.

This near reflex is complicated and details of its pathways are not completely understood. While it is known that it starts at retinal level, its mechanisms are uncertain. Impulses follow the visual path to the striate cortical area of the brain, between the occipital and temporal regions, known as Brodmann's areas 19 and 22. Thence, via the pretectal nucleus, impulses actually reach the Edinger–Westphal nucleus. From the latter III nerve, impulses go to the sphincter muscle of the pupil, to the ciliary muscle and to the medial recti.

Another route for the near reflex impulses has been postulated. This suggests that impulses from the striate cortex reach centres near the frontally-situated Brodmann's area 8 and after that travel to the oculomotor nuclei via the internal capsule. Further research is expected to clarify these reflex paths.

Chapter 5
The Retina

A GENERAL VIEW OF THE RETINA

The retina has several layers, extending over the posterior $\frac{2}{3}$ of the globe. Internally, it is bounded by the vitreous body, while externally it is connected to Bruch's membrane of the choroid. Light which enters the eye is focused on the retinal photoreceptors, stimulating them to produce nerve impulses. These are modified by intermediate retinal cells before the ganglion cells send messages along their axons to the *lateral geniculate body* (or *nucleus*) via the *optic nerve* and the optic tract.

It is necessary for the retina to be in a suitable state to detect light or its absence: it must be able to signal alterations and detect movement. The retina fulfils a double need. One involves detecting light and movement and thereby motion within the visual field. Such functions depend essentially on the *rods*, these photoreceptors being so named on account of the rod-like appearance of their outer segments.

Other important retinal functions include colour vision and good form vision, the latter being associated with the central visual field; the *cones* are responsible for these two functions. Over most of the retina the cones have relatively 'conical' outer segments; hence their name. The retina looks like a thin, transparent membrane, often reddish on account of visual purple (rhodopsin). It bleaches on exposure to light and in the dead eye, after an hour or so, it changes to a grey opaque layer.

Retinal thickness differs between regions. Near the optic disc it is about 0.56 mm, changing to 0.1 mm at the ora serrata. It is thinnest at the *fovea centralis*, where it measures about 0.09 mm. But around this area, in the region of the *macula* (lutea), it is more like 0.35 mm.

The retina comprises three main areas:

- The pars optica.
- The pars ciliaris.
- The pars iridica.

The last two areas are considered to be 'retinal' because of their embryonic origins. The pigment epithelium of the retina covers the ciliary body as its external pigment epithelial layer, the inner cell layer being a continuation of the nervous layers of the retina. Both layers extend over the back surface of the iris, where each is pigmented.

The 'pars optica' has two main layers:

- Pigment epithelium.
- Nervous tissues.

These strata abut each other, the pigment epithelium being attached to Bruch's membrane and the nervous tissues firmly attached at the optic disc and at the ora serrata. Elsewhere, the attachment between the neural layers and the pigment epithelium is very weak, particularly behind the ora serrata.

The *fundus oculi*, the internal background of the eye, seen ophthalmoscopically, has an orange–red colour derived from the choroidal blood vessels and the retinal pigment epithelium. Variations in pigmentation (retinal and choroidal) give rise to many observed alternative appearances; fair subjects reveal much lighter fundi while dark races have characteristically darker, somewhat greyish, fundi. When there is a lack of pigment, white scleral tissue tends to be exposed. In albinos, who may be almost or completely devoid of pigment, one sees the choroidal vessels through the retina.

The optic nerve leaves the eye at the optic disc or *papilla*, which lies about 3 mm medially to and slightly above the posterior pole. The disc appears circular or slightly oval, having a diameter of between 1.5 and 1.9 mm. Centrally, the disc has a depression or excavation called 'physiological cupping', penetrated by the central retinal artery and vein. This cupping appears in different forms and depths: deeper ones usually expose the lamina cribrosa, whitish–grey strands of connective tissue fibres.

The disc is a much lighter pink than the surrounding retina. It is often found that the retinal and/or choroidal pigment does not reach up to the rim of the disc, when a whitish 'scleral arc' (or even ring) can be seen, typically on the temporal side. Pigment rings or arcs may also be seen, formed by local intrusion of retinal pigment epithelium. Because the optic disc is devoid of photoreceptors, its projection into space produces the *blind spot*.

Rather temporal to, and below the posterior pole, the *fovea centralis* is about 1 to 2 mm in diameter. At this point, retinal thinning produces a shallow depression in the surface, where the nerve elements are heaped around, forming *Henle's layer*, the sides sloping as the 'clivus'.

Within the fovea is a central area called the *foveola*, about 0.35 mm in diameter. This region only contains cones.

Around the fovea centralis, with a diameter approximating 5.5 mm, is the *macula lutea* or 'yellow spot', called this because yellowish (xanthophyll) pigment is found in the region. Here, greater density of the underlying pigment epithelium and the choriocapillaris give a darker colour, compared to the surrounding fundus.

The *ora serrata* is a notched line which separates the neural part of the retinal periphery from the ciliary body; it lies some 8.5 mm behind the limbus and approximately 6 mm in front of the equator, its nasal part being about 1 mm nearer to the limbus than the temporal aspect.

Retinal blood vessels form a characteristic pattern on the fundus, arteries

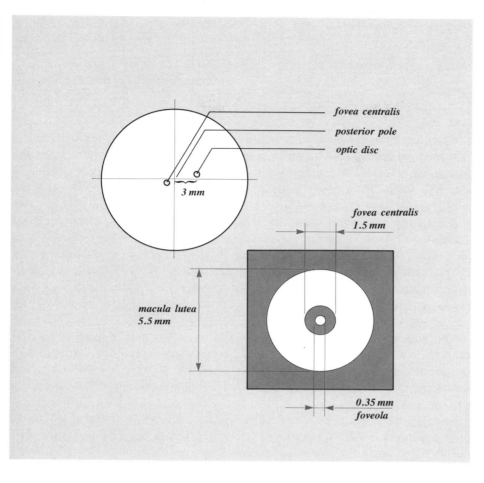

Fig. 5.1 Top: Diagram of fundus features, in the right eye. *Below*: Approximate dimensions of macular region. (*After Wolff.*)

being thinner and of a lighter red than veins. Normally, there are no anastomoses. The fovea is free of obstruction from blood vessels (see Fig. 5.1 and Plate 6).

RETINAL CELLS AND TISSUES

There are four obvious subdivisions in the retina, although careful microscopic viewing with light and dark fields distinguishes ten (Fig. 5.2).

A. The pigment epithelial layer

B. The photoreceptor layer

1. Pigment epithelium.
2. Photoreceptors.
3. External limiting membrane.
4. Outer nuclear or granular layer.
5. Outer plexiform or molecular (synapse) layer.

C. The intermediate cell layer
      6. Inner nuclear or granular layer.
      7. Inner plexiform or molecular layer.

D. The ganglion cell layer
      8. Ganglion cell layer proper.
      9. Nerve fibre layer (ganglion cell axons).
     10. Internal limiting membrane.

The *pigment epithelium* forms a single stratum of epithelial cells, attached to Bruch's membrane, part of which comprises the basement membrane for the hexagonal cells. There are about 5 million in each eye. Somewhat variable in size and form, the cells become most cubical near the fovea, where their diameters and heights are about 14 μm. They are flatter at the retinal periphery, so that near the ora serrata one finds large cells of up to 60 μm in diameter and about 10 μm thick. Pigmented projections intrude between the adjacent rods and cones, protecting the receptors from excessive light, as well as preventing light straying from one photoreceptor to another. Both the cells and their extensions contain melanin pigment but another variety has been seen with fuscin or lipofuscin, likely to be products of phagocytosis of photoreceptor breakdown products.

The pigment cells do not demonstrate mitosis, having the usual organelles found in epithelial cells. Folds in Bruch's membrane enclose the extremities of these cells, where the many mitochondria indicate high metabolic activity and much membrane transport activity. Dead cells have their places occupied by their neighbours.

Each pigment epithelium cell is in contact with an average of up to 45 photoreceptors, possibly a mixture of rods and cones, or just one variety. For example, at the fovea this would be cones alone.

The pigment epithelium has several functions, including absorption of light and removal of heat: it restricts stray light in the retina and protects the receptors from the undesirable effects of light. In addition, the cells give some support to the photoreceptors, which they provide with nourishment and oxygen. They also act as reservoirs of useful substances, among which is vitamin A. They act upon breakdown products of photoreceptors, providing further slow disintegration, this being part of their phagocytotic activity.

Cells within this layer are closely abutted, being attached to each other's cell membrane. Thus they form a barrier against liquids and substances moving between the choroid and the nervous tissues of the retina, the 'blood–retina' barrier. No anatomical connection exists between the pigment epithelium and the receptors and this leads to the ease with which the two layers can be 'detached' in some pathological situations (Fig. 5.3).

The *photoreceptors* are sensory cells which transform light into electrical energy by chemical processes. Impulses then travel along the visual paths. The receptors have a palisade arrangement, being held in position by the external limiting membrane. They are orientated not towards the centre of the eye but pointing at its exit pupil. The distinctive names describe the shapes of the outer

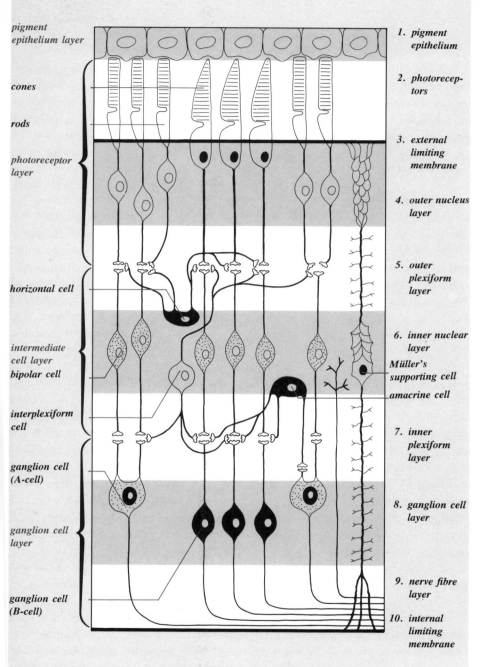

pigment
epithelium layer

cones

rods

photoreceptor
layer

horizontal cell

intermediate
cell layer
bipolar cell

interplexiform
cell

ganglion cell
(A-cell)

ganglion cell
layer

ganglion cell
(B-cell)

1. pigment
   epithelium

2. photorecep-
   tors

3. external
   limiting
   membrane

4. outer nucleus
   layer

5. outer
   plexiform
   layer

6. inner nuclear
   layer
   Müller's
   supporting cell
   amacrine cell

7. inner
   plexiform
   layer

8. ganglion cell
   layer

9. nerve fibre
   layer

10. internal
    limiting
    membrane

Fig. 5.2 Retinal cells
and tissues.

segments, although it is now known that the cones in particular have different forms according to their retinal positions.

The *rods* are long, slender cells about 2 μm thick and between 40 and 60 μm long. Their outer and inner segments differ. Threadlike, hair-type, structures join the two segments. The outer segment is the specially photosensitive part of each cell, containing the photopigment rhodopsin and consisting of 600 to 1000 loosely stacked disc units or lamellae within a cell membrane. Such discs are formed at a rate of one to five an hour at the base of the outer segment, so that the segment builds itself up. Now and then there is a sloughing of groups of about 30 lamellae from the top of the segment. This takes place in the morning or in the light after long periods in the dark. So the lamellae of a rod can be renewed completely over one or two weeks, to undergo phagocytosis by the pigment epithelium.

The molecules of rhodopsin are contained within the membranes of the lamellae. The inner segments of the rods are somewhat thicker than their outer segments. They contain organelles for producing energy and the build up of protein. There is a thin connection between the inner segment, through the external limiting membrane, and the nucleus of the cell (in the outer nuclear layer) through which an axon reaches a spherical ending which itself synapses with dendrites from bipolar cells at the outer plexiform layer.

Rods are very sensitive to light, so they are responsible for vision in very poor lighting conditions (night vision). The sensation which all rods initiate is the same for all wavelengths of light, so they produce colourless vision. It is also true that several rods connect with one bipolar cell, producing considerable convergence of impulses from rods (Fig. 5.4).

Cones are rather shorter but in common with rods have outer and inner segments, joined by cilia. The inner segment resembles that of a rod while the outer segment is thicker and nearly conical, hence the name. At the fovea centralis, cones are more cylindrical, much like rods. Lamellae in the outer segment are attached to the cell membrane and do not peel off as in the rods. There is a similar renewal process but over a longer period of time, such as nine months to one year.

Nuclei of cones lie in their inner segments, together with the organelles. Cone photopigments are of three sorts, each having a distinctive spectral sensitivity. But the chemistry of these pigments resembles that found in rods. The term 'iodopsin' is used for cone pigment and it is located in the lamellae of the outer segment.

Cones can be considered in three categories, according to their photopigments, which differ in their responses to regions of the spectrum. One type is most sensitive to short wavelength (blue), another reacts most to green, while another chiefly responds to red. Yet because cones are not sensitive to small amounts of light, colours are not seen during night vision.

We have already noted several related photopigments. These coloured substances break down in the light and regenerate in the dark. There is good reason to believe that the bleaching process initiates nerve impulses from which

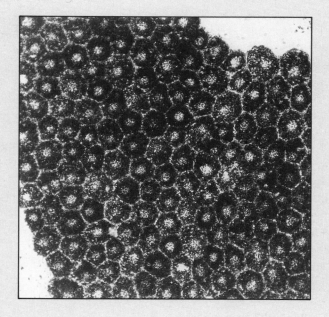

Fig. 5.3   Top: Sketch of retinal pigment epithelium with profile of a single cell. *Bottom:* Sheep pigment epithelium. (*Microphoto: T. Saude.*)

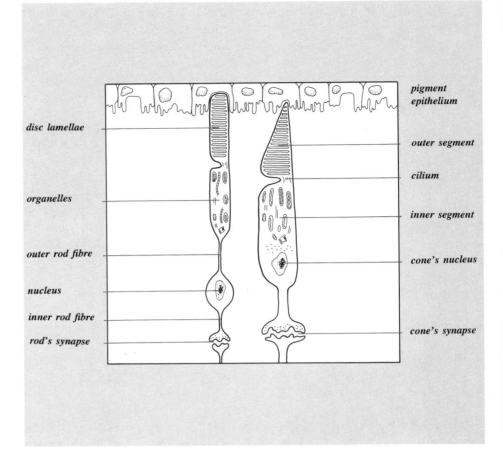

Fig. 5.4 Photoreceptors.

disc lamellae

organelles

outer rod fibre

nucleus

inner rod fibre

rod's synapse

pigment epithelium

outer segment

cilium

inner segment

cone's nucleus

cone's synapse

the brain derives visual information. Cones and rods both connect with the bipolar cells. The cone fibres are substantial and make more direct synapses, while the thinner rod fibres are divided by the rod nuclei.

Fewer cones tend to be connected to a single bipolar cell, making their 'convergence' usually less than that associated with rods. Thus cones provide more specifically localized information, compared to rods, and are responsible for form vision and colour discrimination.

The distribution of cones and rods in different parts of the retina is most important. There are between 110 to 125 million rods and about 6.5 million cones. In the central fovea there are about 147 000 cones per mm^2, this density rapidly decreasing, so that about 0.2 mm away from the foveola it is halved. Ten millimetres from the fovea, the density is some 4000 per mm^2. There are no rods within the small central foveal zone, but 5 to 6 mm away from the fovea there is the maximum concentration of rods, some 160 000 per mm^2. At the ora serrata there is a much decreased number of receptors.

The *outer limiting membrane* is a condensation of cytoplasm, an outcrop of Müller's connective tissue fibres rather than a real membrane. It forms a supporting network around the photoreceptors, holding them in position. In addition, it forms a physiological barrier which limits the flow of liquid between the receptors' outer segments and the other parts of the retina.

The *outer nuclear layer* is formed by the rounded nuclei of the photoreceptors. Cone nuclei are arranged just below the limiting membrane, while rod nuclei are further down and less regularly distributed.

The *outer plexiform layer* is made up of photoreceptor axons and the synapses they form with bipolar cell dendrites. In addition, there are connections between horizontal cells and the photoreceptor synapses. At the foveal region, axons from the receptors move to the side, keeping away from the central fovea and forming Henle's fibre layer. On the basis that the synapses between the photoreceptors and the bipolars are just as dense, there is no indication that some direct connections exist between photoreceptors.

The *inner nuclear layer* contains cell bodies of the following:

- The bipolar cells.
- The horizontal cells.
- The amacrine cells.
- The interplexiform cells.
- Müller's connective fibres.

Bipolar cells have a round nucleus and with their dendrites and axons, form connections between the photoreceptors and the ganglion cells. The synapses are in the outer and inner plexiform layers. Three types of bipolars are distinguished, by means of their synapses with receptors.

Rod bipolars connect with up to 50 rods and as many as four ganglion cells. *Midget or dwarf bipolars* just join with one cone and with one ganglion cell, carrying impulses from the central fovea.

Diffuse bipolars are thus described as they have widespread synaptic connections with several cones (up to seven) and with many ganglion cells. These bipolar cells can operate with both excitatory and inhibitory actions on the impulses from photoreceptors. One type can be hyperpolarizing, another can be depolarizing in connection with the results of the actions of transmitter substances to the photoreceptors.

Horizontal cells send out extended projections horizontally in the retina. They have synapses with photoreceptors as well as with bipolars. Near the fovea it is accepted that three to four horizontal cells may connect with 7 to 12 cones. More peripherally in the retina, the number of cones connected can rise to 30 or 40 per horizontal cell. The horizontal cells can also be connected to each other. Cones have synaptic junctions in the form of dendrites, but rods end in terminal spherules.

It is by no means clear what the functions of horizontal cells are. Probably they act as some intermediate mechanism for impulses from the receptors, through inhibitory or excitatory influences at the level of the synapses with the bipolars.

Amacrine cells are found nearest to the inner plexiform layer, receiving impulses from peripheral bipolars and making synapses with the dendrites of ganglion cells. There are also neural ramifications of amacrines making direct synapses with the bodies of ganglion cells. Little is known of the functions of these cells, also, but research indicates that they have some effect on transmission, or influence impulses coming from the retinal periphery towards the central regions of the retina.

Interplexiform cells. Retinal neural features are so complex that various possibilities exist for interconnections. Many of the processes which permit vision must originate within this network. Evidently some cells operate a 'feed−back' system which modifies the messages from the photoreceptors. Such cells have been called 'interplexiform', making connections not only with the photoreceptor synapses, but also with ganglion cells.

Müller's supporting fibres make up the retinal connective tissue, reaching throughout the entire retina. These ramifications extend into the spaces between the neural elements and also form the external and internal limiting membranes. The Müller type connective fibres also support the network of nerves, producing corresponding astrocytes within the neural tissues. These cells can produce glycogen and probably assist the metabolism of the nerve cells.

The *inner plexiform layer* involves synapses where axons from the bipolar cells connect to dendrites from the ganglion cells. Projections from the amacrine cells also synapse with the ganglion cells in the region.

The *ganglion cell layer* is formed by the bodies of these cells. It is about 10 cells deep near the macula, reducing to single cell thickness peripherally. Four types of cell are found, distinguished by their connections with the bipolars: some have hundreds of such links, while in the region of the fovea, there may be the same number of paths reaching ganglion cells as there are bipolar cells.

It is of interest that photoreceptors are 125 to 130 million in number, compared with just one million ganglion cells. So there is considerable convergence of impulses from the retinal receptors.

Ganglion cells vary in size, being relatively diminutive centrally and larger at the retinal periphery, with a small proportion having intermediate size. *A-cells* (Magno cells) have a big cell body with many dendrites and consequently a large 'receptor field'. Their axons are thick and carry rapid impulses. It appears that A-cells are sensitive to contrasts, helping to interpret light intensities and assisting movement perception. *B-cells* (Parvo-cells) possess smaller bodies, fewer dendrites and thinner axons. As the most numerous, they react most to narrow wave−band light, so they are concerned with colour vision. They have small receptor fields and are therefore involved when high visual acuity is required.

There is a third group of retinal ganglion cells, which involves only some

10% of the total. They are small, with thin axons which leave the optic tract to end in the mid-brain.

The *nerve fibre layer*. In this lie the ganglion cells' axons, carrying nervous impulses via the optic nerve to the lateral geniculate nucleus. The fibres are enveloped by extensions of Müller's fibres and astrocytes. Near the exit of the optic nerve (the disc) the layer is 20–30 μm thick and it is thinner peripherally. Fibres from the nasal part of the retina pass directly to the disc, as do those from the macula (the papillo-macular bundle). Fibres from the temporal retina arch around the macula, forming a horizontal linear separation (or 'raphe') between the macula and the temporal periphery. Fibres from positions above this line run above the macula and vice versa. Such fibres impart a slightly grey, striped appearance to the retina under certain conditions. The axons are normally unmyelinated until they have passed through the lamina cribrosa, but sometimes myelinated (opaque) fibres are found near the disc. Branches of the central retinal artery and the central vein run in the nerve fibre layer (Fig. 5.5).

The *internal limiting membrane* is 1 or 2 μm thick and covers the inner surface

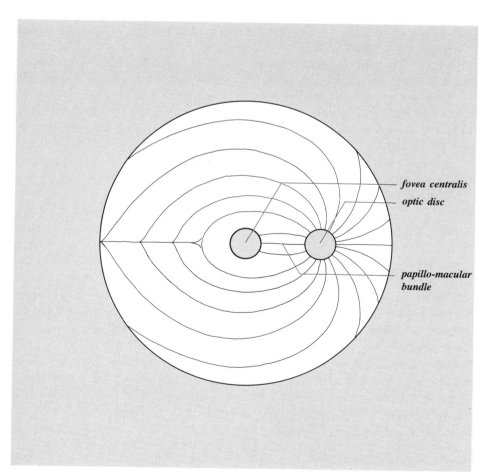

Fig. 5.5 Distribution of retinal nerve fibres.

fovea centralis

optic disc

papillo-macular bundle

of the retina, forming its boundary with the vitreous. It is formed by offshoots of Müller's supporting fibres.

All the retinal layers cease at the optic disc, apart from the nerve fibre layer. The internal limiting membrane is replaced by connective tissue which tends to fill the physiological 'optic cup' (the central meniscus of Kuhnt). At the fovea the 'clivus' is produced as most retinal layers sweep aside. Here, at the fovea, the layers are:

- Pigment epithelium.
- Receptors.
- External limiting membrane.
- Müller's supporting fibres.
- Internal limiting membrane.

Initially, going towards the periphery of the fovea, there are bipolar cells and ganglion cells, which increase in number to the limits of the macular region. The nerve fibre layer of the retina ceases at the ora serrata and here in the retinal periphery the layers are thinner and less regularly arranged, while the glial tissue proliferates. There are no photoreceptors in a zone 1 or 2 mm behind the ora serrata.

Cysts and vacuoles are often present near the ora serrata, mostly in the aged, but at times in young people, appearing most frequently on the temporal side. Usually these cysts are located in the outer plexiform layer, spreading to regions between the two limiting membranes. They are likely to result from reduced metabolism. Such cysts can burst, when retinal detachment may take place.

RETINAL GLIAL CELLS

In addition to the fibres of Müller already considered, the retina has other neuroglia.

Astrocytes, found in the ganglion cell layer and nerve fibre layer, have short and long projections extending in all directions. Some attach themselves to capillaries, while others lie against the outer walls of nerve cells to gain footholds which assist the supporting and protective functions of the astrocytes. These glial cells promote movement of substances from and to the vascular system, hence they are important for local nourishment.

Microglia are small connective cells in many forms. Few are present in healthy tissues, but they proliferate for phagocytosis when there is damage.

RETINAL BLOOD VESSELS

Most of the retinal blood supply comes from the *central retinal artery*. The outer layers, the pigment epithelium, the photoreceptors and the outer nuclear layer are avascular. This applies to some extent to the outer plexiform layer, which derives nutrients and oxygen from the choriocapillaris in the choroid, through Bruch's membrane and the pigment epithelium. The same is true for the fovea, which is completely avascular.

The *central retinal artery*, a slender artery about 0.28 mm in diameter, is a branch of the ophthalmic artery. It enters the optic nerve about 10 to 15 mm behind the eye, then advances in the middle of the nerve to emerge from the optic disc with its accompanying vein, the latter being on the temporal side. While it lies within the optic nerve, the artery sends out tiny branches to gain nourishment for the nerve.

At the optic disc, the main retinal vessels divide into superior and inferior branches, which themselves split into nasal and temporal branches just outside the disc margin. Each of these four branches supplies its own retinal quadrant. There are no anastomoses. Retinal blood vessels lie in the nerve fibre layer near the internal limiting membrane.

Arteries send out capillary networks to two levels of the retina: the nerve fibre layer surface and the region between the inner nuclear and outer plexiform layers. The capillary network is densest near the macula, is absent at the fovea and is also lacking in a small zone 1 to 2 mm to the rear of the ora serrata. The retinal capillaries, which are more densely crowded than elsewhere in the body, make up the actual blood−retina barrier.

Retinal veins tend to accompany their respective arteries some distance away and there are several crossings. Veins are the thicker and darker vessels, usually lying nearer to the vitreous.

The *central retinal vein* exits at the disc, with the central retinal artery to its medial side. It follows the optic nerve backwards in a course which matches that of the artery. Leaving the nerve somewhat further back than the artery, the central retinal vein empties into the *superior ophthalmic vein* or, by a more direct route, straight into the *cavernous sinus*. The *circle of Zinn* (or of Haller and Zinn), which is the circle of arterial points of entry around the optic nerve, is formed by the short posterior ciliary arteries as they penetrate the sclera. Branches leave these vessels to supply the choroid, the optic nerve, the disc and the nearby retina. Some of these arteries anastomose with the central retinal artery in the disc region. One branch (as a 'cilioretinal artery') may reach towards the macula across the fundus, providing larger or smaller subsidiaries to the retina, between the disc and the macula. This is found in about 20% of eyes. If the central retinal artery happens to be occluded, a cilioretinal artery can maintain function in its immediate area.

RETINAL METABOLISM

Nourishment and oxygen are required by the retina and supplied to its tissues from the blood stream. It is well known that the retina ceases to function a few minutes after its blood supply is stopped. This shows how essential are the vegetative processes taking place in the retinal cells if vision is to operate.

Glucose, lipids, amino acids and other provisions, such as vitamins and minerals, are all needed by the retina. An adequate oxygen supply is essential. These items come from the capillaries in the choroid and via the central retinal artery and also, to a small extent, through the circle of Zinn and (probably in trifling amounts) from the vitreous. Carbonic acid and other katabolites return via such routes. Carbohydrates are essential for the production of energy and the retina is sensitive to any fall in sugar concentration within its tissues. It can tolerate a fall in concentration as low as 30 mg/100 ml without any disturbance of activity, but if the concentration becomes any lower, vision suffers. Deprivation of glucose for 8 to 10 minutes results in irreversible cellular damage. Since carbohydrates and oxygen have a close relationship, a similar situation is very likely to occur with a shortage of oxygen.

The production of energy in the retina proceeds in the same way as in other tissues. The most important method of carbohydrate break-down is via *glycolysis* (the Embden−Meyerhof process) to pyruvate and lactate, after that, via the Krebs cycle, to carbonic acid and water.

Glycogen is found stored in the retina, essentially in the glial cells such as Müller's fibres. Such a store serves as a buffer against great changes in the concentration of glucose in the tissues.

Lipids make up an insignificant source of energy for the retina. Some intermediate building blocks are needed in the process of anabolism. Amino acids are also essential for the cells. Above all, proteins are needed for enzymes and for anabolism and katabolism. In the elderly, retinal metabolic processes wane. In addition, external influences, such as ionizing radiation, may lower metabolism.

THE VISUAL PROCESSES IN THE RETINA

THE VISUAL PROCESSES IN THE RETINA

The retina is able to transform light energy into electrical energy which is sent along the visual paths to the brain, where it provides the visual impressions. This transformation requires retinal metabolic activity. So a good supply of nourishment, oxygen and vitamins is needed, in order to support the visual processes. Then the break-down products produced by the cells must be removed.

Retinal photoreceptors are sensitive to wavelengths from about 380 nm to 750 nm within the electromagnetic spectrum. The media of the eye transmit radiation between 300 nm and 1200 nm in wavelength. As age increases, sensitivity decreases, particularly in the shorter wavelength region of the visual spectrum. This is caused primarily by steadily increasing absorption by the crystalline lens, particularly at the blue end of the spectrum.

Light-adapted eyes have a maximum sensitivity for wavelengths of about 550 nm, the response lessening for shorter or longer wavelengths. The classical

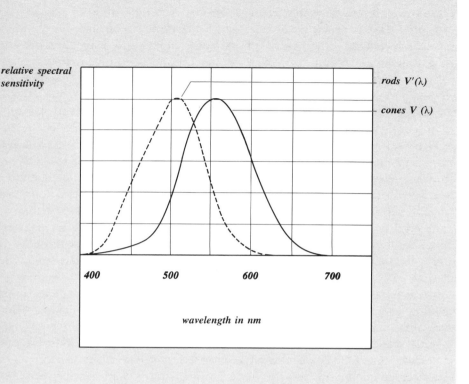

relative spectral
sensitivity

rods $V'(\lambda)$

cones $V(\lambda)$

400   500   600   700

wavelength in nm

Fig. 5.6 Retinal sensitivity across the spectrum.

curve showing this (Fig. 5.6) is called the *photopic relative luminous efficiency curve*.

In the dark-adapted state, visual sensitivity is greatest at about 507 nm and the *scotopic relative luminous efficiency curve* shows the reduction of response on either side of this peak. In the dark-adapted state, the eye does not discriminate colours, seeing different parts of the spectrum in terms of greys. As daylight wanes from photopic towards scotopic levels, the highest retinal sensitivity is progressively reduced from 550 nm to shorter wavelengths. Thus in poor light one sees the blue part of the spectrum better than the red part. The practical manifestation of this is called the *Purkinje phenomenon*. As a result of this alteration of relative sensitivity, the ocular refractive power tends to be more myopic, a situation known as '*twilight myopia*'.

However, there are several alternative theories which explain aspects of twilight (or 'night') myopia, for example spherical aberration. Since dilatation of the pupil (mydriasis) allows more peripheral rays of light to contribute to the total visual impression and since such rays are more strongly deviated, they produce an image in front of the retina. Another possible explanation for twilight myopia is an increase in accommodation with lower light levels, which produces a tendency to myopia. Twilight myopia may result from a combination of these factors.

Photochemical processes

It has long been known that chemical processes form the basis of retinal function which involves the formation and transformation of photopigments. Rhodopsin, or 'visual purple', was the first photopigment to be isolated and is contained within the rods. Rhodopsin is a derivative of carotene called *retinene*, which is attached to a large protein (opsin) and is closely related to vitamin A.

Like most organic compounds, retinene has a three-dimensional structure with a nucleus composed of carbon atoms. These atoms are bound together by single or double 'bindings', formed by one electron from an atom interacting with an electron from a neighbouring atom. It appears that a carbon atom can form two types of such pairs of atoms. One strong connection is called a 'sigma binding' and a weak one is called a 'pi binding'. The single binding is the sigma type whilst double bindings can exist as either the sigma or pi types. Many organic connections are able to alter their structures by rotating part of a molecule around an axis between the carbon atoms. The molecule normally is in a minimal energy state; in the case of retinene this is what is called the 'all-trans' (straight) form (Figs 5.7 and 5.8).

When a photon (of light) is absorbed, the sigma binding between carbon atoms number 11 and 12 breaks and the two parts of the molecule can rotate through 90° over the remaining sigma binding. The pi binding changes with a fresh binding action, which will produce an all-cis (bent) form. In the process the molecule of retinene straightens out and becomes detached from the opsin molecule.

The starting point for the visual process, however, is the electrical impulse which arises when the pi binding breaks and the pair of electrons settle to a temporary position. The simplest situation will be each electron giving to the other half of itself: quantum physics enabling an exchange of halves to be possible. If the two molecules are not symmetrical, displacement of the paired electron will produce a sudden change of double momentum, in about 10 pico seconds. This produces around the molecule a vigorous electrical impulse which escapes through the cell membrane as a nerve impulse.

Rhodopsin is built up and broken down within its own cycle, in which both light and dark play a role. Transitional states develop in several forms, with the possibility of many reactions producing regeneration. Some such reactions are reversible, but others are irreversible, some are rapid and some are slow.

Colour perception involves cone responses, but the differences between the respective retinal cones are slight. This has presented difficulties for the chemical

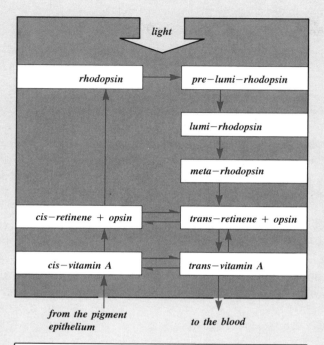

light

| rhodopsin | → | pre−lumi−rhodopsin |

lumi−rhodopsin

meta−rhodopsin

cis−retinene + opsin ← trans−retinene + opsin

cis−vitamin A → trans−vitamin A

from the pigment epithelium

to the blood

Fig. 5.8 Diagram showing how the contorted cis-form from C-atom number 11 is straightened up just at the splitting movement location.

CH3   CH3
C   H   C   H
H2C   C   C   C   C   CH
H2C   C—CH3   H   H
C   CH2   CH3   CH
H2   C
HC   = O

Cis-retinene

CH3   CH3   CH3
C   H   C   H   C   H
H2C   C   C   C   C   C   C   C=O
H2C   C—CH3   H   H   H   H
C   CH2
H2

All-trans-retinene

study of their photochemical processes. Animal studies, however, have revealed how cones also contain pigments related to opsin, with active groups of molecules reminiscent of retinene. It is established that three types of cones exist, each having a special spectral sensitivity according to their respective pigment contents. Their peaks of absorption lie in blue, greenish and red parts of the spectrum.

The processes of adaptation and after images

Changes in light intensity make it necessary for the retinal functions to effect changes in response, or *adaptation*. Assuming that the eye is adapted to a particular level of illumination, which must have been established with the bleaching of rhodopsin, it follows that the relative abundance of rhodopsin at its correct level in the rods, must depend on the light level. Adaptation is also related to the neural elements of the retina. During adaptation to darkness, the eye has great sensitivity to even small light stimuli.

About 60% of the dark adaptation process takes place during the initial five minutes after lights have been extinguished. Complete adaptation takes longer, sometimes up to 30 or 40 minutes. The speed at which this takes place depends on many factors, such as the colour of the light stimulus used for measurement of thresholds, or the intensity and the type of the pre-exposure light. The extent of adaptation also varies according to the retinal area used and its physiological state.

Light adaptation is essentially a faster process, which actually makes it difficult to measure. It partly involves photochemical processes, like dark adaptation, but it has neural aspects. It is over in seconds and normally is virtually complete within a minute.

Phenomena known as *after-images* are also chiefly caused by chemical and neural retinal activities. These after-images are typically experienced as a series of changing visual impressions in a relatively short time following a light stimulus. Chiefly the result of delayed chemical changes, they involve fluctuations in the state of the visual paths and can take the form of 'complementary' (or opposite) colour sensations.

There are two main types of after-image. Hering's after-images are positive and are of short duration, with the same colour appearance as the original light stimulus. There follows a series of possible percepts, some showing different pictures and some similar appearances. Films and TV pictures often show such effects.

Negative after-images (Purkinje's type) develop with colours complementary to those of the initial light. Such complementary after-images probably originate in processes in which photopigments have been bleached or broken down. Hence the tendency for opposite colour percepts to be favoured. Thus red is turned into green and blue becomes yellow as an after-image, etc. Such complementary colours give some credence to the existence of different specialised pigments in the cones. Thus bleaching of a certain pigment should produce one colour sensation, while the process of building it up again would incline to a complementary colour sensation. Much clarification of related neurophysiology is required before this subject can be extended.

Chapter 6
The Visual Paths

Impulses from the retina reach the visual centres in the cortex of the brain through the visual pathways. Some retinal fibres also end in the mid brain. The different parts, in topographical order, are as follows:

- The optic nerve.
- The optic chiasma, where many fibres cross over.
- The optic tract.
- The lateral geniculate nucleus, or body.
- The optic radiations.
- The striate area of the cortex, the highest visual centres.

All the visual paths, including the retina, form part of the central nervous system, having been developed in the embryo from the anterior part of the brain. The visual paths contain the same types of glial cells as are found in the brain and are enveloped by the meningeal coverings, the pia mater, the arachnoidal sheath and the dura mater (Fig. 6.1).

THE OPTIC NERVE

THE OPTIC NERVE

This nerve is comprised of axons from the retinal ganglion cells, which leave at the optic disc and then together form the nerve itself. Within the retina, the nerve fibres are normally unmyelinated, taking up their insulating sheaths after passing through the sclera. There are about one million nerve fibres in the optic nerve and it is some 40 to 55 mm in length, from the papilla to the *optic chiasma*.

Most of the fibres in this nerve are afferent visual fibres but there are also some afferent pupillomotor fibres and some efferent fibres. Little is known of the function of the latter.

The *intra-bulbar* part of the nerve is approximately 0.7 to 1.0 mm long, consisting of the 'papilla' and the neural pathway through the sclera. The papilla or disc lies about 3 mm nasally from the fovea centralis. It is round, or somewhat vertically oval, with a diameter of some 1.5 mm. Lying in the same plane as the rest of the retina, it contains near its centre a small area into which the central retinal blood vessels penetrate. The disc is lighter in colour than most other parts of the retina and because it lacks photoreceptors, its projection into the visual field is the *blind spot*. Normally it is filled with ganglion cells' axons.

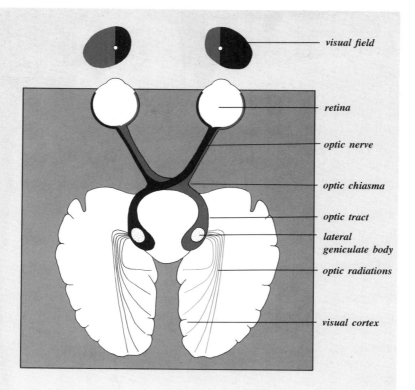

visual field

retina

optic nerve

optic chiasma

optic tract

lateral
geniculate body

optic radiations

visual cortex

Fig. 6.1 The locations
of nerve fibres in the
visual paths, relative to
the retinal projections
onto the visual fields.

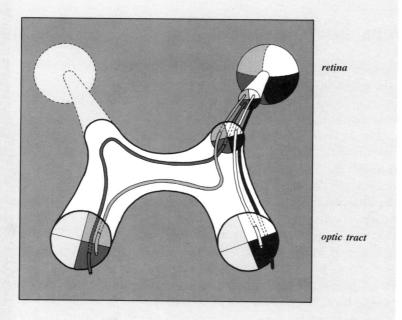

retina

optic tract

Fig. 6.2 The optic
chiasma with the tracks
taken by nerve fibres
from the right eye.

Fibres from the macula region enter the disc laterally, but all other fibres from the temporal retina arrive by arching, either above or below the 'papillo-macular' fibres. Fibres from the nasal retina reach the disc from the medial aspect. Macular area fibres move into the more central parts of the optic nerve, to its intraorbital route, while peripheral retinal fibres take up outer positions in the nerve. It is when the fibres have traversed the *lamina cribrosa* that they are insulated with glial tissue. Thus the nerve increases in thickness from about 1.5 mm at the disc to some 3 mm as it leaves the sclera.

The *intraorbital part* of the nerve extends from its exit from the sclera to the optic canal, being about 25 to 30 mm long and forming an S curve. Since the distance from the globe to the optic canal is only about 18 mm, the 'slack' of between 7 and 10 mm permits ocular rotation.

The *central retinal artery* enters the nerve from below, 10 to 15 mm behind the eye and the *central retinal vein* leaves the nerve rather further back. The nerve is covered here by the three meningeal layers.

The portion of the nerve passing through the *optic canal* is 6 to 7 mm in length and here the dural sheath attaches it firmly to the periosteum. The ophthalmic artery lies underneath the nerve on its way through the canal.

The *intracranial* part of the nerve stretches between 10 and 12 mm from where it leaves the canal to the optic chiasma. Here the nerve loses the outer meninges, being clad only by pia mater and is in company with many large blood vessels. Above the nerve there is the anterior cerebral artery, laterally is the internal carotid and below is the ophthalmic artery.

THE OPTIC
CHIASMA

THE OPTIC CHIASMA

Here there is a crossing of some fibres from the two optic nerves. The chiasma has a transverse diameter of about 12 mm and is some 8 mm in length. It is covered by pia mater and bordered by important structures which will be mentioned briefly.

Anterior to the crossing lies the *anterior cerebral artery* and the *anterior communicating artery*. Behind we see the *tuber cinereum* under which lies the *infundibulum*. The third ventricle lies rostrally. When the *internal carotid artery* has left the *cavernous sinus*, it takes up position lateral to the chiasma. Below the chiasma lie the *diaphragma sellae* which is over the *sella turcica* and the *hypophysis* (or pituitary body). In some people, when the intra cranial part of the nerve is short, the chiasma is situated rather more forward at the *sulcus opticum* at the sphenoidal bone.

Fibres in the optic nerve and the central visual paths are located relative to retinal areas. Fibres from different segments of the retina maintain their distinctive situations in the nerve. Macular fibres lie initially in the lateral part, afterwards moving over more centrally. A vertical line through the fovea can be considered to separate the retina into nasal and temporal halves: nasal retinal fibres crossing at the chiasma while temporal fibres do not. Crossing fibres are more numerous than uncrossed, corresponding to the nasal visual field (the projection of the temporal half of the retina) which is smaller than the temporal field of vision.

Partial crossing of the visual fibres enables stimulation of 'corresponding points' of the two retinas to send simultaneous messages to the visual centres on one side of the brain. Thus fusion of two images to form a single percept is possible. Those animals whose monocular fields of vision are only slightly overlapped, have few uncrossed fibres.

Crossed fibres do not move directly over to the opposite side at the chiasma but loop either backwards or forwards before entering the contralateral tract. Fibres from the lower, medial part of the optic nerve (and retina) bend backward as if going into the opposite optic nerve, before turning into the inferior medial quadrant of the contralateral optic tract. Upper medial fibres move into the upper medial tract via a bend towards the opposite tract, as shown in Fig. 6.2.

THE OPTIC TRACT

This path, on each side, carries nerve impulses up to the *lateral geniculate nucleus or body*. The course of the nerves bends round the brain stem, containing both crossed and uncrossed fibres. On the way, about 10% of the fibres of the visual tract leave. These are predominantly pupillomotor fibres which end in the *pretectal nucleus* which is situated inferiorly to the *superior colliculus* in the *mid brain*. Probably some of these fibres end in the reticular formation in the mid brain and can have an influence on afferent activities.

THE LATERAL GENICULATE NUCLEUS

Also known as the lateral geniculate body (LGN), this is effectively a relay station for visual nerve impulses on their way to the visual cortex. In humans, the LGN receives the greater part of the fibres in the visual paths. It lies laterally to the thalamus and is partly associated with it. Having a complicated laminated structure, it is composed of white and grey substances arranged in six layers.

Layers 1, 4 and 6 layers receive crossed (nasal) fibres, while layers 2, 3 and 5 receive the uncrossed fibres. As they enter the LGN, the nerve fibres divide into several branches which make connections with between four and six cells, corresponding to the local management of the messages from visual impulses (Fig. 6.3).

The LGN cells have a retinotopical arrangement. This ensures that a particular part of the retina is allocated to a region of cells in the LGN. Fibres from the macula are so distributed in the optic tract, that in the LGN they terminate in its middle or back parts. Peripheral retinal fibres end in the anterior part, with

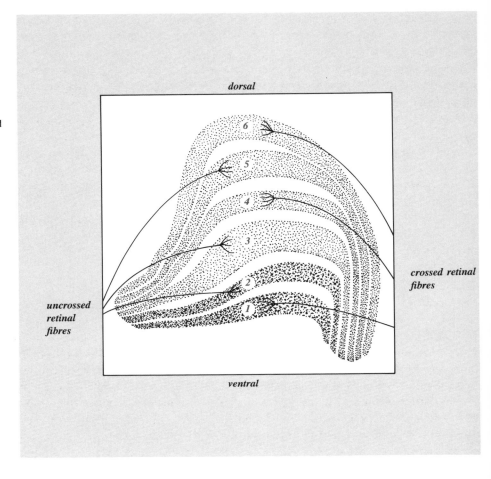

Fig. 6.3 Diagram of the lateral geniculate body. Both layers 1 and 2 are essentially magnocellular, while layers 3 to 6 have parvocellular connections.

the 'upper quadrants' represented medially and the lower ones in the lateral LGN.

There are two main types of cells in the LGN. In layers 1 and 2 (those most ventral) there are substantially large cells (magno cells) and axons from retinal 'A type' cells terminate here. The middle and posterior layers contain small (parvo) cells. Retinal ganglion cells of the B type send axons to end in these four layers. Fibres from every single small part of the retina are accurately situated in relation to each other. Corresponding points from the two half retinas are also represented close together.

The LGN is not merely a relay station for visual impulses. In addition, both excitatory and inhibitory activities take place in relation to such impulses. The nucleus contains many connecting neurones and receives many nerve fibres from the striate cortex, as well as from the reticular formation in the brain stem.

THE OPTIC RADIATIONS

These are the geniculo-calcarine paths, carrying visual impulses to the higher cortical centres. Initially, the fibres pass laterally across the back part of the *internal capsule* in a fan formation, bending backwards and medially. The upper part of the radiations, which serves the superior aspect of the retina, moves steadily back across the outside of the lateral ventricle, to terminate at the top of the *calcarine sulcus*. Below this, the radiations carry fibres from the lower half of the retina, which go underneath and around the posterior horn of the ventricle, to bend backwards and end on the lower part of the calcarine sulcus. Macular fibres travel between these two sets of fibres. As a result, there is a retinotopic arrangement of the nerve fibres.

THE VISUAL CORTEX

The regions of the brain's cortex concerned with vision may be separated into the primary region, Brodmann's area 17, and the secondary region, which includes areas 18 and 19. The primary visual cortex occupies the area around the calcarine sulcus, with the cuneal gyrus above and the lingual gyrus below. On the top, area 17 stretches from the parieto-occipital sulcus backwards, including also part of the posterior-lateral cortical surface. Underneath, it occupies the corresponding region, extending rather further forward here.

The cortex of area 17 is about 1.5 mm thick, thinner than elsewhere in the brain. It has a characteristic white stripe (of Genarri) made up of myelinated nerve fibres. So this region is called the *striate area*. The cortex has six layers of cells, as in the brain generally, each layer having connections with other parts of the brain. These are chiefly with areas 18 and 19, but also with the superior colliculus and some fibres travel back to the LGN.

There is a precise location for bundles of fibres in the striate cortex, hence each retinal area belongs to the appropriate part of the cortex. The macula supplies a relatively large extent, which is located at the back of the calcarine sulcus and a small region at the posterior/lateral aspect of the brain. Peripheral parts of the retina are represented in comparatively small areas, in the anterior parts of the calcarine fissure. Note particularly how the upper quadrants of the retina (projected to the lower visual field) are represented above the calcarine sulcus, impulses from the lower parts of the retina ending at the lower side of the fissure.

Retinal ganglion cells have circular receptor fields, the centres of which are excitatory or inhibitory when light stimulates them, while the encircling zones have reverse characteristics. This is also true in the LGN. Receptor fields in the striate area are rectangular, with one zone excitatory and one inhibitory. The cortical cells have a specific orientation sensitivity, reacting to a linear light stimulus which matches each particular receptor field. Such cells react strongly if the stimulus is moving and this cell reaction depends on the direction in which the stimulus moves. Cells with similar characteristics are organized in groups in the striate area. Such groups do not merely respond to the parts of the visual field which control them, but are selective as to the information the retina sends. As an example, cells which have specific responses to colours are arranged in such groups (Fig. 6.4).

The *secondary cortical areas*, which are areas 18 and 19, encircle the striate area on the medial and lateral sides of the brain's cortex. Here there are also six layers of cortical cells but no stripes of white substance intrude. These regions have been called, respectively, the parastriate and the peristriate areas.

This region receives afferent fibres from area 17 and other cortical areas, as well as from the thalamus and superior colliculus. The secondary cortical region, in common with parts lying further forward, is concerned with visual perception, since it transforms visual impulses from area 17 into perceptual images and conscious impressions. Similarly, other regions of the brain use

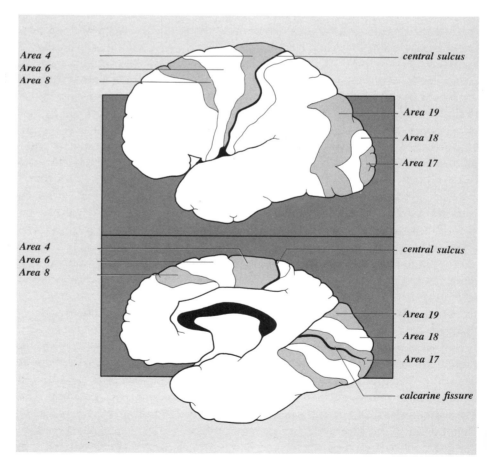

Fig. 6.4 The visual cortex of the brain. *Top*: lateral view. *Below*: medial section.

Area 4
Area 6
Area 8

central sulcus

Area 19

Area 18

Area 17

Area 4
Area 6
Area 8

central sulcus

Area 19

Area 18

Area 17

calcarine fissure

their connections, which include those parts essential for the control of eye movements.

Area 18 has interconnecting fibres with the corpus callosum, across to the visual centres of the other half of the brain. This enables co-ordination of the binocular impressions from two eyes to take place.

THE DISTRIBUTION OF NERVE FIBRES IN THE VISUAL PATHS

The previous descriptions of the different parts of the visual system, show how fibres from various parts of the retina send their messages upwards, with retinotopical representation. Some extra points will now be made, with repetition of the main points.

The visual field is represented, point by point, on the retina. The optics of the eye ensure that the temporal field is the projection of the nasal retina, and vice versa. The upper field, likewise, corresponds to the lower part of the retina.

Axons from ganglion cells converge onto the disc from the whole of the retina. There is a radial pattern of nasal retinal fibres, while on the temporal retina, the papillo-macular bundle travels directly to the disc. Other temporal fibres circumvent that bundle.

Arrangement of fibres within the intrabulbar nerve follows the retinal pattern. Macular fibres, comprising about a third of the optic nerve fibres, initially occupy the lateral aspect of the optic nerve, but soon move more centrally. Nasal retinal fibres then occupy the medial side and temporal fibres are placed laterally. Vertical dispositions of fibres persist as expected.

Nasal retinal fibres, including those from the nasal part of the macula, cross the midline at the optic chiasma. They move to the contralateral optic tract, while temporal fibres continue into the ipsilateral tract. Fibres belonging to lower nasal quadrants of the retina cross one another at the chiasma's lower anterior part. They loop first into the opposite optic nerve, then turn again, into the optic tract in its lower medial quadrant. Fibres from the upper nasal quadrants, on the other hand, extend onwards on the same side. They appear to be going into the ipsilateral tract, before bending medially and crossing to continue into the upper medial quadrant of the contralateral optic tract (Fig. 6.5).

Macular fibres cross more centrally, within the chiasma, compared to peripheral fibres and occupy a large portion of the central chiasma. Nerve fibres in each optic tract are diverted medially, so that fibres from upper temporal retinal quadrants are on the medial side, with those from lower quadrants more laterally disposed. Thus fibres from corresponding parts of the retina become associated here. Fibres from superior nasal retinal regions become juxtaposed to uncrossed superior temporal fibres. Similarly, inferior nasal fibres take up position beside uncrossed inferior temporal fibres.

The front of the LGN receives nerve endings from the retinal periphery,

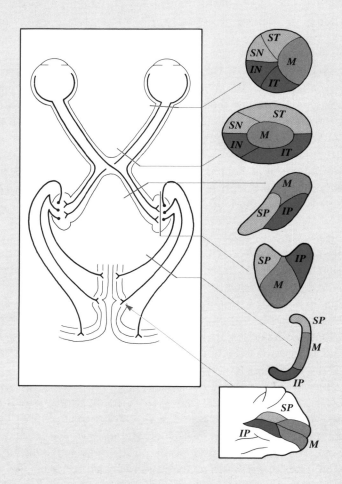

Fig. 6.5 Distribution of fibres from retinal quadrants, at different levels of the visual paths.

M: *macula*
IT: *inferior temporal*
ST: *superior temporal*
SP: *superior peripheral*
SN: *superior nasal*
IP: *inferior peripheral*
IN: *inferior nasal*

those from superior retinal quadrants being medially sited, while lower quadrants end laterally. Macular fibres terminate at the middle and rear of the LGN, temporal uncrossed fibres synapse in layers 2, 3 and 5 and crossed fibres have synapses in layers 1, 4 and 6. Crossed and uncrossed fibres, therefore, do not end in the same layer, but nevertheless fibres from corresponding points of the two retinas do end near each other in adjacent layers.

Each axon from the retina ends in four to six branches in the LGN, each making its synapse in the same layer. Hence each LGN neurone can make synapses with a number of retinal fibres, always from the same eye. Also, it has been established that 'multipolar interneurones' exist, which connect cells between different layers.

The optic radiations are formed by axons from LGN cells. Initially, the fibres bend together, through the back part of the *internal capsule*. After that there is a spreading of the nerves, into upper and lower bands, the uppermost fibres carrying impulses from the superior retina and vice versa. Looping right over the lateral aspect of the lateral ventricle, through parietal and occipital parts of the brain, they eventually reach the striate cortex. Fibres from the lower retina move in the lower parts of the optic radiations, backwards and downwards around the temporal horn of the ventricle, before proceeding straight back to the striate area. Macular fibres are carried in the centre of these neural paths.

BLOOD SUPPLIES OF THE VISUAL PATHS

The circle of Zinn supplies blood to the intraocular part of the optic nerve. This ring of blood vessels lies conveniently around the nerve head, formed by the short posterior ciliary arteries. In its orbital and intracranial parts, the nerve is served by plexi of vessels in the pia mater and the vasculature of connective tissue, which segregates bundles of nerve fibres. Here the pia mater receives branches of the central retinal artery before and during its penetration into the nerve. During the intracranial course of the nerve, the surrounding pia mater supplies it; blood arrives from the internal carotid artery via the anterior superior hypophysial artery or the ophthalmic artery (Fig. 6.6).

The chiasma is also covered with the pia mater, from which it derives its blood supply. Plexi of vessels in the pial tissues take their blood from many neighbouring arteries, including the hypophysial artery, the posterior communicating artery, the anterior cerebral and the anterior communicating arteries (Fig. 6.7).

Branches of the pia mater provide blood to the optic tract, having themselves come from the anterior choroidal artery, the posterior communicating artery and the medial cerebral artery. The LGN derives its supply from the anterior choroidal artery and also from tributaries of the posterior cerebral artery.

The anterior regions of the optic radiations receive blood from the anterior choroidal artery; towards the rear, the supply comes out of the medial cerebral

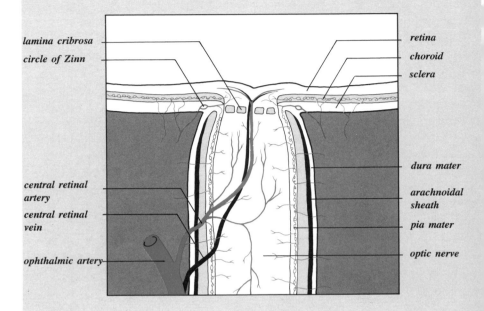

Fig. 6.6 The blood
supply of the optic
nerve and disc.

lamina cribrosa

circle of Zinn

retina

choroid

sclera

central retinal
artery

central retinal
vein

ophthalmic artery

dura mater

arachnoidal
sheath

pia mater

optic nerve

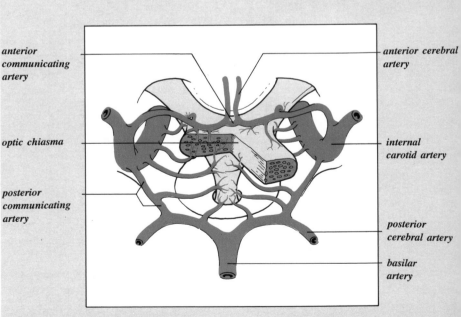

Fig. 6.7 The blood
supply to the optic
chiasma, divisible into
two groups of blood
vessels. The superior
group is from the
anterior cerebral artery
and anterior
communicating artery.
The inferior group is
derived from the
internal carotid artery,
the posterior cerebral
artery and the posterior
communicating artery.

anterior
communicating
artery

optic chiasma

posterior
communicating
artery

anterior cerebral
artery

internal
carotid artery

posterior
cerebral artery

basilar
artery

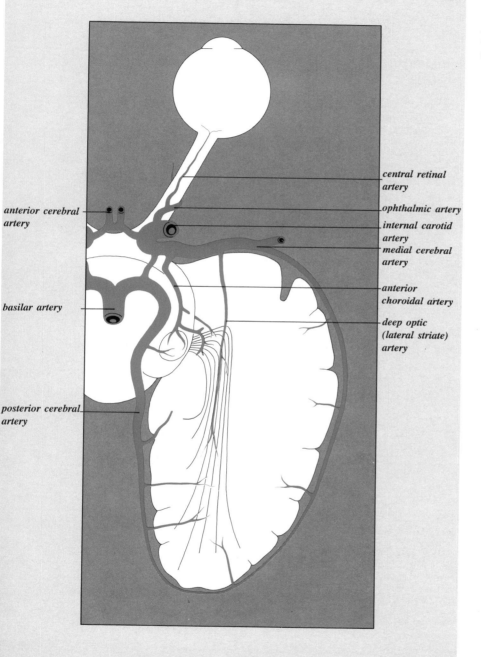

anterior cerebral
artery

basilar artery

posterior cerebral
artery

central retinal
artery

ophthalmic artery

internal carotid
artery

medial cerebral
artery

anterior
choroidal artery

deep optic
(lateral striate)
artery

Fig. 6.8 Cranial blood
vessels associated with
the visual paths.

artery, which has a deep 'optic' branch, as well as from the posterior cerebral artery.

Posterior cerebral arteries on each side nourish the visual cortex, a small area at the anterior aspect of the calcarine sulcus being additionally served by the medial cerebral artery (Fig. 6.8).

THE OCULAR FASCIA

Tenon's capsule (fascia bulbi) is a thin membrane of somewhat elastic fibres, enveloping the globe from the limbus to the optic nerve. It has close contact with the sclera, to which it is bound with fine fibres. Anteriorly, it is firmly attached to the sclera round the limbus and between the two there is a serous interstice. Separation of the layers is difficult, however, limited movement taking place between Tenon's capsule and the sclera. Such movements are impeded by fibrous attachments and by those structures which penetrate the capsule and tend to make it adhere to the sclera. Between the capsule and the *dura mater* cladding of the optic nerve, there are direct fibrous connections. So the capsule really amounts to a continuation of the dura mater around the eyeball.

Through Tenon's capsule pass the following:

- The optic nerve.
- The ciliary nerves.
- The ciliary arteries.
- The vortex veins.
- The tendons of the extraocular muscles.

Beneath the eye, Tenon's capsule is thicker, acting as a suspensory (hammock-like) supporting band, counteracting gravitational displacement of the globe. This is known as the suspensory ligament of Lockwood. The capsule also provides sheaths of connective tissue around the extraocular muscles from where they pass through. These envelopes vary in length in different muscles, attaching themselves to the muscles' fascia and extending strong bands to nearby structures.

The lateral rectus sends a connecting band to the *orbital tubercle* and a similar connection goes from the medial rectus to the lacrimal bone. To some extent these substantial bands limit or oppose the ocular rotations and some have been called 'check' ligaments.

The band of fibres from the superior rectus is fastened to the levator muscle of the upper eyelid, which assists in co-ordinating movements of the two muscles. So when the superior rectus elevates the eye, the upper lid tends to be raised.

From the inferior rectus, fibrous tissue extends forwards over the inferior oblique muscle as far as the lower lid, to fasten into the tarsal plate. Because the fibres penetrate up to 2 mm, the lower lid adjusts its position when the eye looks down.

Each tendon of the appropriate muscles makes a connection with the conjunctival fornix, so the conjunctiva is stretched as the eye rotates. Fatty tissues occupy spaces within the orbit. The consistency and connective tissue content of this material differs from place to place and it is organized in patches, within connective tissue coverings. Between individual external muscles of the eye, there are fatty and membranous connections, divided into central and peripheral parts. But these are less prominent towards the orbital apex. The eye itself and other orbital structures enjoy a yielding and flexible environment on account of this fatty material.

THE EYEBROW
REGION

THE EYEBROW REGION

The eyebrows and lids are an important part of the structure of the face and their movements are linked to some of the muscles of expression. There is a bony ridge in the frontal bone, where the eyebrows separate the forehead from the eyelids. The bone here is covered with connective tissue and muscle, and is less pronounced in females. The hairs of the eyebrows grow from follicles contained in the skin, making an arch which on the medial side, comes beneath the orbital margin but which is above it laterally (see Plate 8).

Three main types of hairs are present: a delicate, unpigmented, downy sort and a rather coarser and partly pigmented variety. However, the eyebrow hairs themselves are thicker and stronger and can be particularly long in the elderly: even as much as 8 to 10 cm if not trimmed! There is no smooth muscle associated with these follicles and no sweat glands but there are many sebaceous glands.

The eyebrows are moved by means of these muscles (Fig. 7.1):

- The frontalis muscle, which raises the brows.
- The corrugator supercilii, which draws the brows together.
- The depressor supercilii, which lowers the forehead in menace towards the nose.
- The orbicularis (orbital part), which lowers the brows and squeezes the lids together.

The eyebrows have several functions: they shield the eye from strong light and act in important facial expressions. Since their hairs grow laterally and many sebaceous glands are present, the eyebrows stop sweat running from the forehead into the eyes. These hairs are also highly sensitive, because their follicles have a rich nerve supply. Therefore they have a marked protective function.

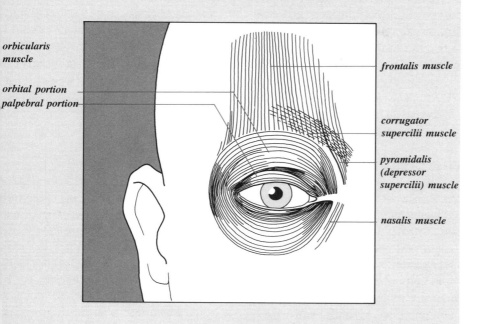

orbicularis
muscle

orbital portion
palpebral portion

frontalis muscle

corrugator
supercilii muscle

pyramidalis
(depressor
supercilii) muscle

nasalis muscle

Fig. 7.1 The
periorbital muscles of
facial expression.

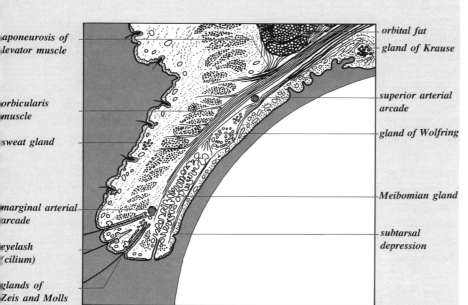

aponeurosis of
levator muscle

orbicularis
muscle

sweat gland

marginal arterial
arcade

eyelash
(cilium)

glands of
Zeis and Molls

orbital fat

gland of Krause

superior arterial
arcade

gland of Wolfring

Meibomian gland

subtarsal
depression

Fig. 7.2 Upper eyelid,
sagittal section.

THE EYELIDS

The palpebrae protect the eye against injury and excessive light. During eye movements, the lids move across the cornea, distributing tears liquid with blinking actions and also assisting the movement of tears into the drainage canals by pumping movements. During closure of the eye, the capillary network beneath the lids is a source of nourishment to the cornea.

The upper eyelid has its top boundary near the eyebrow, in the form of a horizontal furrow known as the *superior palpebral furrow or sulcus*. This divides it into an orbital part and a tarsal part. The lower lid has no distinct boundary at the cheek. In the elderly, there are extra furrows extending from the outer (lateral) canthus and down medially to meet the naso-jugal fold, which comes across from the bridge of the nose. Each lid is very flexible and elastic, which is important as far as contact lens wear is concerned.

The upper eyelid has more mobility than the lower one and the two meet at the temporal and nasal angles or *canthi*. The outer canthus makes an angle of between 30° to 40°, but the inner (medial) one is not so distinct. The lower margin is approximately horizontal, with a medial ridge, formed by the medial palpebral ligament.

The *caruncle* is a small, reddish elevation within the inner canthus. It is essentially a lump of skin, which contains sweat glands and sebaceous glands, their openings being in tiny hair follicles. There are between 15 and 20 small hairs growing medially which provide a trap for impurities in the tears liquid (see Plate 6).

The *plica semilunaris* is a folded mucous membrane and part of the bulbar conjunctiva. It is sometimes described as analogous to the third eyelid. This is more vascular than the rest of the conjunctiva, so it is light red. It stretches during eye movements and has connections with the medial rectus. Each of the *lacrimal papillae* is an avascular, whitish elevation at the medial end of each lid. They contain the initial, vertical, part of the *lacrimal canaliculus*, the upper one being slightly medial to its lower counterpart. A *lacrimal punctum* is found on each papilla, this being an opening about 0.3 mm in diameter into each lacrimal canaliculus (Plate 9).

The *palpebral margin* or the edge of the eyelid, is about 2 mm wide and 30 mm long. Its back angle is relatively sharp, while at the front the edge is more rounded. Each lid has a ciliary portion and a lacrimal part, separated by the papilla. The former division has the eyelashes, or cilia, which are arrayed in three or four rows in the upper lid and two in the lower one. These cilia have no smooth muscles, but are well supplied with nerves. They grow and are renewed two or three times a year.

The tarsal glands open onto the lid margin, their orifices forming the barrier between the mucous membrane of the conjunctiva and the dry skin of the front of the eyelid. The *lacrimal margin* is devoid of cilia and tends to be more rounded.

The *palpebral fissure* is small at birth, but enlarges vertically after the first few days of life, as the head becomes bigger. Its width increases in adulthood.

Tissues of the eyelids

Tissues of the eyelid are shown in Fig. 7.2. These include the following:

- The epithelial layer of the skin.
- Underlying skin layers.
- A layer of striped muscle.
- Sub muscular tissue.
- Fibrous layer.
- A layer of smooth muscle.
- Conjunctiva.

The *superficial skin* is unusually thin, being among the most delicate in the body. Easily wrinkled and very elastic, it is almost transparent. It contains both sweat and sebaceous glands, as well as downy hairs and their follicles, as elsewhere in the body.

The *underlying layer* is made of loose connective tissues, rich in elastic fibres and thus very flexible, making it easy (as in oedema) to raise the skin from the layers beneath. These layers are, uncharacteristically, devoid of fatty deposits.

The *muscle layer* is comprised of the *orbicularis*, which is the sphincter of the eyelids. This is one of the muscles of facial expression, so it is controlled by the VIIth cranial or *facial nerve*. It runs in an oval around the palpebral fissure, covering the lid and orbit up to the eyebrow. Here there is an interweaving of fibres with the frontalis muscle, so both can move the eyebrow.

The orbicularis arises from the medial palpebral ligament region, at the medial part of the orbital margin where the upper jaw and forehead meet. A small part comes from the posterior lacrimal crest, as Horner's muscle or the *lacrimal portion*. Such fibres travel laterally behind the lacrimal sac and have some attachment at the sac. Hence this muscle contributes to pumping away the tears.

Orbicularis fibres move laterally to fasten onto the band of tendon called the lateral palpebral raphe, at the external (lateral) canthus and near the orbital tubercle. The muscle is divided into 'orbital' and 'palpebral' parts.

The *palpebral part*, some one third of the muscle thickness, gives a voluntary or blink reflex lid closure. Tonus here retains the lid against the eye.

The *orbital part* occupies the periphery, covering those parts of the forehead and upper jaw which lie nearby. On contraction, it closes the eye and pulls the surrounding skin medially.

The *sub muscular layer* is made of loose connective tissue, through which extend fibres of the *levator muscle*. These penetrate the orbicularis to be

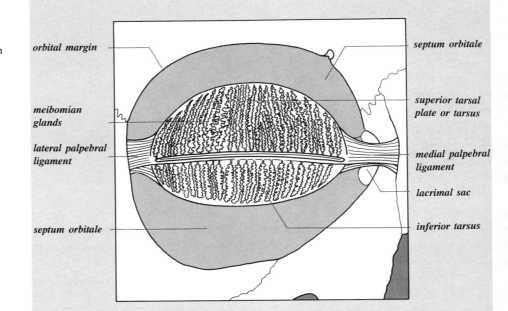

Fig. 7.3 Layers of palpebral tissue, including Meibomian glands.

orbital margin

septum orbitale

meibomian glands

superior tarsal plate or tarsus

lateral palpebral ligament

medial palpebral ligament

lacrimal sac

septum orbitale

inferior tarsus

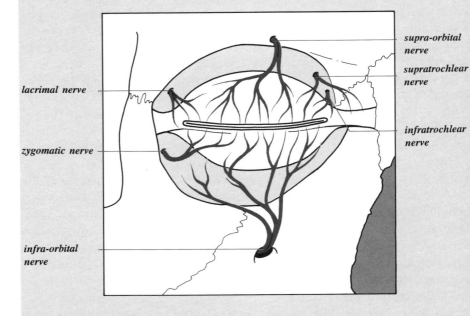

Fig. 7.4 The nerve supply to the eyelids.

supra-orbital nerve

supratrochlear nerve

lacrimal nerve

infratrochlear nerve

zygomatic nerve

infra-orbital nerve

mbedded in the skin. This layer of the lids also carries blood vessels and nerves.

The fibrous layer acts as a ' skeleton' or stiffener for the lid and includes:

The tarsal plates (superior and inferior).
The orbital septum (septum orbitale).
The medial and lateral palpebral ligaments.

Each *tarsal plate* is made of dense connective tissue (not cartilage) and gives form to the lid, being about 29 mm wide, like a D on its side. The upper tarsal plate is about 11 mm vertically, with the lower one some 5 mm. They are about mm thick and the rims progressively thin out to form the fascia of the lids. The Meibomian or tarsal glands lie within the tarsal plates. The *palpebral fascia*, a loose membranous structure, stretches from the tarsal plates to the orbital margins, where it is attached to the periosteum. The orbital septum forms a division between the eyelids and the orbital contents.

The *medial palpebral ligament* extends from the medial edge of the tarsal plates to its attachment at the *anterior lacrimal crest* by the suture between the maxilla and the frontal bone. This ligament divides into two lateral parts which belong, respectively, to the upper and lower tarsal plates. The posterior (deeper) parts of the layer have connections with the lacrimal sac.

The *lateral palpebral ligament* is somewhat looser. It runs from the lateral border of the tarsal plates, to be fastened at the orbital tubercle. The two ligaments act together to hold the tarsal plates in position.

The *unstriped muscle* layer is under sympathetic nerve control and is called Müller's muscle. In the upper lid, these muscle fibres amalgamate with the tarsal plate and the tendon of the levator muscle. In the lower lid, there are associations with the tarsal plate and the inferior rectus tendon. The layer diminishes medially and laterally. Little is known about its function, but some suggest it contributes to maintain lid posture and opening. A later section will be devoted to the conjunctiva.

The glands of the eyelids

The tarsal or *Meibomian* glands are within the tarsal plates, numbering about 25 in the upper lid and 20 below. The glands have extended central canals, served by small secretory sacs. They emerge onto the rim of the lids at the boundary between the dry and mucous surfaces. Sebum is secreted, giving an oily layer to the film of tears liquid. This fatty secretion prevents tears from overflowing and giving trouble on the dry skin of the cheek. There is the possibility of blockage of these glands, which raises lumps on the inside of the lids and can be a source of corneal irritation or pressure.

The sebaceous glands of *Zeis* open into the hair follicles of the eyelashes. The glands of *Moll* are small sweat glands with a spiral formation, lying parallel to, and in contact with, the eyelashes' follicles, particularly at the rims of the lids. They do not have glomeruli.

The blood supply of the lids

This comes principally from branches of the ophthalmic artery. Medially, the area is served by the two tributaries of the *medial palpebral artery*, one to each lid. These arteries anastomose with the *lateral palpebral artery*, which is itself an offshoot of the lacrimal artery. These arteries form marginal arcades around the palpebral fissure, one superior and one inferior. There are also anastomoses with arteries of the face, mainly with the facial artery itself. The upper lid also has an incomplete peripheral arterial arcade or ring (Plate 10).

Veins of the eyelids are bigger and more numerous than arteries and are of two sorts. Divisions of the ophthalmic vein receive blood from the conjunctiva and pretarsal drainage goes to the angular vein and the superficial temporal vein.

Lymphatic vessels form subcutaneous and subconjunctival plexi which empty laterally into the superficial parotid lymph nodes and medially to the submandibular nodes.

The nerve supply

The sensory supply of the eyelids is by the V cranial or trigeminal nerve. The upper lid is served by several branches of the ophthalmic or first division, while the lower lid is innervated by the maxillary or second division (Fig. 7.4).

THE CONJUNCTIVA

This is a thin covering of skin which continues from the lids to the eyeball. Thus it forms a barrier which prevents ingress to the orbit from outside. It has a *palpebral* part, a *fornix* and a *bulbar* portion.

The palpebral part is subdivided into two zones. The *marginal zone* extends from the opening of the glands at the lid rim, across the border of the lid as far as the *subtarsal furrow*, which is about 2 mm up, on the back of the eyelid. At this point, the tarsal glands and the lacrimal punctum emerge. This region is covered with tissue which can withstand much wear. The tissues are not smooth or even, having minor ridges or elevations. These provide slight friction over the cornea and the tears liquid can run across the depressions between the ridges.

The *tarsal zone* is thin and vascular and is light red in colour. It has a good attachment to the underlying tissues, being transparent so that the Meibomian glands can be seen from the rear as yellow streaks.

The *orbital zone* is loosely attached to the tissues below, lying in horizontal folds.

The *conjunctival fornix* forms a linear sac folded, above, below and laterally and extending along the margin of the orbit. This fold prevents stretching when the eye moves. Medially, the *plica semilunaris* has a corresponding function. In order to avoid a collapse of the fornix as the globe rotates, there are appropriate connections of tissue with the superior, inferior and lateral recti. Thus the fornix follows movements of these muscles. The plica semilunaris has corresponding connections with the medial rectus.

The *bulbar conjunctiva* is thin and transparent, attached loosely to the tissue beneath, except around the limbus in a 3 mm wide zone, where it is fastened firmly. The palisades of Vogt are found in the limbal conjunctiva, as little radial ridges about 0.5 mm wide and one or two millimetres long. They are light elevations, often with pigment in the furrows and are most distinct at the lower limbal areas.

Conjunctival tissues

The main structures are surface epithelium and underlying connective tissue. At the marginal region there is many-layered, non-keratinized squamous epithelium, resistant to 'wear and tear'. The epithelium extends from its origin near the Meibomian gland outlets, around the back edge of the lid margin and up to the subtarsal furrow, which lies some 2 mm up on the back of the lid. This furrow is a narrow depression, or fold, in the conjunctiva, its length matching the spread of the eyelashes, less than 1 mm deep. It is an excellent trap for materials which would befoul the cornea and assists small specks of debris covered in mucus to move nasally with blinks, for collection by the hairs of the caruncle.

The epithelium of the tarsal region consists of two or three layers of more columnar cells. Because it forms a very thin, uneven layer, with ridges and grooves, it reduces friction, but simultaneously ensures a useful collection area for debris and bacteria.

The epithelium of the fornix consists of three or four layers of cubical cells, growing in number from the bulbar conjunctiva. Around the limbus a stratified layer appears, between 8 and 10 cells thick, with additional squamous epithelium which is very robust. The surface layer cells of the conjunctiva have microvilli similar to those of the cornea.

The *stroma* has a superficial adenoid layer containing lymphocytes. It forms three or four months after birth, and is laid on a deeper and thicker subconjunctival connective tissue stratum, both ending at the limbus. It appears reticulated and is thickest at the fornix, being thinner elsewhere but absent at the marginal and tarsal zones. Nerves and vessels reach the conjunctiva in the fibrous layer.

Conjunctival bacteria

From the first week of life the conjunctiva carries bacteria. The amount is usually equal within both eyes, although this is subject to individual variations. These bacteria resemble those common to the skin.

Conjunctival glands

Goblet cells are present, as monocellular mucus-producing glands, which are found in the basal epithelial layer. They rise within the layer to discharge their secretions on the surface, although it is uncertain whether, after secreting mucus, the cells are able to replenish their supplies. About 1.5 million cells are found in each conjunctival sac, most authorities suggesting that the distribution is greatest near the fornices, with fewer in the tarsal conjunctiva. The number of cells is reduced as the blood vessels thin out. The mucus from these cells contributes greatly to the content of the tears liquid.

The *glands of Krause* have been called accessory lacrimal glands, since their secretion resembles that of the lacrimal gland. About 42 are found in each upper fornix, with some six or eight in the lower fornix.

The *glands of Wolfring*, also of the serous accessory lacrimal type, are larger but fewer than those of Krause. Up to five of these are found near the upper region of the tarsus, with rather fewer below the lower lid. Since there is no nervous control of these glands, they maintain a constant level of tears.

Conjunctival blood vessels

These arise from the palpebral arterial arcades, which produce the posterior palpebral arteries, reaching backwards via the fornices to the limbus. Here they anastomose with the anterior ciliary arteries, themselves producing in this region the deep plexus of vessels in the scleral tissues. The veins closely accompany the arteries, emptying into the venous network of the lids. The conjunctiva is rich in lymphatics, which also drain through the vascular arcades of the eyelids.

When there is inflammation of the cornea or conjunctiva, these conjunctival vessels dilate, making the tissues become light red. Note how 'injected' conjunctival vessels can be moved with the conjunctiva, for distinction from 'ciliary injection'. The latter condition, accompanying inflammation of the iris or ciliary body (or sometimes narrow angle glaucoma), involves deeper vessels of the scleral network and exhibits a perilimbal ring of darker purple. These dilated vessels cannot be moved with the conjunctiva and are less distinct. In serious conditions, both layers can be inflamed.

The nerve supply to the conjunctiva

Sensory innervation for the bulbar conjunctiva is from the long ciliary nerves which are branches of the nasociliary nerve. The upper fornix and palpebral conjunctiva are served by the frontal and trochlear divisions of the ophthalmic nerve, while the lacrimal nerve covers the region of the outer canthus. The conjunctiva of the lower eyelid is innervated by the infraorbital nerve.

Chapter 8
The Lacrimal Apparatus

SECRETION OF THE TEARS

The two main parts of the lacrimal system are those involved in tear production and tear drainage. There is also the matter of tear distribution over the cornea, which ensures that this film of liquid and its important components, covers the cornea (Fig. 8.1).

The *lacrimal gland* is found at the upper, temporal aspect of the orbit, just behind the orbital rim. It weighs about one gram and is a flat, acinous, gland. It is associated with the tendon of the *levator muscle*, which almost divides it into two parts: the upper $\frac{2}{3}$, or orbital part, is attached to the orbital roof, while the lower (palpebral) section, rests loosely in the nearby tissues. There are between 10 and 12 outlets, mostly below the upper lid, which empty into the region opposite the tarsal plates.

The gland is essentially acinous, with a microscopic appearance like that of the parotid gland. It comprises two types of secretory cells which have typical, grainy, cytoplasm. One type of cell appears to secrete mucus, the other a serous product. In the liquid, there is lysozyme and other proteins. The tubules contain contractile myoepithelial cells which assist in expressing the secretions, which arise in the acinous cells and are collected into a system of ducts. Here other components are contributed by cells en route.

The final product has a proteinous content, with a bactericidal property, supplied by lysozyme, and immunoglobulin, for example. And the gland, together with its accessory glands, also contributes the aqueous layer of the tears film.

The gland is supplied with blood from the *lacrimal artery*, which is drained by the *lacrimal vein* to the ophthalmic vein. The *accessory lacrimal glands*, some 60 in number, are located in the two eyelids. As indicated in the section on the conjunctiva, their secretions resemble those of the main gland.

The innervation of the lacrimal gland

Both sympathetic and parasympathetic systems contribute. The literature mentions a secretory 'centre' in, or near, the *superior salivary nucleus* in the pons. Parasympathetic innervation comes from this salivary nucleus, via the *intermediate nerve* (the parasympathetic branch of the VII nerve) to the *geniculate ganglion* and then through the *major petrosal nerve*. These pre-ganglionic fibres end in the *pterygopalatine ganglion*. From this parasympathetic ganglion, the route follows the *zygomatic nerve*, laterally and forwards in the orbit via the *lacrimal nerve* to the lacrimal gland. Here there is contact by the parasympathetic fibres, with the secretory cells and the cells of the outgoing ducts.

Since the classical accounts of the parasympathetic innervation of the lacrimal gland, many new ideas have been advanced. Ruskell (1971) described the retrobulbar plexus which receives nerve fibres from the pterygopalatine ganglion. From this plexus, non-myelinated fibres reach the lacrimal gland via lacrimal rami.

The sympathetic innervation from the secretion centre moves along to the *superior cervical ganglion* of the sympathetic chain. The post ganglionic fibres follow the *internal carotid artery* upwards in the brain and along its distribution of nerves to the *major petrosal nerve*. From here both the sympathetic and parasympathetic messages follow the same path to the gland. The sympathetic fibres end at blood vessels and thus have a regulatory effect on the gland's blood supply. It is possible, also, that the gland has sympathetic innervation from fibres accompanying the lacrimal artery.

The pontine secretory centre is under the influence of several parts of the brain, which may respond to mechanical irritation, emotional disturbances, smell or taste (Fig. 8.2). Secretion of tears may occur as part of the normal flow, as the result of emotional weeping or as a reflex action. This last phenomenon is often called 'lacrimation'.

Normal flow of tears appears to be under sympathetic control, being chiefly a matter of regulation of the gland's blood supply. Strong light or air pollution tend to increase lacrimation, while a dry atmosphere seems to have little effect.

Emotional weeping, which is a unique human characteristic, probably originates from some parasympathetic regulation within the gland itself, particularly associated with the outflow mechanism. The secretory centre is affected by many parts of the brain, such as the frontal cortex, the basal ganglia, the thalamus and the hypothalamus. In the neonate, there is little secretion of tears, since the parasympathetic innervation is imperfectly developed, hence for some time there is no emotional weeping.

Reflex lacrimation arises from corneal or conjunctival irritation, coughing, sneezing, taste or smell. The new born have a minimal output of tears from these causes.

There are some individuals who experience a marked flow of tears during a meal. These have been called 'crocodile' tears. They arise from a faulty nervous connection which diverts impulses to the salivary glands to the lacrimal gland as well.

DRAINAGE OF THE TEARS

The *lacrimal puncta* are small round openings, about 0.3 mm in diameter, leading to the *canaliculi*, or tear canals. One of these orifices is at each papilla, one of the pair of avascular structures about 5 mm lateral to the inner canthus.

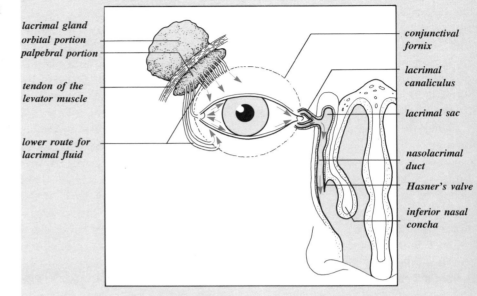

Fig. 8.1 The lacrimal apparatus.

lacrimal gland
orbital portion
palpebral portion

tendon of the
levator muscle

lower route for
lacrimal fluid

conjunctival
fornix

lacrimal
canaliculus

lacrimal sac

nasolacrimal
duct

Hasner's valve

inferior nasal
concha

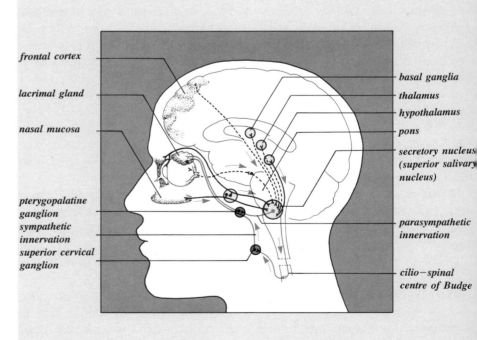

Fig. 8.2 Nervous control of the lacrimal gland.

frontal cortex

lacrimal gland

nasal mucosa

pterygopalatine
ganglion
sympathetic
innervation
superior cervical
ganglion

basal ganglia

thalamus

hypothalamus

pons

secretory nucleus
(superior salivary
nucleus)

parasympathetic
innervation

cilio–spinal
centre of Budge

Each papilla rises about 1 mm above the lid margin and they are directed rather backwards, just dipping into the *lacrimal lake* formed by the tears liquid, near the inner canthus. Note how the upper papilla is more medially located.

The tear canals are about 10 mm long, after a sharp bend. Before this bend, their initial two millimetres after the papilla run vertically, upwards in the top lid and downwards in the lower lid. Then the two passages bend sharply into the *lacrimal sac*.

The *lacrimal ampulla* comes where the canal changes directions; sometimes the canal and the sac may amalgamate with vague distinctions. The canals lie behind the medial palpebral ligament, being enclosed in fibres from the palpebral section of the orbicularis muscle (Horner's muscle).

The *lacrimal sac* occupies the *lacrimal fossa*, behind the medial palpebral ligament. It is about 12 mm long, somewhat flattened in the sagittal plane, and its lumen is stretched open on account of the thin surrounding layer of connective tissue, the *lacrimal fascia*. This fascia is attached anteriorly to the anterior lacrimal crest and to the posterior lacrimal crest behind. In front, there is also a connection to the medial palpebral ligament, but at its back the lacrimal sac has fibrous attachments with Horner's muscle. Thus contraction of that muscle dilates the sac.

The lacrimal sac merges gently with the *nasolacrimal duct*, itself emptying out into the *inferior nasal meatus*. The whole passage is about 15 mm long, moving downwards and laterally. The mucous membrane of the region which opens into the nose produces a fold, the *plica lacrimalis*, or Hasner's valve, which overhangs the area where the nasal passage begins. This valve stops air, etc., moving upwards when the nose is blown, although the valve's action may be imperfect.

The whole of these passages consist of connective tissues, internally covered by two layers of epithelium with mucus-producing goblet cells.

KINETICS OF THE TEARS

Tears liquid forms a thin film over both cornea and conjunctiva. At the ciliary margin of the lower lid (and to some extent along the upper lid) there is a linear pool or strip of tears. This can be called the tears 'meniscus', 'prism' or 'river'. A lacrimal 'lake' is found at the inner canthus and plica semilunaris, a collection of tears liquid with which the puncta make contact.

The tears liquid comes out of the exit canals of the main and accessory lacrimal glands, flowing across the eye to reach the marginal tears prism of both lids. At each blink, the tears prism is moved upwards and downwards across the conjunctiva and cornea, to refurbish the precorneal tear film. A continuous stream also comes from the temporal side towards the puncta. Closure of the palpebral fissure takes place initially on the temporal side, sweeping tears towards the inner canthus. Each punctum is kept open by strong, fibrous coatings, so the 0.3 mm diameter orifice uses capillary attraction to take in liquid. Fibres of the lacrimal portion of the orbicularis make closure movements of the lower lid, pressing on the ampulla and shortening the canaliculi. This encourages the flow of liquid to the lacrimal sac. When blinking takes place, the canaliculi are pressed medially by the surrounding muscle fibres' contraction, raising the pressure in the canals, which can vary between about 6 and 8 mm Hg. Closing the lids raises the pressure and vice versa. Variations of the direction of gaze can also produce such pressure changes. At the same time, muscles close to the sac itself expand it from its flattened resting state. Such suction draws tears into the sac and its opening results in a disturbance of the tissues, closing the valve of Hasner. This stops air from rushing up from the nose.

There is a reduction of orbicularis tonus as the eyes open. Then the lacrimal sac flattens and the ampulla expands, producing suction to bring in fresh liquid.

Tears liquid flows from the lacrimal sac through the *nasolacrimal duct* under several influences. These include the effects of gravity on the liquid and air pressure in the nose. A negative pressure is induced on inspiration, opening Hasner's valve and drawing tears through the passages to the nose. This vacuum increases with sneezing or strong inspirations of other types. Expiration increases pressure in the nasal passages, when Hasner's valve closes, preventing air and mucus from moving up to the lacrimal passages. Normally most of the tears are absorbed, however, by the mucosa of the lacrimal passages.

In some 5% of people, Hasner's valve works incompletely and they have the ability to blow bubbles out of their puncta, as air emerges through the lacrimal ducts!

THE TEAR FILM

This is a very specialized, thin film, covering the conjunctiva and cornea. It is bordered by the lid margins, where it is restrained by the Meibomian secretions and where the mucous membrane of the conjunctiva meets the dry skin of the eyelids. The liquid keeps the conjunctiva moist and has an emollient effect, reducing friction during blinking actions and when the eyes move. The cornea receives additional oxygen through the film of tears, which also fills up minor irregularities in the cornea to provide a good optical surface.

The tear film over the cornea is thickest just after blinking, when it measures about 9 μm. It reduces gradually, so that after some 30 seconds a minimum thickness of 4 μm is reached. When blinking is restrained, the tear film 'breaks up', so that dry patches appear on the cornea.

Under usual conditions, some two drops of tears liquid are present in the conjunctival sac, very little of this covering the cornea. The amount is greatest in young adults, decreasing steadily with age, so that by the age of 70, perhaps barely 10% is present, compared to in youth. However, this reduction apparently has little actual effect on normal ocular function in most cases.

It is the strip of lipid along the lid margin which produces the tears meniscus. The tear film moves at the same time as the eye, since there is a thin strip which connects them. A corresponding region exists round the edge of a contact lens, in situ on the eye.

There is a watery layer in the 'precorneal' tear film, produced by the lacrimal gland system. Behind this is a mucous layer, comprising conjunctival goblet cell products, while on the front, an oily layer from the Meibomian glands is present.

The lipid layer covers both the cornea and the conjunctiva, having a thickness of about 0.1 μm. As it covers the precorneal film, the layer reduces evaporation by up to 90%, according to some researchers. The Meibomian gland secretions consist of a cholesterol ester and phospholipids, mingled with small amounts of fatty acids. The bulk of the secretion consists of non-polarized lipid molecules, which alone are unable to spread over an aqueous surface, on account of surface tension. So surfactant substances are essential additional components. Such elements come from the conjunctival mucus.

Meibomian secretions probably reach the cornea through the tear film, being massaged into the corneal surface cells by the lid movements. This would also assist local epithelial metabolism. The combination of lacrimal secretions with mucus from goblet cells thus gives the tear film the required hydrophilic features to help it spread itself.

Secretions from this range of lacrimal glands serve the aqueous layer. The pH varies from 7.1 to 8.6, but the variation is lower for the product of 'reflex' lacrimation. In a normal eye, the osmotic pressure (potential) of the tears is between 0.9 and 1.0 equivalent NaCl. The tear film temperature with open lids is between 30° and 35°C, being considerably influenced by external temperature and wind conditions. In extreme cold or wind, the temperature of both the tears liquid and the corneal tissues can drop so much that this handicaps corneal metabolism.

In the open eye, the oxygen pressure varies between 140 and 160 mm Hg, under normal conditions. The tears liquid contains small admixtures of urea, inorganic salts and lactate. The glucose content is as low as $\frac{1}{10}$ of the blood plasma level.

A range of proteins is found in human tears, chiefly albumin, globulin and lysozyme. These proteins have several effects, including lowering the tear film's surface tension and enabling it to spread over the cornea and conjunctiva. Molecules of protein also act as transport molecules, as well as maintaining the osmotic pressure and buffering against large changes in pH. Protein molecules also have a significant bactericidal function.

Albumin constitutes some 40% of the total protein content of the tears liquid, going a long way to maintain the liquid's osmotic stability. Its content drops during reflex lacrimation, perhaps even halving, so this lowers the osmotic pressure and is likely to contribute to corneal oedema.

Lysozyme is probably the most important protein constituent of the normal tears, and is present at a concentration of about 170 mg/100 ml. Since its production is constant, this concentration tends to drop on lacrimation. It is a good bactericide, particularly against gram−positive bacteria, by attacking the cell envelopes. While their mechanism is obscure, other proteins in the tears also have deleterious effects on gram−negative organisms.

Immunoglobulin, normally present in small amounts within the tears liquid, is chiefly of types A and G, with traces of other types. Its concentration is reduced during reflex lacrimation, showing that little immunoglobulin originates from the lacrimal gland. Its constant supply comes chiefly from the plasma cells in the conjunctival lymphatics. Immunoglobulin provides an effective defence mechanism against the invasion of microbes at the surface tissues of the cornea and conjunctiva. The activity of the immunoglobulin system, together with phagocytes in the tears liquid, maximizes protection against infection.

There are many other types of cell in the tear film, some living and some dead. These include fragmented cells from the cornea, the conjunctival epithelium, blood vessels and the conjunctival lymphatic tissues. Most of these cells are epithelial or lymphocytes and other leucocytes. Many of the cells are trapped within the mucus beneath the lower eyelid, being urged medially to end up enmeshed in the tiny hairs of the caruncle.

The tears film relies on a steady replenishment of mucus with the appropriate chemical and physical characteristics to maintain the normal features of the corneal covering and of the conjunctiva's mucous membrane. Goblet cells provide mucus to the conjunctiva and have several other important functions, such as reducing friction when the lids move (as when blinking) by a greasy lubrication. As has been seen above, their modification of the surface tension of the tears liquid is vital to its distribution over the anterior ocular surface. The mucus is also very useful in enveloping dirt and foreign bodies and removing them from the cornea.

Cell debris is mixed within gelatinous, thin threads and stringy mucoid accumulations which are made to amalgamate by the movements of the lids within the fornices, pushing them to the inner canthus by blinks. The surface area of this conglomeration of varied materials can be estimated at between 3 and 5 mm^2. Fortunately, such chains of mucoid debris do not reach the tears drainage channels, but are washed up on the caruncle.

The surface of the cornea is covered with tiny microvilli, like those found on the conjunctiva. It is, however, hardly possible that these microvilli play any part in the spread of the tears across the cornea. For this would involve a high surface tension of the cornea itself, accompanied by a relatively low tension of the tears liquid, whilst the intermediate region between them would require the lowest possible tension. As already mentioned, between the corneal microvilli, there are phospholipids and small amounts of cholesterol, with free fatty acids, arising from Meibomian secretions. Such materials provide the required surface layer to form a good basis for the tear film, and the mucus of the tears' basal layer serves to encourage suitable spreading across the cornea.

Normally, the tear film completely covers the cornea and is renewed with each blink. Holding the lids apart, to prevent blinking, causes this film to develop small patchy losses. The time lapse from the last blink to such a loss of continuity is called the 'break up time' (BUT). This is usually about 30 seconds in adults and if it is as low as 10 seconds it is classified as 'abnormal'. Such breaking up of the tear film is accompanied by its rapid thinning, following each initial wetting. The thickness of the film after blinking is probably between 8 and 9 μm, but this is reduced by about half at break-up. The phenomenon of break-up can appear over the whole cornea, or local patches can alter from one blink to another. However, wind and temperature conditions seem to have little effect on BUT and there is no correlation between BUT and the size of the palpebral aperture.

Goblet cell mucus production is very significant for tear film stability and the diminution of these cells' activity in the elderly is a condition which militates against a stable tear film. As soon as dry areas of cornea appear, there is irritation and reflex lacrimation.

THE MECHANISM OF BLINKING

The eye is protected by lid closure, which includes blinks, as well as by the tears. It is the blinking mechanism which is responsible for the maintenance of corneal and conjunctival moisture by the tears liquid. We have seen also how blinks assist tears to drain away. However, many blinks are incomplete so that they neither completely cover the pupil nor interfere completely with sight, although some upward eye movements may accompany blinks.

Closure of the lids results from contraction of the palpebral portion of the orbicularis, while opening the palpebral aperture is by means of the levator muscle. Thus, these muscles have antagonistic functions in blinking. Blinking can be voluntary or involuntary, the latter type being subdivided into spontaneous and reflex types.

Spontaneous blinks, as the term suggests, do not require external stimuli. They probably arise in the 'blink centre' in the basal ganglia, but little is known about this. The frequency of blinking during waking hours is between 15 and 20 times a minute; however, great variations are possible according to the state of attention or activity of the individual. When awake, a person tends normally to have a constant, individualistic, blink rate. Some suggest that men and women have similar rates. Extremely dry air, wind, emotional stress, surprise, anger or fright can considerably augment the blink rate. It is likely that a lower blink frequency will occur during stressful visual tasks. Drying of the cornea can also affect the blink rate, although this is not the most significant influence.

Reflex blinking is the result of a direct stimulus. Such stimuli can include flashes of light, or mechanical contact with the cornea, conjunctiva or eyelids. Strong, sudden sounds or violent blasts of air, can likewise produce reflex blinks.

Voluntary blinking takes place when a deliberate closure of the palpebral aperture takes place; this may be contrasted to the alternate blinking of each eye. The time that such blinking actions takes is capable of being controlled, as is the degree of lid closure.

Closing of the eyelids during blinking is likely to be accompanied by a movement of the eye, to which the term 'Bell's phenomenon' has been applied. Here there is a co-ordinated reflex, involving the nuclei of the facial and oculomotor nerves. As the eyes close, there is a decrease of tonus in the levator muscle and electrical activity ceases. There is next an immediate increase in activity in the superior rectus, as well as a decrease in that of the inferior rectus which results in upwards movement of the two eyes. This movement assists in the maintenance of corneal moisture, so it is important where there is incomplete eye closure during blinking. The action also tends to remove the centre of the cornea from danger of flying particles, as in an explosion.

Chapter 9
The Extrinsic Ocular Muscles

GENERAL FEATURES

It is a basic requirement for the maintenance of binocular vision that corresponding points in each retina shall be stimulated by the same external object. This presupposes the normal situation in which movements of both eyes are co-ordinated, whether such movements consist of slow following actions, rapid saccades or refixations.

Such accurately co-ordinated ocular rotations depend upon a complex system of motor control, to activate these movements, as well as various influences. Ocular rotations therefore obey impulses reaching the terminations of certain cranial nerves, originating in the brain's cortex, the cerebellum and the brain stem. The final activity in the motor neurone takes place in an effector-organ. As a result, the muscle rotates the globe. We use the term *'extra-ocular' (or extrinsic)* for the muscles under consideration, to distinguish them from the internal ocular muscles.

OCULAR MOVEMENTS

A suitable analogy for these movements is the rotation of a ball, around a certain axis. Three distinct axes, at 90° to each other, provide a useful co-ordinate system, with the place where the three axes intersect being regarded as a point around which the eye rotates, or 'centre of rotation'. All movements are then considered as rotation around one or other of these axes, sometimes involving more than one (Fig. 9.1).

It is useful for reference to use the fixed, simplified co-ordinates suggested. Thus, it should be considered that when the eye is in a primary position, the equator of the eye is approximately in the frontal plane. (However, it should be remembered that the real centre of rotation is theoretical, and does not remain stationary but moves slightly as the eye changes position relative to the orbit.)

Each movement can be considered to arise from a starting point or *primary position*, for which the head is assumed to be erect and level, with the object of visual regard being in the distance. Thus the line of sight, or visual axis, coincides with the sagittal axis of the eye, this axis being the Y axis of the co-ordinates used. At the same time, the horizontal plane through the eye cuts the centre of rotation, the eye being in the primary position. The horizontal axis is the X co-ordinate axis and the Z axis corresponds to the vertical axis through the eye.

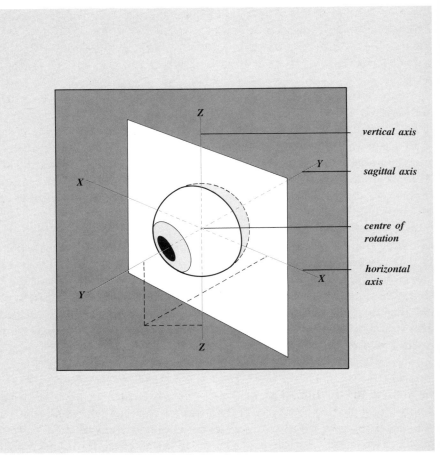

When the eye simply rotates around either the X axis or the Z axis, it takes up a *secondary position*. If the ocular rotation uses both the X and Z axes, it looks in an oblique direction and comes into a *tertiary position*. Of course, the eye may also rotate around the Y axis, in which case there is an ocular 'torsion' or cyclo-rotation.

A movement of the eye nasally, round the Z or vertical axis, is called an *adduction*, a movement temporally being known as an *abduction*. An ocular rotation around the horizontal X axis, produces either an upwards or downwards movement, called respectively *elevation* and *depression*. Rotation around the sagittal Y axis is with respect to the 12 o'clock position on the cornea. Nasal rotation of this point is called an *intorsion* (incyclo-rotation) while a temporal rotation is an *extorsion* (excyclo-rotation).

The extrinsic muscles have fixed origins within the orbit, the four recti and the superior oblique muscle having a forward course in the orbit to reach the eye. The somewhat conical form of the orbit, causes these muscles to diverge from each other long before they become attached to the eyeball. Since the medial walls of the two orbits are almost parallel to the sagittal plane, their lateral walls make an angle of about 45° with this plane. A central line, equidistant from the two walls of each orbit is thus at 22.5° to the sagittal plane (see Fig. 1.1).

As the four rectus muscles advance to their insertions on the eye, each is at an angle to the line of sight, the sizes of these angles (which depend on the places their ring of insertions occupy on the sclera) having decisive effects on ocular rotations.

At the terminal 4 to 9 mm of each extrinsic muscle, a tendinous band flattens out to merge with the sclera at the insertion. In each case, the extent of this tendon varies with individuals, the difference between the tendons of the respective muscles being relatively constant.

MACROANATOMY

There are seven extrinsic muscles, six of which rotate the eye, while one raises the upper eyelid. The latter, the levator muscle, is not able to move the eye, so it is not usually included when the extraocular muscles are considered.

Just as with other voluntary, striated, skeletal muscles, the extrinsic ocular muscles are made of cylindrical cells, rich in nuclei, called muscle fibres. Each muscle consists of 10 000 to 40 000 such muscle fibres, the diameters of which vary from 10 to 50 μm. The medial rectus has most muscle fibres, while the inferior oblique muscle has least. These fibres run parallel to the length of the muscle, being mingled to some extent with connective tissue. The belly of the muscle is covered with a layer of connective tissue, called the *epimysium*. From this epimysium, which has the thickest stratum of connective tissue, a network of much finer connective tissue fibres, known as the *perimysium*, extends into the middle of the muscle, dividing the muscle fibres into bundles. A very delicate *endomysium* is found as a connective tissue layer around individual muscle fibres.

Less perimysium is found in the extrinsic ocular muscles than in the skeletal muscles of the rest of the body. It also happens that the bundle construction of the muscles within the perimysium is less pronounced. The controlled amount of connective tissue between the bundles of muscle gives the muscles greater elasticity. Another special feature is the large quantity of endomysium surrounding each muscle fibre, relative to the striped musculature elsewhere.

One of the main purposes of this connective tissue is to encourage the parts of the muscle to work as a unit, by mutual pulling. Even if such a muscle is relatively short overall, about 40 mm in adults, not all of the muscle fibres are as long as the muscle itself. Thus it is important to have some transmission of activity between muscle fibres and this is aided by the connective tissue.

Muscles which are attached to opposite sides of the eye must have opposing effects on ocular rotation when they act and so are called antagonists. The symmetrical insertion points of the extrinsic ocular muscles round the eye provide three pairs of antagonists.

- The medial and lateral recti.
- The superior and inferior recti.
- The superior and inferior obliques.

The origins of the muscles at the annulus of Zinn

The four recti originate at an annular structure of connective tissue at the rear of the orbit, called the *annulus of Zinn* (circle of Zinn). From this foothold these muscles pass forward to attach themselves to the sclera, a few millimetres from the limbus. The superior oblique muscle originates from a position just above and medial to the annulus of Zinn. Then it runs forward to the *trochlea*, through this small tendinous 'pulley' and continues backwards to become attached at the posterior lateral half of the upper part of the globe. The inferior oblique muscle has its origin on the medial posterior lower region of the orbit at the maxilla. It is then inserted at the posterior lateral side of the lower part of the eyeball. The *annulus of Zinn* is a ring of tendon attached to the connective tissue around the optic canal, extending over the medial part of the superior orbital fissure.

In section, it is approximately oval, its upper part acting as the origins for the superior rectus and the levator muscle, with the medial rectus commencing on the medial aspect. Where some of the annulus extends across the superior orbital fissure, there is the origin of the lateral rectus. Rather below the optic canal, the lower section of the annulus of Zinn is fastened onto the sphenoid bone. As seen in Plate 1, this is where the inferior rectus has its origin.

Dura mater, which lines the optic canal, meets the periorbital tissue at the opening of the canal and at their junction they provide a suitably thick attachment for the annulus of Zinn. In cases of retrobulbal neuritis, this fibrous amalgamation with the dura can be responsible for pain during eye movements.

The periorbital covering forms a protective barrier around the superior orbital fissure, through which pass a succession of nerves and vessels. Part of this fissure is covered by the annulus of Zinn, therefore some individual nerves go through the annulus (as the oculomotor foramen) while some pass outside it (Fig. 9.2).

THE INSERTIONS OF THE EXTRINSIC MUSCLES

The four recti are inserted at different distances from the limbus, the superior rectus being furthest away, as follows:

- Superior rectus at about 7.9 mm.
- Lateral rectus at about 7.0 mm.

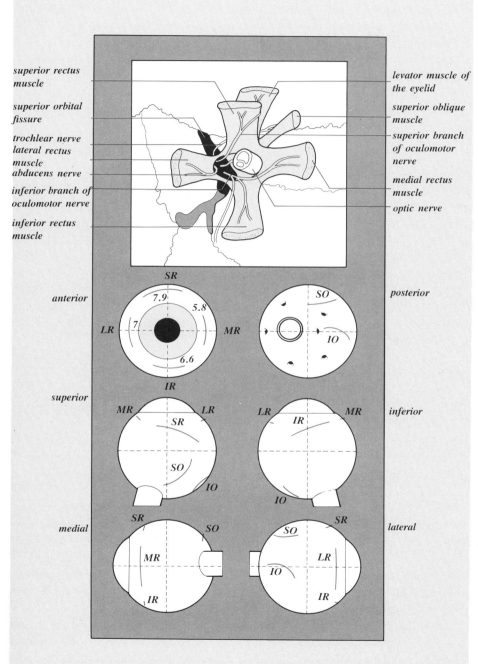

superior rectus muscle

superior orbital fissure

trochlear nerve
lateral rectus muscle
abducens nerve

inferior branch of oculomotor nerve

inferior rectus muscle

levator muscle of the eyelid

superior oblique muscle

superior branch of oculomotor nerve

medial rectus muscle

optic nerve

anterior

SR
7.9
5.8
LR — 7 — MR
6.6
IR

posterior

SO
IO

superior

MR — SR — LR
SO
IO

inferior

LR — IR — MR
IO

medial

SR — SO
MR
IR

lateral

SO — SR
IO — LR
IR

Fig. 9.2 Above: The origins of the extrinsic muscles at the apex of the orbit. *Below*: The insertions of the muscles on the eyeball, as seen from different directions.
SR: superior rectus.
MR: medial rectus.
IR: inferior rectus.
SO: superior oblique.
LR: lateral rectus.
IO: inferior oblique.

- Inferior rectus at about 6.6 mm.
- Medial rectus at about 5.8 mm.

The anterior part of each muscle consists of a tendon which spreads, fan-like, to attach itself into the sclera. The end of this tendon is set at 90° to the length of the muscle.

A circle, or rather a spiral, is formed by the positions where the tendons are inserted. This is sometimes known as the spiral of Tallaux.

Angles with respect to the visual axis, made by these muscles at their insertions, vary with each muscle and between individuals. Such angles have some bearing upon ocular rotations.

The superior rectus

This muscle originates in the annulus of Zinn, above the optic canal, where it blends with the dura around the optic nerve. It then moves anteriorly and laterally in the orbit *over* the attachment of the superior oblique and the equator. Above it is the levator of the upper lid. The superior rectus is inserted into the sclera some 7.9 mm from the limbus. It varies in thickness, being wider in the middle and towards its insertion where the muscle continues into its tendonous insertion. This tendon is about 5.8 mm long. As the rectus makes a somewhat lopsided angle of insertion, relative to the line of sight, this insertion is itself rather obliquely placed.

The muscle's blood supply is from the lateral muscle branch of the ophthalmic artery, and it is innervated by the superior branch of the oculomotor or III cranial nerve.

When the eye is in the primary position, the visual axis and the line of the muscle are at about 23°. Contraction of the muscle when the eye is thus placed, produces elevation, as well as adduction and intorsion. The main action is elevation, since the muscle is attached at the upper half of the eye and its direction of pull is backwards. However, we have seen how the direction is not exactly backwards, because of the 23° angle. Thus a small vector operates medially. In addition, the insertion is in advance of the centre of rotation, but the direction of pull is to the medial side of this centre. Hence, taking into account the insertion on the upper globe, there are supplementary rotational effects.

It follows that movement of the eye takes place around the vertical (Z) axis, nasally, or by adduction. Correspondingly, a rotation using the sagittal (Y) axis gives an intorsion.

The action of the superior rectus alters according to the eye's position, so that when, during abduction, the angle of the visual axis to the muscle axis becomes zero, then the chief result is elevation, additional actions such as intorsion and adduction being eliminated. Pure elevation arises when the superior rectus muscle pulls thus. In the same way, with the eye adducted, this muscle has its elevating power reduced, while the supplementary actions increase, particularly intorsion (Fig. 9.3).

The inferior rectus

From its origin at the annulus of Zinn, this muscle extends forwards and laterally. In common with the superior rectus, it makes an angle of about 23° with the visual axis. The tendon of the inferior rectus is approximately 5.5 mm long and is inserted into the sclera about 6.6 mm from the limbus. Above the muscle lie the optic nerve and the oculomotor nerve, embedded in orbital fat. Below is the orbital floor and, at the anterior end of the muscle, the inferior oblique.

The muscle receives its blood supply from the medial muscular branch of the ophthalmic artery; innervation is from the lower division of the oculomotor nerve.

The line of traction of the inferior rectus lies almost parallel to that of the superior rectus, the insertions of the two muscles being symmetrically placed above and below the globe. These muscles are antagonists. Thus the inferior rectus gives adduction and torsion as secondary actions, from the primary position of the eye. Its chief action is depression; after all, it is inserted at the lower part of the eye. Yet its adductive vector resembles that of the superior rectus. Rotation around the vertical (Z) axis would have the same effect, whether such pull is from above or below the eyeball, viz adduction. However, the muscle under consideration, being inserted below, produces extorsion around the sagittal axis. This, it will be recalled, rotates the corneal reference point of 12 o'clock temporally. Just as for the superior rectus, the main action of the inferior rectus is depression which is greater when the eye abducts, whereas during adduction the subsidiary actions, such as extorsion, are accentuated while the primary action diminishes (Fig. 9.4).

The medial rectus

Containing the greatest number of muscle fibres, this is consequently the thickest and strongest of the extraocular muscles. Its origin is at the medial aspect of the annulus of Zinn, also having connective tissue association with the dura mater around the optic nerve. The muscle advances along the medial wall of the orbit, to the scleral insertion at the intersection of the upper and lower quadrants of the eye, about 5.8 mm from the limbus. This insertion is comparatively short, at some 3.7 mm. Above this muscle is the superior oblique and between the bellies of the two muscles lie the ophthalmic artery, the superior ophthalmic vein and the nasociliary nerve.

The muscle is provided with blood from the medial muscular division of the

Fig. 9.3 The superior rectus muscle.

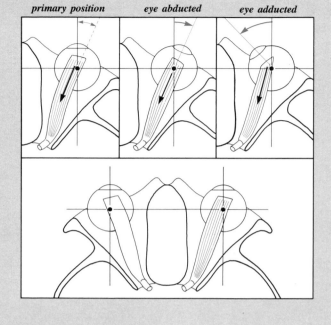

Fig. 9.4 The inferior rectus muscle.

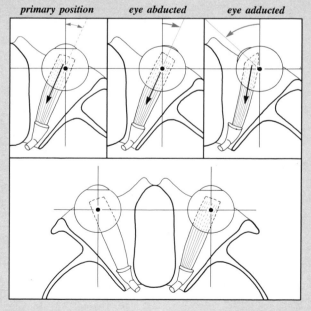

ophthalmic artery, and with nerve impulses by the inferior branch of the oculomotor nerve.

The direction of the muscle, which is forward to its insertion on the eye, is such that in the primary position, contraction has the effect of a pull parallel to the line of sight. Among the extrinsic muscles, only the medial and lateral recti have no secondary effects (in the primary position) on ocular rotation. The reasons for this are the coincidence of direction with the visual axis and the fact that the vector operates over the centre of rotation.

Starting with the primary position, the medial rectus moves the eye around a vertical (Z) axis, to produce adduction. On the other hand, the eye would elevate or be depressed were the muscle axis to depart from the position over the centre of rotation, when the line of traction would be at an angle with the visual axis, producing a secondary action. Were the visual axis to be in a depressed position as the muscle contracts, in addition to the primary action there would be a contribution to further ocular depression. Then the muscle would be operating from a line lower than the centre of rotation and assisting a turning round the X axis.

In a corresponding manner, an elevation will be encouraged as a secondary action when visual regard is upwards, bringing the muscle axis and action above the centre of rotation (Fig. 9.5).

The lateral rectus

This muscle has its origin on the lateral side of the annulus of Zinn, emerging from a bridge of tendon over the superior orbital fissure. In addition, it has a small lateral attachment on the great wing of the sphenoid bone, to the temporal side of the annulus. As it advances, the muscle follows the lateral wall of the orbit and is inserted in the sclera about 7.0 mm from the limbus, its tendon being approximately 8.8 mm in width. The lacrimal artery and the lacrimal nerve are above the muscle and the orbital floor lies below.

Blood comes from both the lateral muscular division of the ophthalmic artery and the lacrimal artery, while the VI cranial nerve, the abducent, provides a nerve supply.

As a pure antagonist to the medial rectus, the lateral rectus has a traction line which lies parallel to the line of sight. Both pull in the sagittal plane, the lateral rectus on the lateral side of the orbit. This lateral wall is set at about 45° to the medial wall, making the surface of contact between eye and muscle longer on the temporal side than medially. Thus the tendon of the lateral rectus is considerably longer than others. If the lateral rectus contracts, the eye being in the primary position, there is an uncomplicated abduction. However, just as in the case of the medial rectus, secondary action is possible. Elevation occurs when the visual axis is raised and depression is augmented during vision below the horizontal (Fig. 9.6).

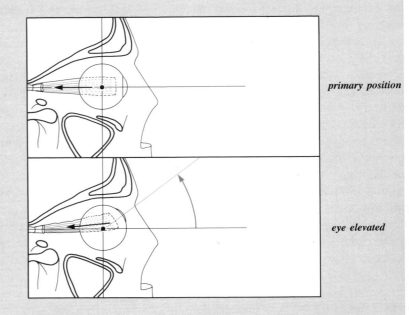

primary position

eye elevated

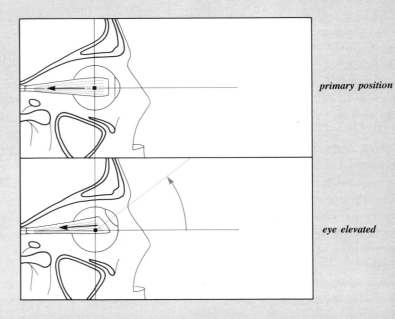

primary position

eye elevated

The superior oblique

This is a long, slender muscle, being the longest of the extraocular muscles. It starts above and medially to the origin of the superior rectus and then extends anteriorly along the medial orbital wall, rather above the medial rectus to the *trochlea*. The trochlea is a small loop of connective tissue attached to the frontal bone on the upper medial aspect of the orbit, a little behind the orbital rim. Muscle fibres of the superior oblique give way to a tendon before the latter goes through the trochlea. So the part traversing the trochlea has no muscle fibres. The muscle passes back from the trochlea, to make an angle of about 54° with the visual axis, then goes under the superior rectus to become inserted on the upper, posterior and lateral quadrant of the globe.

The muscle is supplied with blood by the lateral, muscular branch of the ophthalmic artery, while the IV cranial nerve, the trochlear nerve, provides innervation.

On account of its insertion and the fact that the angle of 54° exists for the primary position, as described above, the muscle's primary action is intorsion. The traction from the direction of the trochlea also makes the eye rotate around the horizontal (X) axis, giving depression as a secondary effect. Since the line of pull is effective from the rear of the vertical (Z) axis, another secondary action is abduction.

If the eye is adducted, the visual axis and the muscle line of action approach each other, so during adduction the main function of the superior oblique becomes depression.

Therefore downwards movement of the eye, caused by the inferior rectus, is supplemented by the superior oblique when the eye is adducted. On the other hand, during abduction, there is a lessening of the influence on depression, but intorsional and abductive effects are enhanced (Fig. 9.7).

The inferior oblique

This, a thin small muscle, is the only extrinsic muscle not to have its origin at the rear of the orbit, as it stems from the front, medial, floor of the orbit just behind the rim. The muscle stretches backward and upward, initially passing between the orbital floor and the inferior rectus, then between the lateral rectus and the eye itself. The insertion is at the lower ocular quadrant, which is on the lateral aspect at the back. Its tendon and that of the superior oblique, lie in the same direction, forming a loop around the back, lateral, part of the globe.

The medial muscular branch of the ophthalmic artery and the infraorbital artery both serve the muscle, its innervation being from the lowest part of the inferior division of the oculomotor nerve.

If the eye is in its primary position, there is an angle of about 51° between the muscle and the line of sight, when the primary action is extorsion. Because of the correspondence of course with the superior oblique, the inferior oblique has supplementary actions of elevation and abduction. Some increase of the effect on elevation is to be expected during adduction, with lessening of extorsion and abduction. During ocular adduction, the inferior oblique should supersede and replace the contribution the superior rectus makes to elevation. During abduction, this oblique muscle increases its actions of extorsion and abduction (Fig. 9.8).

The levator muscle of the upper lid

This, the 'levator palpebrae', may not properly be considered as an oculo-rotatory muscle, but it is both conventional and suitable to treat its actions in this context.

It has its origin at the rear of the orbit, at the lesser wing of the sphenoid bone, just above the origin of the superior rectus. These two muscles therefore have some common tissue at that point. A flattened belly then takes the course of the muscle forward along the roof of the orbit, just above the superior rectus, to about 10 mm behind the orbital septum. At this point the muscle terminates by fanning out into a tendinous aponeurosis, almost extending across the front part of the orbit. While there is a generally horizontal direction to the muscle, the tendinous part is bowed, so that this part ends up almost vertically disposed, as it continues forwards and down to where the spread tendons fasten into several parts of the upper lid.

The main attachment of the levator is at the upper lid's skin, below the superior palpebral furrow, the tendon fibres going through the orbicularis muscle. Some of the spread fibres of the tendon fasten into the upper tarsal plate, but the greatest amount of connection is through the smooth musculature of Müller's muscle. There are also attachments at the superior conjunctival fornix, which draw the conjunctiva up to follow the eye. At the outer canthus, the aponeurosis has an osseous attachment or 'horn'. This extends laterally, between the orbital and palpebral sections of the lacrimal gland and is attached at the orbital tubercle (on the zygoma) as well as being contiguous with the lateral palpebral ligament. A less robust medial horn moves into the medial palpebral ligament and lacrimal bone for its insertion.

The muscle receives its blood supply from the lateral muscular branch of the ophthalmic artery and its innervation from the superior division of the oculomotor nerve.

Since the levator action is to raise the upper lid, it is an antagonist to the orbicularis. On account of the intimate connective tissue association between the levator and the superior rectus, there is elevation of the lid as the eye moves upwards. (See the relevant passage concerning Tenon's capsule.)

Ptosis is a condition in which one or both of the upper lids cannot lift adequately, the resultant drooping covering most of the cornea. Sometimes the condition is congenital, or it may be the result of defective innervation or

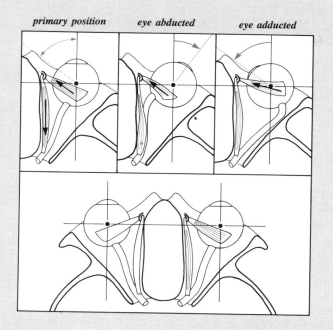

Fig. 9.7 The superior oblique muscle.

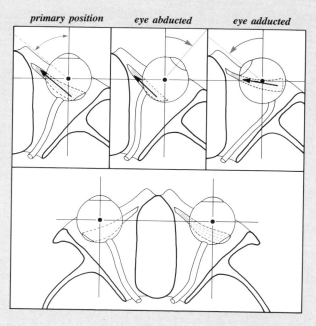

Fig. 9.8 The inferior oblique muscle.

diminished strength of the levator muscle. Innervational ptosis is most commonly unilateral, being the sequel to oculomotor nerve damage. Such damage is usually accompanied by interference with the position of the eye and faulty ocular movements.

The blood supply

The extraocular muscles are richly supplied with blood giving them the greatest muscle blood flow in the body. We have seen how each muscle is served by two small branches of the ophthalmic artery; for example, the lacrimal artery serves the lateral rectus. Frequently, the infraorbital artery sends branches to the inferior oblique. To summarize:

- The lateral muscular branch of the ophthalmic artery supplies the superior rectus, the lateral rectus, the superior oblique and the levator.
- The medial branch supplies most of the needs of the inferior rectus, the medial rectus and the inferior oblique.

These arteries enter the extraocular muscles, together with the appropriate nerves. The veins, too, usually use the same part of the muscle (see Chapter 10). There are branches from the arteries to the muscles which give rise to the anterior ciliary arteries.

MICROANATOM-
ICAL DETAILS

MICROANATOMICAL DETAILS

It is the positioning and power of the extrinsic muscles which produce ocular movements. But these extraocular muscles cannot be compared with ordinary skeletal muscle elsewhere in the body because they are unique in both structure and function. It has been known for a long time that the extraocular muscles contain more than one type of muscle fibre. Classical investigations have categorized the fibres in different groups on the basis of size. In such work from 1914, Thulin described two different types of extraocular muscle fibre in monkeys and in humans. One sort had irregular myofibrils of various sizes, with a special form of nerve terminal. The other type had evenly distributed fibrils, with more cytoplasm.

Thulin's categories can be considered to be the first accounts of the muscle fibres which later were described with the terms *felderstruktur* and *fibrillestruktur*. In a later study, Kato (1938) applied himself to the division of the muscle fibres. Those fibres having the largest diameters were found to be concentrated at the centre of the muscle, surrounded by smaller fibres out at the periphery. Electron microscopic study by Hess (1961) showed that there were distinct morphological differences between the two types of fibre. Hess and Pilar (1963) took these studies further, claiming on the basis of the fibres' anatomy that they had different physiological properties. Hess and Pilar found the felder fibres to be of a slow and tonic type, with many motor nerve terminals and without the capacity to generate an action potential over the complete muscle fibre, just near the nerve terminal. Fibrille fibres were of a rapid twitch type, more similar to other skeletal muscles as far as innervation and action potential responses were concerned.

This classification of muscle fibres into two main groups has been generally adopted and incorporated into the relevant literature and is still accepted.

Subsequently, more groups of muscle fibres have been distinguished, as a result of pharmacological, electrophysiological and histochemical studies. However, there is some disagreement as to how wide suitable groups or sub-groups should be in the classical divisions. Without ascertaining which of these classifications is closest to the truth, even with light microscopy it is possible to establish a quite genuine difference between at least two groups of fibres.

Transverse sections of muscle (across fibres) give us an idea of the total number of fibres in a muscle. These fibres lie in bundles, separated by the perimysium of the muscle. This division into bundles is not as pronounced as in other striated muscles and it diminishes towards the centre of the muscle. In this region, it is also difficult to separate one muscle fibre from another. As found by Kato, the diameter of fibres in the centre of the muscle is larger than those found more peripherally, the latter being a somewhat darker colour.

A cross section of a muscle fibre shows, with light microscopy, many small rounded fibrils making up the fibre. The space between individual fibrils varies with the type of fibre, on account of the differences in sarcoplasmic reticulum. From this, came the initial classification of such fibres, which are said to have a fibrille structure. In other words, they have more sarcoplasmic reticulum and show a light colour when standard histological methods are used (Fig. 9.9).

Any tissue section along the direction of the muscle fibres shows their myofibrils. It is the fibrils which are the contractile elements of the muscle and they consist of myofilaments, actin and myosin. Light and dark bands are produced by differing types of protein, so a transverse striped appearance exists along the whole length of the muscle fibres. Hence the name 'striated' muscle.

The I band and H band will vary, depending on the muscle's state of contraction. The length of the A band, which represents the myofilament, thus remains constant. Comparison between A bands of the different muscle fibres, within the fibrillar structure shows that they have different lengths, which suggests there are actually sub-groups (Fig. 9.10).

In the felder fibres it is difficult to distinguish between individual myofibrils, the entire muscle fibre acting uniformly as a single unit. There are Z lines, cross-partitioning the microfibrils, which are so densely packed, that there appear to be continuous lines crossing the width of the muscle fibres.

In the fibrille fibres, the interstices between individual Z lines are such that neighbouring myofibrils can be distinguished from each other. The Z lines are straighter, but do not necessarily close up to where the adjoining Z line begins.

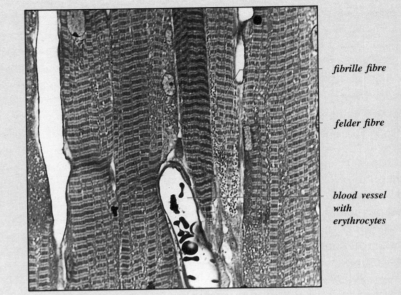

Fig. 9.9 A muscle fibre in an extraocular muscle. (*Microphoto: J.R. Bruenech.*)

fibrille fibre

felder fibre

blood vessel with erythrocytes

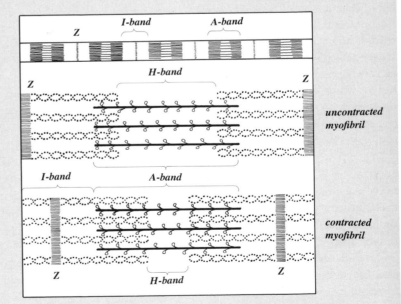

Fig. 9.10 Sarcoma in uncontracted state and in contracted state.

Z   I-band   A-band

Z   H-band   Z

uncontracted myofibril

I-band   A-band

contracted myofibril

Z   H-band   Z

As a result, there are irregular dividing lines. The differences between the two fibre types lie in their amounts of sarcoplasmic reticulum.

Contraction of a muscle depends on the transport of Ca^{++} ions. A rapid passage of ions following absorption, produces correspondingly rapid contraction, controlled by the sarcoplasmic reticulum. The big difference in amounts of sarcoplasmic reticulum between the dark, thin felder fibres and the lighter, thick fibrille fibres shows that the latter can respond more rapidly.

Another differing characteristic of the two types of fibre is the prevalence of mitochondria. These well known organelles have the capacity to convert effectively chemical energy from cytoplasm into energy which is useful to the cell itself (ATP). When the cell possesses many mitochondria, it has constant access to energy. Resembling red and white cross-striated skeletal muscles, the fibres of the extraocular muscles possess varying amounts of mitochondria. Looking at the size, abundance and distribution of the mitochondria in the extrinsic muscles, their classical division does appear to be rather an over-simplification, because there are huge variations between fibres which to all appearances have identical ultrastructures. This has also led to sub-divisions among fibres which were formerly lumped together in the same group.

Motor nerve terminals of these muscles fall into two main categories. One type has a distinct striation similar to the classical motor end plates found in other striped muscles, its one or two dark boundaries being clearly visible. The other type has many small oval 'felder', which are spread along the length of the fibre and are known as 'en grappe' since they resemble bunches of grapes. Every time the appertinent motor nerve winds itself round the surface of the fibre, it sends out such terminals.

There are grounds for belief that there are different varieties of activity within the extraocular muscles, because these many types of muscle fibre exist. Hess and Pilar (1963) were the first to differentiate between fibres on the basis of physiological performance. Greatest differences are found between muscle fibres whose systems of innervation are distinctive.

Fibrille fibres use a classical motor end plate and thus produce an action potential which depolarizes along the length of the muscle fibre, resulting in a rapid and uniform contraction, called the 'twitch' contraction.

In the case of felder fibres, where no action potential arises, depolarization is very parochial, being confined to a small region a few millimetres from the nerve terminal. The muscle fibres, similarly, pull at the same time, because there are many small terminals along the fibre. This simultaneous activity is therefore produced gradually, depending on how strongly the depolarization builds up (Fig. 9.11).

Parallels between the physiological characteristics of different muscle fibres and the distinctive types of eye movement have been made successfully for some time. After Hess and Pilar pointed out their discovery of 'rapid' and 'slow' types of fibre, many theories were introduced. It was natural to suggest that for slower ocular movements, such as when the eyes drift or make sustained fixations, the slow felder structure fibres would be involved. Such movements

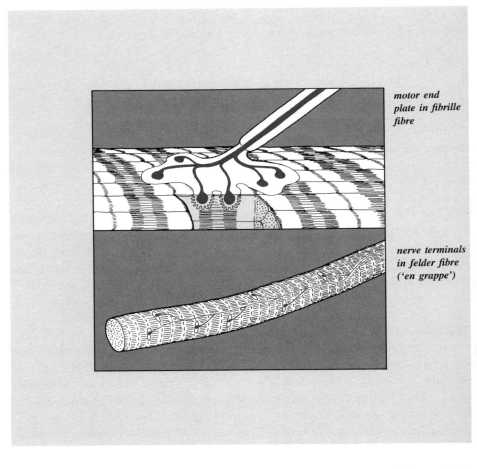

Fig. 9.11 Nerve terminals in an extraocular muscle fibre.

motor end plate in fibrille fibre

nerve terminals in felder fibre ('en grappe')

would not call for rapid contractions, but require enduring conditions, which exactly match the known habits of this type of fibre.

Saccadic eye movements might be assumed to be caused by rapid fibrille fibres because their action potential allows immediate depolarization to be effected, and provides the means for a rapid and powerful contraction. Electromyographic measurements, however, have shown that such theories are a simplification of the actual situation. Apparently, all groups of fibres are active with every type of ocular movement and there is no group of fibres which acts in isolation. At the same time, it is true that not all fibres contract as much as each other during different excursions of the eyes. Even if one could detect activity in every type of fibre during a saccade, there is little doubt that it is summation of the rapid fibrille fibres' effects, which produces the rotation. Contraction of the felder fibres is too weak to make a contribution worthy of mention in connection with such fast movements.

The role of different types of muscle fibre is a matter of sustained debate in the context of oculomotor action. It has been discovered that alterations occur in the ultra structure of fibres in patients with particular forms of strabismus.

But it is not understood how the distinctions between various types of fibres are involved, in this case.

INNERVATION OF THE EXTRAOCULAR MUSCLES

The oculomotor nerve innervates the superior, inferior and medial recti with the inferior oblique. The trochlear or IVth cranial nerve, controls the superior oblique, while the lateral rectus is supplied by the VIth cranial or abducent nerve. Each of these nerves enter their respective muscles about midway between the origin and the tendon. All have striated fibres and their effector organs are typical ones; innervation is by nerves carrying both sensory and motor fibres.

The nerve to a single muscle contains between two and three thousand nerve fibres of different thicknesses. These range from thick myelinated nerve fibres whose diameter is up to 15 μm, to lesser unmyelinated fibres with diameters down to 0.5 μm.

Motor innervation

A motor unit consists of a motor neuron, the axon and all the muscle fibres with which it is in contact. When the neuron produces stimulation, all these muscle fibres contract, hence the name 'unit'. A motor neuron which innervates the extraocular muscles, controls only a small number of muscle fibres, about 6 to 10. Thus there are proportionally more small motor units within the extraocular muscle than in other body muscles whose motor units may be linked to up to a couple of thousand muscle fibres.

Some muscle fibres can operate independently. Indeed, the delicate motility seen in high grade binocular vision, would not be possible without small motor units. Each motor nerve reaches its muscle by advancing parallel to that muscle until it reaches its point of entry (close to the middle zone) after which it branches into many small nerve fibres which move in both proximal and distal directions. The concentration of motor end plates is greatest in the middle zone of the muscle.

In the case of the normal neuromuscular junction, a transmitter substance initiates the action potential in the muscle fibre. This leads on to a rapid depolarizing of the muscle's resting potential and a quick, uniform, contraction of the muscle fibre. Fibrille fibres also react to innervation like this.

Felder fibres, on the other hand, react only with a local depolarization. So each single terminal gives only one contraction to a restricted length of muscle fibre. However, this is compensated by the fact that each fibre receives many terminals from the same nerve, so the final result may also be a contraction of the whole muscle fibre.

Sensory innervation

In order to operate the delicate motor control of the extraocular muscles, the central nervous system relies upon 'feed-back' messages. The body's muscles usually receive information gained through the sensory nerves, which come from receptors in the muscles and muscle spindle to the central nervous system. There are receptors in the extraocular muscles which have distinct morphological and physiological resemblances with the receptors found in other types of striated muscle. And there is actually a large number of muscle spindles in the extraocular muscles. Indeed, Sunderland (1950) reported up to 71 in a single muscle. Usually there is one muscle spindle to about eight encapsuled muscle fibres. These so-called 'intrafusal' muscle fibres are normally thinner than the remaining muscle fibres, which are known as 'extrafusal'. A 'gamma system' provides motor innervation to the intrafusal fibres, at the ending of each fibre, while the middle section receives a sensory nerve branch which coils itself several times around the middle of the fibre. When the muscle contracts the muscle spindle also reacts: this is known as an 'alpha/gamma' composite activity. Intrafusal muscle fibres in the extrinsic ocular muscles, however, do not have the same type of modification. They have nearly the same diameters as the extrafusal fibres and therefore less inbuilt freedom of movement. The condition for correct 'feed-back' is that the intrafusal fibres' contraction is independent of that of the extrafusal fibres. Such a condition is only partially fulfilled in the muscle spindles of the extraocular muscles. Also, the intrafusal fibres can be stained after degeneration.

These factors, together with additional morphological variations, have made researchers question whether there is any proprioceptive function in the extraocular muscles. Others claim that in early life, the muscle spindles' function is to develop binocular vision after which, visual stimuli are adequate and supplant such proprioceptive data. A sufficiently large disparity between the two cortical visual impressions is able to initiate appropriate motor impulses to the extraocular muscles.

TESTING OCULAR MOTILITY

It is possible for the tonus in a muscle to lessen, perhaps because of muscle or nerve damage. This would alter the effects which the unaffected muscles have on the eye. Thus, if there is sufficient disturbance of the relative actions, the eye will change its position. This means that the eye's position and/or function relative to the unaffected eye will be unbalanced. In fact, there will be an anomaly of binocular control.

When the eye is in the primary position, several muscles are in action, so it is difficult to detect which of them may be faulty. Yet it is possible to determine a fixation direction in which an individual muscle should be working alone, so that its action can be investigated. Motility tests rely on this principle. The test uses a pattern of ocular movements with which the action of every muscle in turn can be isolated. This is done by comparing the relative positions of the two eyes in a given direction of gaze, whereby the eye and then the muscle at fault can be detected (Fig. 9.12).

The cover test is a simple test of binocular vision, which involves covering one eye at a time, while observing the resulting movements of the eyes. Combined with a motility test, the cover test enables us to detect whether the condition is concomitant (any ocular deviation is the same in all directions of gaze) or incomitant (where the deviation will alter with direction of gaze).

The principle behind the motility test is involved in any full evaluation of binocularity; for example, when measuring heterophoria.

Take the case of a vertical strabismus, where there is a larger deviation for distance vision than for near vision. This gives a clear indication of which group of muscles is involved. During distance vision, it is the superior rectus which has the strongest effect on elevation, while for near vision it is the inferior oblique. One merely has to decide which eye has the affected muscle.

In heterotropias, which arise as the result of a reduced muscle function, most cases will show an incomitant condition, the angle of squint altering according to the direction of fixation. Such patients suffer from double vision (diplopia) whose extent will alter in accordance with the angle of strabismus.

Many clinicians take advantage of these facts by asking patients 'In which direction of gaze do you find the greatest amount of double vision?' The diplopia would obviously be greatest in the position which corresponds to the primary action of the affected muscle. Patients with diplopia often try to compensate this situation by turning their heads into unnatural positions. The head is turned towards the side where the defective muscle normally makes least contribution.

A patient with a 'paresis' of the lateral rectus in the left eye will have an esotropia in the primary position. When the patient looks left, the angle of squint will increase, because horizontal rotation of the two eyes to the left requires the actions of the right medial rectus and the left lateral rectus. If there is a greater need for co-operation of the defective muscle, there will be a greater angle of strabismus.

Now suppose the same patient looks right. This should involve the right lateral rectus and the left medial rectus, so the defective muscle is not involved in the movement. Thus, there will be a reduction of the tropia, or it will be completely removed. To reinforce this observation, it is possible to notice also how the patient moves the head to the left in this situation, as the gaze moves to the right. This head movement should be in the direction of the defective muscle. Corresponding effects can be noticed when patients have vertical or torsional anomalies (see Fig. 9.13).

A patient with a hypertropia may be able to compensate for the situation by moving the head forward or backward. If the defective muscle is one with an elevation action, the head will be moved so that the activity of the depressor muscles is increased. It is worth-while noting how horizontal anomalies can

Fig. 9.12 The motility test. Arrows indicate directions of primary action of extraocular muscles for eye movements.

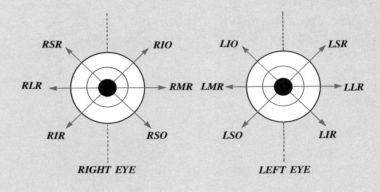

RIGHT EYE   LEFT EYE

Fig. 9.13 On the left: Normal eyes making torsional rotations as the head leans to one side. *On the right*: Paresis of left superior oblique muscle, producing diplopia. As the head leans to the right, the diplopia lessens and perhaps disappears, on account of postural reflexes.

also produce a raising or lowering of the head. Most people have the so-called V syndrome, in which the two eyes tend to converge more when the eyes look down. Those with an 'exo' condition (exotropia or exophoria) should benefit from that 'V' tendency during near vision and the opposite is the case for those with an 'eso' condition. The best way to compensate eso conditions, is to hold a book high and depress the head forwards so that the gaze is upward. As an example, a person may find it more agreeable to lie on the floor, face nearest to the set, when watching television.

Abnormalities of torsion may be compensated by leaning the head to one side, down towards the shoulder. For example, if the left superior oblique has a paresis, the result is extorsion. By holding the head down towards the right shoulder the patient can produce a relative intorsion of the right eye. Thus, the relative difference between the rotations about the Y axis for the two eyes will be reduced and there will be a more tolerable outcome.

Chapter 10
The Orbital Blood Vessels

The *ophthalmic artery* arises from the *internal carotid artery*, first moving vertically and bending forward to pass through the *optic canal* underneath the *optic nerve*. The artery emerges into the orbit laterally to the nerve, but almost immediately crosses over to the medial side. Together with the nasociliary nerve, it extends forwards within the orbit on the medial side, between the bellies of the *medial rectus* and the *superior oblique*. Somewhat behind the septum orbitale it divides into two terminal branches, the dorsal nasal artery and the supratrochlear artery.

The ophthalmic artery supplies the orbit, neighbouring structures of the forehead and the region of the nose, having many anastomoses with the *external carotid* through the facial arteries. During its course forwards within the orbit it sends out numerous branches to the different orbital structures.

DIVISIONS OF THE OPHTHALMIC ARTERY

The *central retinal artery* leaves the ophthalmic artery when its anterior part is still under the optic nerve. It then follows underneath the nerve until at about 10 to 15 mm behind the globe, it strikes into the nerve at about the same point as the central retinal vein leaves it, the latter having brought blood from the optic disc. The artery nourishes the anterior aspect of the optic nerve and the retina.

The *short posterior ciliary arteries* originate from the ophthalmic artery, where the anterior part of the ophthalmic artery lies below the optic nerve. These arteries produce between 10 and 20 tributaries which penetrate the eyeball in a ring around the optic nerve. After this, small episcleral vessels are supplied and there is a network of vessels formed in the choroid. Branches of the short ciliary arteries also form the circle of Zinn.

The *long posterior ciliary arteries* arise from the ophthalmic artery near its crossing of the optic nerve, as two, long, thin arteries entering the sclera on each side of the nerve, rather lateral to the short ciliaries. Advancing through and forwards between the sclera and the choroid they do not branch here but produce the *major arterial circle* (of the iris). This arterial annulus, lying almost at the root of the iris, supplies the ciliary body and iris with blood. Through branches which pass backward, the circle anastomoses with choroidal arteries (Fig. 10.1).

The *anterior ciliary arteries* come from the muscular arteries of the four recti. As a rule, each rectus carries two arteries, but the lateral rectus has only one.

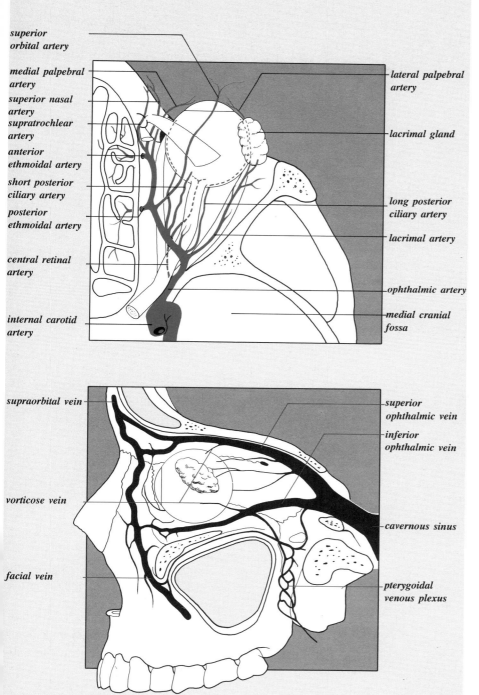

superior
orbital artery

medial palpebral
artery

superior nasal
artery

supratrochlear
artery

anterior
ethmoidal artery

short posterior
ciliary artery

posterior
ethmoidal artery

central retinal
artery

internal carotid
artery

lateral palpebral
artery

lacrimal gland

long posterior
ciliary artery

lacrimal artery

ophthalmic artery

medial cranial
fossa

Fig. 10.1 The orbital arteries.

supraorbital vein

vorticose vein

facial vein

superior
ophthalmic vein

inferior
ophthalmic vein

cavernous sinus

pterygoidal
venous plexus

Fig. 10.2 The more important orbital veins.

The anterior ciliary arteries form the limbal plexus in the sclera and have anastomoses with the plexi in the conjunctival and limbal region. Branches from the anterior ciliary arteries bore through the sclera and supply blood to the major arterial circle.

The *lacrimal artery* is an important one, arising from the ophthalmic artery, just after the latter leaves the optic canal. It travels laterally along the orbit, along the upper edge of the lateral rectus muscle, together with the lacrimal nerve, to reach the gland. The lacrimal artery's branches include its terminal lateral palpebral artery. This supplies the upper and lower lids on their lateral sides, where the medial palpebral artery and the arterial arcades of the lids are situated. The lacrimal artery sends a branch to the lateral rectus and while still at the rear of the orbit, it has a meningeal branch, which anastomoses with the *medial meningeal artery*.

Muscular branches from the ophthalmic artery consist of two which supply the extraocular muscles with blood. The lateral branch goes to the lateral rectus, the superior rectus, the levator and the superior oblique muscles. The medial branch supplies the inferior rectus, the medial rectus and the inferior oblique.

The *supraorbital artery* leaves the ophthalmic artery near the passage over the optic nerve, advancing along the orbital roof, first medially and later above the levator. The artery passes through the supraorbital foramen to provide a blood supply to the upper eyelid and forehead, then produces branches to the levator, the periorbital and bony tissues. Anastomoses are made with the temporal and supratrochlear arteries.

The *posterior ethmoidal artery* moves with its corresponding nerve into the posterior ethmoidal air cells, supplying them and the nasal mucous membranes with blood. It also supplies part of the dura mater in the anterior part of the skull.

The *anterior ethmoidal artery* is larger than those just mentioned. It travels through the anterior ethmoidal cavity to the anterior ethmoidal cells, from where it moves up into the front bones of the skull, and gives off a meningeal offshoot. The artery continues down through the spongy plates of the region to the nasal cavity, the mucous membrane and its skin.

The *medial palpebral arteries* are two vessels which leave the ophthalmic artery in the anterior part of the orbit, just under the trochlea. They pass respectively under and over the medial palpebral ligament and travel to the upper and lower lids. Here they join the palpebral arcades and the lateral palpebral artery.

The *nasal artery* forms one of the terminations of the ophthalmic artery, passing through the septum orbitale rather above the medial palpebral ligament. This artery supplies the root of the nose and the lacrimal sac, anastomosing with the facial arteries.

Another of the ophthalmic artery's terminations is the *supratrochlear artery*, which penetrates the septum orbitale above the trochlea together with its accompanying nerve. It ascends onto the forehead at the medial part of the

orbital rim and supplies the skin, muscle and periosteum there. It also anastomoses with adjoining arteries on the same side and with tributaries of the
supraorbital artery.

VEINS

The veins of the orbit are extensive and have many anastomoses, which also
have many extensions to venous plexi in the neighbourhood of the orbit. Most
orbital veins drain into the *cavernous sinus* via the *superior ophthalmic vein*.
The *inferior ophthalmic vein* is also large, usually emptying into the superior
vein, so it can be treated as a branch of that. Orbital veins have no valves, but
produce widespread anastomoses with facial veins, with the *pterygoid venous
plexus* and with the nasal venous plexus. Most veins match the corresponding
arteries and drain the appropriate structures. Only those which show distinct
departures from this principle are now to be described in detail (Fig. 10.2).

The *superior ophthalmic vein* arises from the plexus near the medial corner
of the orbit. It passes backward with the ophthalmic artery and receives
tributaries corresponding to the arterial system. Close to the apex of the orbit,
it receives the central retinal vein and here the inferior ophthalmic vein joins
the main stream. The superior ophthalmic vein also takes in the upper vortex
veins from the globe, then crosses over the optic nerve with the artery and
traverses the *superior orbital fissure*, before emptying into the *cavernous sinus*.

The *inferior ophthalmic vein* starts from the plexus near the front edge of the
orbital floor, moves back with the inferior rectus and empties into the superior
ophthalmic vein, or directly into the cavernous sinus. It has anastomoses with
the facial veins and the pterygoid plexus. The vein joins branches from the
inferior rectus, the lateral rectus, the inferior oblique, the lacrimal sac and the
lower vortex veins.

The *cavernous sinus* is situated on each side of the *sella turcica* in the central
depression of the skull. In common with other intracranial venous sinuses, the
cavernous sinus occupies a cavity between the two leaves of the dura mater.
The sinus has virtually a spongiform construction, since it contains extensive
connective tissue fibres. It is from this appearance that the sinus derives its
name. The abducent nerve and the internal carotid artery traverse the sinus
and many structures are attached to its lateral wall. Above and below are
located various nerves: the oculomotor, the trochlear, the ophthalmic and
maxillary. Rather laterally to the cavernous sinus, lies the semilunar (Gasserian)
ganglion. The sinus collects venous blood from the anterior, lower, part of the
brain and from the orbit (Plate 11).

THE CRANIAL NERVES

Nerves to the orbit convey motor, sensory and autonomic impulses. Most of the innervation is concerned with cranial nerves, six of the twelve having actions connected with the visual system. The somatic–motor innervation is from cranial nerves III, IV and VI, with a branch of VII being concerned with closing the eyelids. Sensory impulses from the eye and orbit follow the V cranial nerve's first and second divisions. Parasympathetic innervation for the eye and orbit is through fibres in cranial nerves III and VII, while sympathetic innervation comes from the *superior cervical ganglion*. The postganglionic fibres reach the orbit via the sympathetic nerve plexus along the *internal carotid artery*.

Of the twelve cranial nerves, only the few with activity relevant to vision are now to be considered. The optic nerve (cranial nerve II) was dealt with in Chapter 6.

The oculomotor or III cranial nerve

This nerve emerges from the front of the brain stem in the cisterna or fossa interpeduncularis, coming from its nucleus in the mesencephalon. It advances in the middle depression of the cranium, covered with pia mater. The nerve lies in the supra-arachnoidal space here, later penetrating the dura mater to become fixed in the lateral wall of the cavernous sinus. On the way, it receives sensory fibres from the ophthalmic nerve and sympathetic fibres from the plexus around the internal carotid. Before it enters the orbit, it divides into a smaller superior branch and a larger inferior branch. These two branches pass into the orbit via the superior orbital fissure, rather medially, in that part of the fissure which holds the fibrous annulus of Zinn. This region around the optic canal has been called the 'oculomotor foramen' (see Fig. 11.1 and Plate 1).

The *superior division* of the third nerve ascends to enter the rear half of the superior rectus muscle. Having produced this supply, the nerve continues through this muscle to supply the levator muscle which is on top. Now and then, branches may be sent to the levator, via the medial side of the superior rectus, instead of through it.

The *inferior division* itself divides into three small nerves to supply the medial and inferior recti and the inferior oblique. The nerve to the medial rectus travels medially under the optic nerve and pushes in at the back section

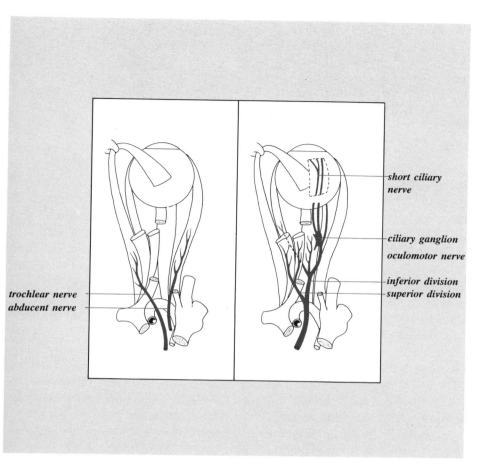

trochlear nerve
abducent nerve

short ciliary nerve

ciliary ganglion
oculomotor nerve

inferior division
superior division

Fig. 11.1 Cranial nerves innervating the extraocular muscles.

of the muscle on its lateral side. The branch to the inferior rectus moves forward on the upper surface of the muscle to enter its belly in the back half. The longest of the three branches travels to the inferior oblique muscle, moves forwards along the orbital floor and lateral to the inferior rectus. Then it uses the typical position of entry to the muscle.

The nerve to the inferior oblique sends a thick but short root to the ciliary ganglion. This transmits III nerve parasympathetic fibres which synapse in the ganglion. The postganglionic fibres follow the short ciliary nerves to the globe.

The third cranial nerve is very large in relation to the number of muscle fibres which it supplies. Holding some 24 000 nerve fibres, it is the largest of the motor nerves to supply the extrinsic muscles of the eye. It also carries thin parasympathetic fibres to the ciliary ganglion.

The oculomotor nerve nucleus lies in the brain stem within the anterior part of the grey matter around the aqueduct and at the top of the superior colliculus. The nucleus consists of a somatic, motor, section which controls voluntary muscles and a parasympathetic part, the Edinger−Westphal sub-nucleus, which supplies parasympathetic innervation to the eye.

If there is complete paralysis of the oculomotor nerve, the eye is unable to move upwards, downwards or inwards. It will suffer a divergent strabismus because of the tonus of the lateral rectus and also depression of the eye, which comes from the tonus of the superior oblique. The upper lid will droop over the upper cornea (ptosis), since the levator muscle will be paralysed. The pupil will be dilated and there will be paralysis of accommodation, caused by damage to the eye's parasympathetic innervation. In partial lesions of the nerve, one or more of these effects can appear.

The trochlear or IV cranial nerve

This is the thinnest of the cranial nerves, containing only about 3400 fibres. It leaves the brain stem at the back, just under the inferior colliculus. Before it emerges, it crosses over from one side to the other. The nerve goes round the brain stem, moving forward on the ventral side. It is covered with pia mater and advances within the subarachnoidal space, then passes through the dura mater just under the oculomotor nerve, to the cavernous sinus. When the nerve leaves the sinus it bends upward and crosses the oculomotor on its lateral side. The trochlear nerve enters the orbit through the superior orbital fissure, above the annulus of Zinn. Within the orbit, the nerve progresses medially, above the levator and near the top of the rear of the superior oblique muscle. Here it splits into a number of small terminals and penetrates the muscle.

The trochlear nerve has its nucleus in the brain stem, near but below the oculomotor nucleus, and abreast of the inferior colliculus.

In cases of trochlear nerve paralysis there is overaction of the inferior oblique muscle and consequently hypertropia and extorsion. If the lesion is unilateral, the patient can unconsciously tilt the head towards the unaffected side, as well as forward, in order to avoid diplopia.

The trigeminal or V cranial nerve

As a somatic afferent nerve, this deals with sensory impulses from the face and its surrounds. In addition, it has a motor part which is involved with mastication.

The trigeminal nerve emerges from the lateral aspect of the pons, immediately forming the *semilunar* or *Gasserian ganglion* in the middle fossa of the skull, rather lateral to the cavernous sinus. The semilunar ganglion is sensory and corresponds to the chain of spinal ganglia. The nerve's nucleus is extended, the sensory part stretching throughout the brain stem, while the motor section lies in the pons, a little below the IV nerve nucleus.

Three divisions of the nerve extend from the semilunar ganglion:

- The ophthalmic.
- The maxillary.
- The mandibular.

The orbital divisions of the ophthalmic nerve

The nerve advances within the lateral wall of the cavernous sinus, below the trochlear nerve and over the maxillary nerve. On the way, it receives a sympathetic supply from the carotid plexus and sends (proprioceptive) sensory fibres to the cranial nerves III, IV and VI. It also gives out meningeal branches to the *cerebellar tentorium*. Just before it enters the superior orbital fissure, the nerve divides into three parts to form:

- The lacrimal nerve.
- The frontal nerve.
- The naso-ciliary nerve.

The *lacrimal nerve*, as the smallest of the three branches, comes into the orbit at the lateral aspect of the fissure, above the annulus of Zinn. It moves forwards in the orbit laterally along the upper part of the lateral rectus, together with the lacrimal artery. During its course, it receives from the zygomatic nerve some secretory fibres. The lacrimal nerve innervates the lacrimal gland, the skin around the outer canthus, and the lateral parts of the upper eyelid and conjunctiva.

The *frontal nerve*, the largest of these branches, enters the superior orbital fissure just to the medial side of the lacrimal nerve, outside the annulus of Zinn. It then follows the roof of the orbit on the upper surface of the levator muscle. However, halfway along the orbit, it bifurcates into a larger supraorbital part and a lesser supratrochlear division.

The *supraorbital nerve* also follows the orbital roof, above the levator and leaves the orbit through the supraorbital foramen. It supplies the upper lid, the conjunctiva, the forehead and parts of the mucous membrane in the frontal sinus.

The *supratrochlear nerve* progresses medially and forward. It passes above the trochlea and, with the supratrochlear artery, moves up on to the forehead, innervating the upper lid, conjunctiva and the medial parts of the skin of the forehead.

The *nasociliary* nerve enters the orbit through the 'oculomotor foramen'. It bends medially, passes over the optic nerve and advances along the medial orbital wall between the bellies of the medial rectus and the superior oblique muscles. It produces many branches:

- The long sensory root of the ciliary ganglion.
- The two long ciliary nerves.
- The posterior ethmoidal nerve.
- The anterior ethmoidal nerve.
- The infratrochlear nerve.

The *sensory root* of the *ciliary ganglion* leaves the naso-ciliary soon after it enters the orbit. The fibres traverse the ganglion and go to the eye with the short ciliary nerves, to receive sensory impulses.

The *long ciliary nerves* both leave the naso-ciliary close to its passage over the optic nerve. They then travel together with the nerves from the ciliary ganglion, to penetrate the sclera near the optic nerve. Without dividing on the way, the fibres reach the anterior part of the eye through the suprachoroidea. There the nerves carry sympathetic fibres to the pupil dilatator muscle and sensory fibres from the cornea.

The *posterior ethmoidal nerve* parts company with the naso-ciliary to pass through the posterior ethmoidal foramen. It innervates the mucous membrane in the posterior ethmoidal bony cavities.

The *anterior ethmoidal nerve*, one of the two end terminals of the naso-ciliary nerve, enters the anterior ethmoidal foramen, goes into the anterior ethmoidal sinuses and innervates the membranes there. It continues up the anterior cranial depression, with its corresponding artery and moves further on into the nasal cavity. Here it supplies the nasal mucous membrane and the skin at the lower part of the nose.

The *infratrochlear nerve*, the other terminal, continues forward over the medial rectus, passes under the trochlea and penetrates the septum orbitale to reach the inner canthus. It innervates the lacrimal sac, nearby conjunctiva and the region's skin, including that of the upper nose.

The ophthalmic nerve may be infected by the 'varicella zoster' virus, one of the herpes virus group. This virus lies latent in the nerve ganglion, but with provocation can infect the structures served by the sensory nerve. Ophthalmic herpes zoster, or 'shingles', is an acute, one-sided, inflammation which often affects the elderly. It can extend over the complete area supplied by the ophthalmic nerve, or it can just affect a single branch (Fig. 11.2).

The maxillary nerve or upper jaw branch of V

This leaves the semilunar ganglion to advance into the side of the cavernous sinus, under the ophthalmic nerve. It leaves the cranium via the *foramen rotundum* then reaches the *pterygopalatine fossa* where it produces branches to the spheno-palatine (Meckel's) ganglion. Then two divisions move into the orbit through the inferior orbital fissure.

The *infraorbital nerve* extends forward by a groove or canal in the orbital floor, known as the infraorbital sulcus. On its way, it gives off several branches to innervate the teeth and the gums of the upper cheek, also the mucous membrane of the maxillary sinus. The nerve reaches forward onto the cheek through the infraorbital foramen to innervate the skin, parts of the face and nose, the lower lid and nearby conjunctiva.

The *zygomatic nerve* advances along the lateral orbital wall to provide secretory fibres to the lacrimal gland, through the lacrimal nerve. Then it

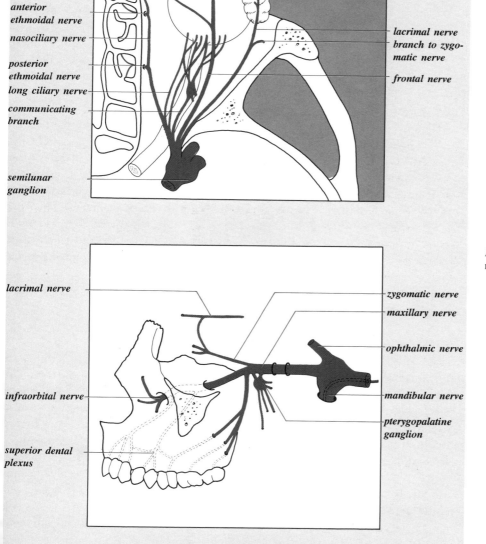

supratrochlear nerve

infratrochlear nerve

anterior ethmoidal nerve

nasociliary nerve

posterior ethmoidal nerve

long ciliary nerve

communicating branch

semilunar ganglion

supraorbital nerve

lacrimal nerve

branch to zygomatic nerve

frontal nerve

Fig. 11.2 The ophthalmic nerve.

lacrimal nerve

infraorbital nerve

superior dental plexus

zygomatic nerve

maxillary nerve

ophthalmic nerve

mandibular nerve

pterygopalatine ganglion

Fig. 11.3 The maxillary nerve.

leaves the orbit via the zygomatic foramen. It innervates the skin of the temple and the chin and sends a branch to the outer canthus (Fig. 11.3).

The mandibular nerve

The *mandibular nerve* leaves the cranial cavity through the foramen ovale and goes to the infratemporal fossa, where it branches copiously. Motor fibres control mastication muscles and various neck muscles. Sensory innervation is supplied to the skin of the temple and the oral cavity (including tongue membranes). A long branch, the inferior alveolar nerve, passes into the mandibular foramen through the mandibular canal and comes forward by way of a notch through the mental foramen. The branch innervates teeth and gums in the lower cheek region, skin (via a notch) and the lower lip.

The VI cranial or abducent nerve

This emerges from the brain stem between the pons and the lateral side of the pyramid. It then passes upwards and forward in the subarachnoidal space, enveloped in pia mater. Slightly behind the dorsum cellae, it penetrates the dura mater and bends straight over the acute angle in the petrosal part of the temporal bone. The nerve moves on through the cavernous sinus, close to the internal carotid. Its entry into the orbit is via the superior orbital fissure, inside the oculomotor foramen. Within the orbit, it moves laterally and forward to enter the lateral rectus on the medial aspect of its rear portion. Note that the nerve only innervates this muscle.

The abducent nerve is small, comprising between six and seven thousand fibres. Its nucleus is in the pons, slightly below the motor nucleus of the trigeminal nerve.

These nerves, which govern the ocular movements, are vulnerable to lesions resulting from excessive pressure within the brain. This applies particularly to the abducent nerve, since its passage over the sharp angle of the petrosal section, makes it particularly liable to damage by displacement of brain tissues when pressure is excessive. Paralysis of the lateral rectus is a common result.

In the case of such paralysis of the abducent nerve, the eye cannot turn laterally. When the patient looks in the primary position, there is esotropia, caused by the tonus of the medial rectus.

The VII cranial or facial nerve

This is also called the nerve of facial movement, since it controls the facial muscles of expression, by sending motor fibres to them. It also has a visceral part, the intermediate nerve, which contains afferent fibres for taste from the tongue and efferent parasympathetic fibres to glands in the region of the face.

Both the facial and intermediate nerves emerge from the lower lateral aspect of the pons, very near the VIII cranial nerve. Both of these cranial nerves leave the cranial bowl through the internal acoustic meatus, the facial nerve following the VIII nerve inwards towards the inner ear. Each in individual canals, they run out of the base of the skull somewhat in front of, and to the inside of, the protuberance of the ear. The motor part of the nerve sends out several branches which spread out actively in order to innervate the muscles of expression, including the orbicularis (Fig. 11.4).

The visceral section of the facial nerve, the intermediate, follows the motor part to the inner ear. Here afferent fibres form a small ganglion, known as the *geniculate ganglion*, from which they accompany the visceral fibres' own distribution.

Parasympathetic nerve fibres from the geniculate ganglion form the *superficial petrosal nerve* which extends forwards to the middle bones of the skull. Here the nerve combines with sympathetic fibres (in the 'profundus' petrosal nerve)

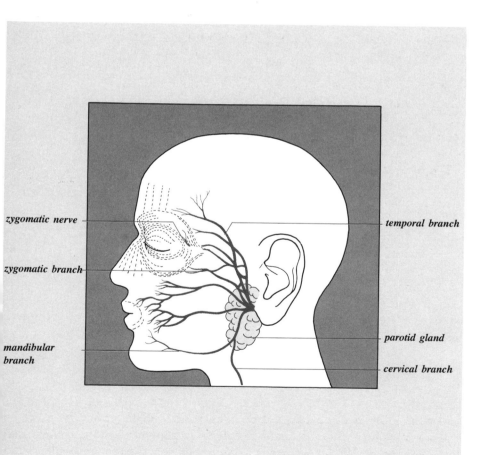

Fig. 11.4 Branches of the facial nerve to the muscles of facial expression.

zygomatic nerve

zygomatic branch

mandibular branch

temporal branch

parotid gland

cervical branch

derived from the carotid plexus, to form the *major petrosal nerve*. This leaves the cranium to terminate in the pterygopalatine ganglion. This ganglion sends post-ganglionic fibres (sympathetic and parasympathetic) via the zygomatic nerve and the lacrimal nerve, to the lacrimal gland. It also innervates the mucous membranes of the nose and mouth.

VISCERAL GANGLIA

The *ciliary ganglion* is a small, reddish grey parasympathetic ganglion, measuring about 2 mm by 1 mm. It is situated towards the rear of the orbit, between the optic nerve and the lateral rectus and some 10 mm in front of the optic canal. It has three roots. A long afferent root, from the nasociliary nerve, carries sensory fibres from the globe. There is also an efferent, parasympathetic, motor root from the III nerve which sends parasympathetic fibres (synapsing in the ganglion) to the eyeball. The third is an efferent sympathetic root which comes from the network of sympathetic fibres around the internal carotid artery, reaching the ganglion via the superior orbital fissure and supplying the eye with sympathetic innervation.

Six to ten short, ciliary nerves emerge from the ganglion, advancing in the orbit and interconnecting with each other and with the long ciliary nerves until they penetrate the globe in a circle around the optic nerve. After these nerves reach the inside of the globe, they move in the suprachoroideal space, to innervate the ciliary body, the iris and the cornea.

The *pterygopalatine ganglion* is another related parasympathetic ganglion, which lies in the upper part of the pterygopalatine fossa. It has three roots. The first is sensory, and comes from the maxillary nerve just where it enters the orbit. There is also a parasympathetic root from the VII cranial nerve (superficial petrosal nerve) and a sympathetic root derived from the greater petrosal nerve (from the carotid plexus).

The ganglion sends out many branches to innervate the membranes of the nose, the palate and the throat. Fibres from the ganglion to the lacrimal gland follow the zygomatic nerve, before passing laterally within the orbit, above the lacrimal nerve to end in the lacrimal gland.

NERVOUS CONTROL OF OCULAR MOVEMENTS

Types of eye movement

To maintain fixation of the eyes, there is an accurate control mechanism for ocular movements. The gaze must be able to move rapidly from one point of fixation to another, but must retain the ability to maintain steady fixation, even in the presence of head movements. The eye also has to combine voluntary and involuntary (reflex) movements, so several parts of the brain need to be involved in this control system.

Conjugate eye movements may be classified as being either saccadic or steady pursuit movements. Somewhere between these is a type of eye movement termed *nystagmus*, of the physiological variety.

Saccades are rapid, conjugate, movements taking the eyes from one fixation point to another. They may be voluntary or reflex. Saccades operate when one views a landscape, changing the gaze from one point to another. Smooth following, tracking or pursuit eye movements arise when the gaze attempts to follow the movement of an object, in order to maintain a constant position of its retinal image. It is possible that such an image can be maintained both by eye movements and by head movements.

Nystagmus is something of a mixture between saccades and following movements. One variety is the 'optokinetic' type, such as when the head is still but the field of vision moves. The classical situation is when one looks out of the window of a moving train. Nystagmus may also be of the 'vestibular' type, such as when the head is rotated relative to fixed surroundings and the semicircular canals are involved.

Convergence type movements involve the point of fixation approaching the observer, while the lines of sight change position to maintain the binocular images on corresponding retinal points. This is vital, both for simultaneous vision with foveal fixation and for stereoscopic vision.

The principal reflexes controlling eye movements arise from retinal responses to light. This fixation reflex causes the eyes to turn towards a bright, or other, object to make the appropriate retinal images fall on the foveas. Reflex movements are usually regarded as more or less unconscious. These visual reactions, however, involve the most specialized aspects of our visual processes and therefore have been classified under the heading of 'psycho-optical' or optokinetic reflexes.

Such psycho-optical reflexes develop at an early stage. A baby tends to look towards a light even a few days after birth. Binocular fixation, however, is not likely to develop until several months later.

Psycho-optical reflexes are divided into:

- Fixation reflexes.
- Fusion reflexes.

Fixation reflexes are saccades or steady following movements, arising from retinal stimulation. Saccadic movements are caused by a peripheral stimulus which attracts attention and produces swift eye movements. The function of these steady following movements is to maintain the images of the object of fixation within the two foveal regions, while the object is moving. An even following movement is able to cope with an object's velocity of up to 30° per second. Fusion reflexes are critical requirements for good binocular vision. Motor control ensures that the images of an object fall on corresponding points of the two retinas (binocular fixation) while the sensorium fuses the two impressions in the brain as a single, integrated percept.

Postural reflexes, otherwise known as vestibulo-ocular reflexes, are saccades, or steady following movements involved when the head moves and the object of regard remains still. Such postural reflexes allow fixation to be maintained upon an object, despite head or bodily movements. The eye is enabled to move continuously in the opposite direction to the bodily movements. The latent time of this type of reflex is very short, so there is immediate compensation for the variation in body position.

The nerve nuclei involved with ocular movements

Motor innervation of the ocular muscles, as mentioned before, is controlled from nuclei in the brain stem. The oculomotor nerve has its nucleus in the upper part of the midbrain, rather below the superior colliculus and level with the aqueduct. It was formerly believed that this nucleus could be divided into a series of well defined sub-nuclear parts, but subsequent research has shown that matters are more complicated. The nucleus produces somatic efferent neurones, serving the appropriate extraocular muscles but it also includes a parasympathetic nucleus (the Edinger—Westphal nucleus) which innervates the ciliary and pupil sphincter muscles (see Fig. 11.5).

The nucleus for the *trochlear nerve* is situated below and rather behind the oculomotor nucleus. A small nucleus, it lies within the grey matter in the floor of the aqueduct, level with the inferior colliculus.

The *abducent nerve* has its nucleus in the pons, at the floor of the fourth ventricle (see Fig. 11.6).

All ocular movements arise from the activities of the nuclei concerned with these three cranial nerves. Exact and well—differentiated movements of the eyes are the outcome of a very complex network of connections. The nuclei are closely interconnected, mainly through the medial longitudinal fasciculus (bundle). This is the nervous pathway travelling medially along the brain stem. When conjugate eye movements are made, necessitating appropriate muscular exertions, there is excitatory innervation which simultaneously inhibits the correct antagonistic muscles. Thus there are connections for both excitation and inhibition between the different parts of the nuclei.

Nervous control centres for eye movements

In the brain there are many regions concerned with such control. There are also inbuilt connections, both direct and indirect. In one way or another they all share involvement with the activities of the nuclei which control the extra-ocular muscles.

The complexities of the oculomotor control system and the neural paths

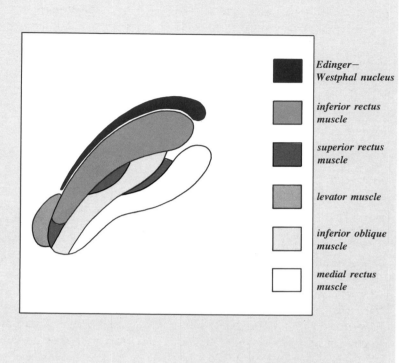

■	Edinger—Westphal nucleus
▨	inferior rectus muscle
■	superior rectus muscle
▨	levator muscle
□	inferior oblique muscle
□	medial rectus muscle

Fig. 11.5 Divisions of the third nerve nucleus in the mid brain, seen from the lateral side.

involved are not completely understood. Thus, the account which follows is necessarily both schematic and simplified. However, it should provide some insight into the neurological aspects of this control system, and contribute to an understanding of how anomalies of oculomotor balance can arise.

The control system for ocular movements must involve both an afferent element, with sensory data received and united, and the composite efferent functions, which produce ocular movements. It is not only the motor 'centres' which dictate eye movements: several parts of the central nervous system are also involved. The particular region controlling a movement depends on the sort of movement involved. For example, a swift saccade is not under the same cerebral control centre as a slow following movement. But although the oculomotor system generally acts as a unified whole, it has some parts which preserve their independent, specialized functions. There are roughly three such divisions.

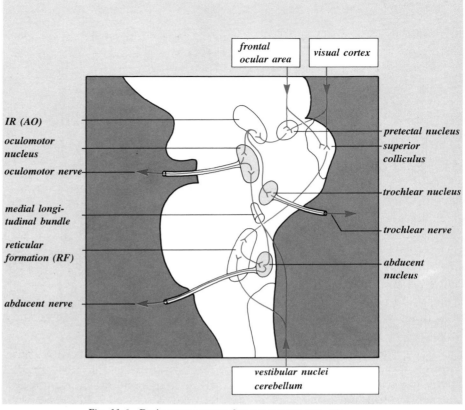

Fig. 11.6 Brain stem centres for eye movements. Many
nerve routes are localized, some being illustrated here.
Nerve trunks run from the visual cortex to the superior
colliculus, having connections with the RF (reticular
formation). Neurones to the abducent nucleus pass from
the RF, which sends impulses to the lateral rectus and has
connections with the oculomotor nucleus. These links are
principally with the part of the nucleus controlling the
medial rectus. Efferent fibres also connect the pretectal
nucleus with the oculomotor nucleus, via the interstitial
nucleus (of Cajal) in the accessory oculomotor nucleus
region (IR and AO). This path ends in the area of the
nucleus controlling the superior rectus, the inferior rectus
and the inferior oblique. Another connection from the
pretectal nucleus goes past AO to the visceral part of the
oculomotor nucleus, or Edinger Westphal nucleus. This
AO additionally connects with the trochlear nucleus
through the medial longitudinal bundle.

Vestibular nuclei and the cerebellum both connect
directly and indirectly with the cranial nerve nuclei.

The brain stem

Here there are many nuclei and 'centres', closely connected to ocular movements. These include the *superior colliculus*, the *reticular substance* and the *pretectal nucleus*, together with the triad of cranial nerve nuclei concerned with innervating the extrinsic ocular muscles.

The *reticular substance* is a column of cells occupying a central position in the brain stem. It extends from the upper part of the mid brain down to the medulla oblongata. It has ill−defined boundaries, being composed of cells of different sizes. These cells are multipolar and have many far reaching extensions. The reticular substance thus consists of a mixture of white and grey substances arranged in a network. There are many important bodily functions with which the reticular substance is concerned. However, it also has important nuclei which are involved with oculomotor functions.

Close to the abducent nucleus in the pons, there is a nucleus known as the paramedian pontine reticular formation (PPRF), which is a centre concerned with horizontal eye movements. It is appropriate to describe the PPRF as a 'centre' as it is known that it receives large amounts of data from other areas of nuclei in the central nervous system. Impulses from the frontal 'eye related' lobes (area 8) are received by the PPRF, laying the foundation for saccadic activity.

The *superior colliculus* accepts visual information directly from the visual pathways and the visual cortex. Impulses sent further still to the PPRF by the superior colliculus are certainly important regulating factors for horizontal eye movements. Both the cerebellar and vestibular nuclei are in contact with the PPRF.

The efferent neural paths from the PPRF initially go to the abducent nucleus on the same (homolateral) side as motor neurones operating the contraction of the lateral rectus, whereas intermediate neurones contribute inhibitory impulses to the oculomotor nucleus on the opposite side, thus activating the medial rectus muscle. At the same time, the lateral rectus, the corresponding antagonist, is inhibited.

The extrinsic muscles which produce vertical movements are controlled by pre-motor nuclei. These are connected with the reticular substance near the oculomotor nucleus in the mid brain. A region known as the rostral interstitial nucleus of the medial longitudinal fasciculus (riNMLF) is included in this control system. The nearby Cajal's nucleus is probably also involved. Another term for this control area is the 'assistant oculomotor (AO) nucleus'.

These nuclei send efferent impulses directly to the nuclei of the cranial nerves III and IV, via the medial longitudinal bundle. And it appears that a similar type of influence is exerted upon vertical eye movements as the PPRF has on horizontal ones. These nuclei also have connections with the same part of the brain as does the PPRF.

Very many ocular movements are not purely horizontal or vertical but are combinations of such movements. The two centres must therefore communicate closely with each other, in order to achieve co-ordination of all such movements.

The *superior colliculus* has often been called the 'optic tectum'. The area's function is better understood and has greater significance for the oculomotor system in the case of lower animals, than for humans. The superior colliculus consists of many cell layers: the outer layers only receive visual impulses, the middle layers receive visual, somatic and acoustic impulses, while the deeper layers are non-visual and have significant responsibility for rapid eye movements.

The superior colliculus plays an important role in controlling ocular movements, especially those co-ordinated with other bodily movements. It may be considered to be the centre for ocular reflex movements in response to visual stimuli. The superior colliculus receives visual information directly via the visual paths and indirectly from the visual cortex. Because there are no direct connections with the nuclei concerned with the ocular muscles, the efferent fibres from the superior colliculus actually run via the contralateral PPRF and AO nuclei.

The *pretectal nucleus* lies ventrally and rostrally in relation to the superior colliculus. The function of this region of nucleus has long been associated with the light reflex of the pupil. Formerly, it was considered that the region was also involved with part of the oculomotor system. The pretectum, just like the tectum, receives visual information from the visual paths and it has connections with the III nerve nucleus via the AO. There is another connection with the visual paths which goes through the AO and directly to the visceral (Edinger–Westphal) part of the III nerve nucleus. Both the tectum and the pretectum receive impulses from the frontal 'eye field' (see Fig. 11.6).

The vestibular nuclei register all head movements, thus identifying the head position taken up at any one time. Such information is derived from the labyrinth in the inner ear and is transferred to the vestibular nuclei in the pons, via part of the VIII cranial nerve. From here, impulses are sent on to parts of the central nervous system which are responsible for balance and the bodily equilibrium.

The vestibular nuclei are directly connected with those cranial nerve nuclei which are concerned with rotations of the eyes. The vestibular system co-operates with the oculomotor system in many ways, the most obvious being the 'vestibulo-ocular' reflexes.

These reflexes enable us to fixate a stationary object while moving our heads. This takes place by contra-rotation of the eyes in relation to the movement of the head. The three semicircular canals in the labyrinth are set at 90° to each other, so they register movements in every plane. The vestibulo-ocular reflex therefore occurs independently of the direction of head movement. On the other hand, there is a distinct connection between the direction of this movement and the particular muscles which rotate the eye.

When an object is fixated right in front of someone whose head is simultaneously moved to the left, the lateral and medial recti are involved. The medial rectus of the left eye and the lateral rectus of the right eye receive facilitating innervation, and both pull at the same time. Simultaneously, the left lateral rectus and the right medial rectus receive inhibitory impulses which reduce these muscles' tonus. This results in the eyes maintaining their position with respect to their surroundings, whilst rotating in relation to the head. The same type of reflex takes place when the head is raised or lowered, in which case the vertically acting muscles are obviously involved.

The vestibulo-ocular motor effect is also operative when the head is tilted to one side, towards a shoulder. If the head tilts towards the left shoulder, the eyes suffer a torsional rotation to the right. Thus sometimes a condition of a rather crooked ('wry') neck, produced by head movement, is compensated for by the ocular apparatus. The contra-rotation which is accomplished is, however, less complete in humans than is found in many species of lower animals.

Torsional effects in humans are usually strong enough for patients with binocular vision anomalies to be able to compensate for their condition with abnormal positions of the head, for example a patient with a paralysis (or paresis) of the superior oblique. This muscle has the effect of intorsion when the eye is in the primary position, and if the muscle is affected the patient experiences diplopia because of the resulting extorsion. By holding the head towards the unaffected side, the patient's vestibular system is enabled to introduce an intorsion of the eye. The difference between the relative rotations around the Y axis between the two eyes will then be lessened and the patient's diplopia consequently reduced (see Fig. 9.13).

The vestibulo-ocular reflexes arrange the stabilization of an object's image. The quality of the retinal image is actually better under such conditions, than when the head is held still and the object moves. One may compare two situations: one with the head held still, while the object moves in front at a rapid speed. The other is with the object held still, while the head is moved instead, at the object's former speed. The difference between the two visual impressions is great. Connections between the vestibular nuclei and the nuclei controlling the extrinsic muscles of the eye take place through the medial longitudinal bundle (or fasciculus). This is known as the FLM. There is also an indirect pathway through the PPRF.

The cerebellum

The cerebellum or 'small brain' consists of a midline part called the *vermis*, with a hemispherical lateral mass on either side. To the ventral side, lies the flocculonodular lobe (also called the archicerebellum or 'vestibulo-cerebellum'). These three divisions are all involved in control of the extraocular muscles.

Visual stimuli activate parts of the vermis, which are also collectively known as the *oculomotor vermis*, and the region receives indirect projections of data from the vestibular nuclei, probably via the reticular substance. The cerebellum's two hemispheres are believed to be able to produce both saccadic and pursuit movements. In addition, the reticular substance uses this area as an important relay station for impulses to the nuclei serving the extraocular muscles.

The flocculonodular lobe controls all regions which receive direct information from the vestibular nuclei. And from here there are efferent impulses which reach the nuclei for the extrinsic eye muscles, through the vestibular nuclei and FLM.

The cerebellum also makes connections with other central nervous system nuclei operating ocular motility. Among these are small groups of nuclei which are given the all-embracing term: '*perihypoglossal nuclei*'. They are situated near to those concerned with the ocular muscles. The one best associated with oculomotor function is probably the '*nucleus prepositus*'. As with the cerebellum, these nuclei are connected with the vestibular nuclei, the PPRF and the assistant oculomotor nuclei. Communications between these nuclei, however, are not entirely understood.

The cortical system

Much work has been done to elucidate the cortical control of ocular movements, which is restricted to the area in front of the pre central gyrus, corresponding to Brodmann's area 8. This is the 'frontal eye-field'.

The *frontal eye-fields* play a significant role in advanced types of ocular movement control. This was discovered some time ago during studies of experimental and pathological damage to this area which resulted in difficulties in controlling voluntary saccades. Thus a patient with a lesion of the frontal eye-fields of the left cerebral hemisphere, is unable to look to the right on request.

The fact that such a contralateral effect exists, indicates that there is a crossing over of the neural routes, between the frontal eye-fields and the PPRF which is the centre for co-ordination of horizontal ocular movements. Saccadic movements are not only controlled by the frontal eye-fields; the superior colliculus, connected to the control centre, is also associated with saccades. Inability to perform saccades is most likely when both the frontal eye-fields and the superior colliculus suffer lesions. The frontal eye-fields comprise the chief centre controlling the extraocular muscles and this centre has associations with the visual cortex and the pretectal nucleus.

The *visual cortex* occupies the parts around the calcarine fissure, including Brodmann's areas 17, 18 and 19. Most visual information arrives here, through the visual pathways, so it is essentially sensory. Yet this region is also connected to the frontal eye-fields, to the superior colliculus and to the pretectal nucleus (see Fig. 6.4).

The visual cortex is primarily a sensory area and it is not certain at what level, or by which route, it sends oculomotor signals. It is likely that steady following movements, in particular, are essentially controlled from the region. Someone with normal binocular vision has no difficulty in tracking a moving object, such as a fly in flight because their eyes can make suitable sustained movements. But if an individual is commanded to make repeated movements in the absence of an object to follow, the eyes can certainly describe the route indicated, but only with many jerky saccades. Thus, in the absence of a visual point of reference from an object, the eyes are no longer able to produce steady pursuit movements.

The extraocular muscles alone have such accurate control mechanism for their movements, but like other striated skeletal muscles, they have many muscle spindles. The extent to which these (extraocular) muscle spindles contribute by way of proprioceptive impulses is very debatable. A few authorities suggest that visual information is the most important factor.

We can now summarize the different central nervous system functions concerned with the oculomotor system.

Normal eyes can move in a variety of ways. An eye can rotate fast and spasmodically in order to change fixation from one object to another. Alternatively, it may have an even and slow movement in order to follow a moving object. Body and head movements are also able to stimulate ocular rotations. The different movements which the eye can perform are controlled by very diverse centres in the central nervous system. Saccades are chiefly determined by the reticular substance's PPRF nuclei and by the frontal eye-fields. The superior colliculus is more involved with saccades commanded by visual stimuli. The vermis of the cerebellum is also involved in controlling saccades which are directed at specific objects.

The visual cortex controls slow following movements or 'smooth pursuit movements'. This cortex is a sensory centre. Exactly where and how the sensory impulses overlap with motor activity is uncertain, but the connections between the visual cortex and other, motor, areas are reasonably well known.

As in musculature in other parts of the body, there is a strong influence from the vestibular system on the extraocular muscles. The vestibular nuclei have direct connections with the nuclei activating these muscles, as well as indirect routes through the PPRF.

Chapter 12
Embryology

GENERAL EMBRYOLOGY – OUTLINE

Several aspects of normal ocular structure and of abnormalities are best under-stood through a knowledge of embryological development. This chapter gives only the more important aspects of general and ocular development. Embryology is the study of ante-natal development, which is divided into stages such as initial cell division, the embryo period and the ultimate foetal stage.

The cell division stage

Fertilization of the ovum takes place in the upper third of the oviduct. The *zygote* immediately begins mitotic division, forming a clump of cells. At this stage, this clump of cells in which two cavities form, is known as a *blastocyst*. The cells between the two spaces are the forerunners of the actual foetus. After about one week, the blastocyst has reached the mucous membrane of the uterus onto which it becomes attached. This stage is *implantation*.

The embryo stage

During the early weeks, cell development, which is controlled by genes, is rapid, cells becoming specialized and developing into the various organs. In the course of the next week after fertilization, an elongated plate is laid down, which consists of two layers of cells, known as the *ectoderm* and *endoderm*. During the third week an intermediate layer develops between these two, called the *mesoderm*. Every individual tissue in the body is derived from this primordium. The ectoderm produces skin and nervous tissues. Mesoderm is responsible for connective tissue, muscles, bone and tissues in the blood vessels and lymphatic system. From the endoderm come the epithelial surfaces of the alimentary tract and related structures.

Next, the embryonic plate, or disc, starts to bend, while below it develops a body stalk. At one end the cells grow rapidly and a thickening develops, which after four weeks can be seen to resemble a head. At the other end of the plate of cells, an enlargement appears which can be likened to a tail. The majority of organ systems appear during the first six weeks of pregnancy, after which stage the embryo has something of a human appearance and is called a *foetus* (Fig. 12.1).

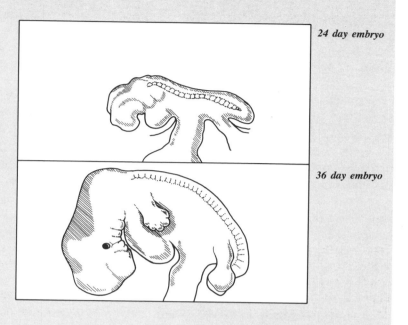

24 day embryo

36 day embryo

Fig. 12.1 Foetal development.

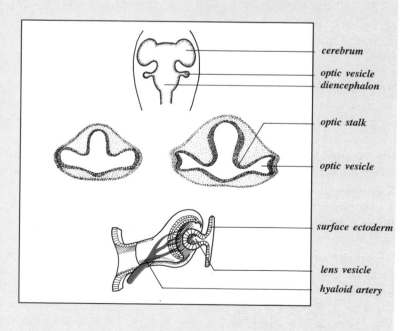

dorsal

horizontal section

the optic cup

cerebrum

optic vesicle
diencephalon

optic stalk

optic vesicle

surface ectoderm

lens vesicle
hyaloid artery

Fig. 12.2 Development of both optic vesicle and optic cup.

The foetal stage

This period is considered to last from when the foetus is six weeks to 38 weeks old. During this time it grows from about 3.5 cm, to approximately 50 cm and the different organs grow and mature. At 35 weeks of age, the foetus is about 35 cm long and it weighs about one kilogram. By then, it has developed so well that, providing it has special care, it would be able to survive outside the uterus. If birth took place earlier there is little possibility of survival.

OCULAR EMBRYOLOGY

The different tissues of the eye are produced both from ectoderm and mesoderm. Ectoderm from the *neural tube* gives rise to the retina, nerve fibres of the optic nerve and the smooth muscles of the iris. The surface ectoderm of the head is responsible for the cornea and the conjunctival epithelium. The lens, the lacrimal glands and tarsal glands are also derived from this tissue.

Mesoderm produces the corneal stroma and endothelium, the sclera, the choroid and part of the iris. In addition, the ciliary muscle and parts of the vitreous humour come from mesoderm.

The central nervous system is derived from a thickening of the ectoderm which appears initially as a groove and later develops into a canal or *neural tube*. This separates from the surface ectoderm and later produces the brain and spinal cord. At the head end, by rapid development, five vesicles are formed. The foremost produces the cerebrum, the next the diencephalon, the third the mesencephalon, the fourth the pons and cerebellum while the fifth develops into the medulla oblongata.

From the brain vesicle, out of which the diencephalon will emerge, a smaller vesicle develops on each side, to the front lateral aspect. These become narrower proximally, eventually forming the optic stalks and optic vesicles (primary optic vesicles). At about the same time, the surface ectoderm lying outside these new vesicles thickens and begins another invagination which afterward will become the lens vesicle. The latter gradually pushes into the optic vesicle, and as an invagination forms the optic cup, which becomes partially filled with the growing lens vesicle (Fig. 12.2).

Such formation of the optic cup therefore brings about two layers of tissue, one outside the other. The inferior border of the optic cup is retarded in its formation, so that here there is a rapid development of a groove or slit reaching back from the rim, known as the *choroidal (foetal) fissure*. Into this fissure there is a growth of vascularized mesoderm, forming the *hyaloid artery*. Later on, the edges of the fissure close around the artery and by the seventh week of pregnancy, the artery is enclosed and forms a canal entering the optic stalk.

Incomplete closure of the choroidal fissure results in a *coloboma*, which can involve the iris, the ciliary body, and/or the choroid and retina (Fig. 12.3 and Plate 12).

The cornea

Mesoderm grows forward from the borders of the optic cup, between the newly formed lens vesicle and the ectoderm. This produces the corneal endothelium and, later on, the stroma is developed in the same way. The corneal epithelium comes from the surface ectoderm. Descemet's membrane appears during the 4th month of development, as a secretion from the endothelial cells, while Bowman's layer is a condensation of the stroma. The cornea is transparent from the start.

The sclera

This is essentially a condensation of mesoderm around the optic cup, starting anteriorly, evidently because it is here that the extrinsic muscles are attached. The limbus is initially rather further back, at about the point where the ciliary body would be. But it gradually moves forward, as the embryonic development continues.

The *fascia bulbi*, or Tenon's capsule, is produced in the same way as the sclera, but somewhat later on.

The choroid

Formed by mesoderm around the optic cup, it becomes dark fairly early. By about the 20th week the choroid has fully developed all its tissues.

The ciliary body

From the borders of the optic cup, mesoderm differentiates into the connective tissue of the ciliary body, the ciliary muscle and the capsule of the lens. The two layers of neural ectoderm of the optic cup grow forwards, forming the double layer of surface epithelium over the mesodermal parts of the ciliary body (Fig. 12.4).

The iris

There is a condensation of connective tissue in the iris and a 'pupillary membrane' which arise from mesoderm associated with the rim of the optic cup.

Fig. 12.3 The closure of the choroidal fissure.

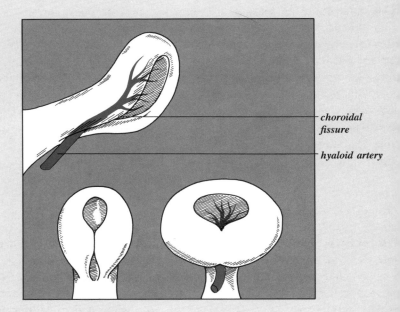

choroidal fissure

hyaloid artery

Fig. 12.4 Development of the anterior part of the eye.

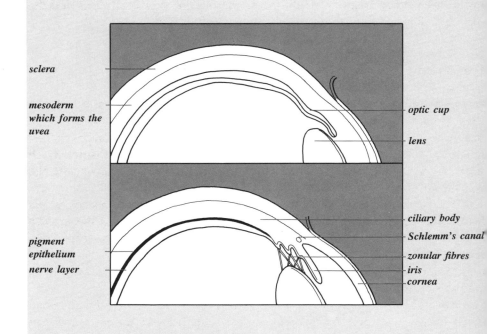

sclera

mesoderm which forms the uvea

optic cup

lens

ciliary body

Schlemm's canal

pigment epithelium nerve layer

zonular fibres

iris

cornea

The two layers of the neural ectoderm which clads the ciliary body move forwards to form the pigment epithelium of the posterior side of the iris, right up to the pupil margin. It is from this pigment epithelium that the pupil sphincter muscle and the dilatator muscle are formed whereas the iris connective tissue and its rich series of blood vessels come from mesoderm. There is some migration of pigment cells from the pigment epithelium into the connective tissue. In the central region of the iris there is the pupillary aperture, but this is initially occluded by the pupillary membrane. This membrane, at first attached to the margin of the pupil, later normally disappears around the pupil rim. But it retains an annular attachment to the anterior surface of the iris at the collarette. At about 32 weeks of pregnancy, the membrane degenerates and then disappears. However, it is not unusual for careful observation to reveal some remnants of this membrane in the neonate. And a small number of adults carry some strands, of it, attached at the collarette, throughout life.

The anterior and posterior chambers

The anterior chamber begins as a split in the mesoderm between the cornea and iris which separate it from the lens and the pupillary membrane. The anterior chamber is shallow until birth and the filtration angle is made up of mesodermal connective tissue, which vanishes in due time. Schlemm's canal is present from about 12 to 13 weeks gestation, when it is filled with blood. The posterior chamber arises as a split in the mesoderm between the iris and the lens, later becoming partitioned into zones by the zonular system.

The vitreous humour

This optical medium is formed between the optic cup and the lens. A *primary vitreous* comes first, composed of a network of thin, cytoplasmic processes made from ectodermal cells of the lens and from neural, ectodermal cells of the optic cup. There is some mesodermal invasion via the choroidal fissure, which brings the hyaloid artery. This comes into somewhat uncertain contact with the primary vitreous.

The secondary vitreous arises from the retina as an homogeneous gel, which displaces the primary vitreous forwards against the lens. Around the hyaloid artery and the remainder of the primary vitreous, the gel condenses and eventually the hyaloid canal develops. The final consistency of the vitreous arises from this network of collagenous fibres and simultaneously the fibrous zonular system is formed.

The *hyaloid artery* branches off the ophthalmic artery, entering the optic cup at the choroidal fissure. As this fissure closes, the artery becomes embedded within the optic stalk. This artery nourishes internal ocular structures and produces a delicate net of vessels over the back surface of the lens. The central retinal artery itself branches from the hyaloid artery, the latter being at its peak size during the third month of gestation and commencing to wither one or two months later. This process is complete at around the eighth month.

The crystalline lens

Development of the lens commences as a thickening of the surface ectoderm opposite the optic cup. This region forms a vesicle, consisting of a single layer of cells complete with a basal membrane. This lens vesicle moves into the optic cup. Then the posterior layer of cells elongates, producing long fibres which later lose their nuclei. These are the *primary lens fibres*, which grow forward until they touch the front cell layer of the lens. During this stage, the lens gradually assumes a more ovoid form. *The secondary lens fibres* are produced directly from the cells of the anterior epithelial layer, new fibres arising throughout life (see Fig. 12.5).

The secondary lens fibres which are formed from cells near the equator of the lens, grow both forward and backward and lens sutures are produced where fibres meet end on. During foetal development, right through early childhood, these sutures are seen in the form of a Y, anteriorly, but as an inverted letter Y posteriorly. Older eyes produce irregular additional sutures.

During foetal life, there is rapid growth of the lens, since it has an active blood supply through the hyaloid system. It is plastic and almost spherical. At birth its axial thickness is similar to the adult dimension but the equatorial diameter is about $\frac{2}{3}$ of the adult size. The capsule of the lens is derived from the surrounding mesoderm.

The retina

This is formed from the optic cup, being divided into the pigment layer and the neural layer. The *pigment layer* is the outer part of the optic cup, which is made up of cubical epithelial cells, which later become pigmented. The more internal wall of the cup is the neural primordium. This lies as far forward as the ora serrata, where the cells are not differentiated and produce the double layer of epithelial cells covering the ciliary body and the back of the iris.

The inner layer in the future retinal region consists of cylindrical cells which soon develop an outer nuclear zone and an inner 'marginal' zone. From the nuclear zone there is an invasion of cells into the marginal zone, from which arise the so-called *inner and outer neuroblastic layers*, separated by a fairly non-nucleated layer (of Chevitz). The more internal layer will produce the ganglion cells, amacrines and Müller's connective cells. The outer layer is transformed into rods and cones, horizontal cells and bipolars.

During about the 25th week of pregnancy, the macular region is seen to commence its special development. Initially, there is a migration from the

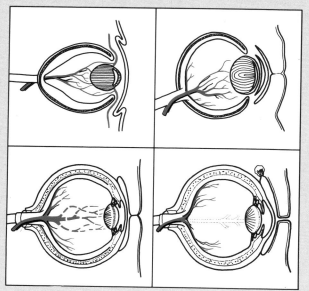

early foetal stage (5 to 10 weeks)

late foetal stage (7 to 8 months)

Fig. 12.5 Different stages of ocular development.

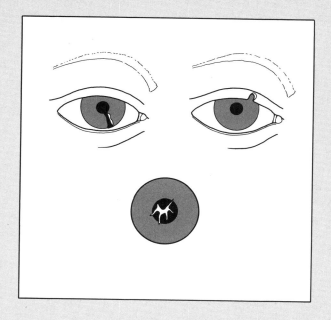

Fig. 12.6 Three ocular abnormalities. *Top left*: Coloboma of the iris. *Top right*: Notch in the upper eyelid. *Below*: Pupillary membrane remnant.

centre of cells in the ganglion cell layer and afterward a depression is formed, which becomes the fovea centralis. Thus, there is a reduction of the ganglion cell layer at the fovea to a single layer which only disappears after birth. The foveal cones decrease in thickness, with elongation of their outer segments, but their density increases. These foveal cones become developed later than the remainder of the retina, to become fully formed about five months after birth, which accounts for the poor central fixation of the eye at birth.

The optic nerve

Axons grow from the retinal ganglion cells, to the region where the optic stalk is producing the optic cup, the latter being a later formation than the optic disc. These axons extend from the optic stalk, via the chiasma, up to the mid brain. Within the optic stalk, cells produce neuroglial supporting tissues. The optic nerve is formed from the ganglion cell axons within the optic stalk. Myelination of the axons is soon begun, although the process is only completed some weeks after birth. The hyaloid artery and its vein produce the central retinal artery and vein (Fig. 12.5).

The extra ocular muscles

Mesoderm around the globe produces these muscles. Initially they take the form of a condensed and connected mass of tissue, which later develops into individual muscles. These firstly form their connections with the eyeball, while there is a later formation backwards to the muscle 'origins'. The levator of the upper lid is the last muscle to be fully formed, as it separates from the mesoderm which produces the superior rectus. During this development, the association of the muscles with the cranial nerves, III, IV and VI takes place.

The lids

These commence as folds of the surface ectoderm. For much of the antenatal period they are attached to each other, remaining thus until about the 20th week, when separation begins. The separation process is completed by about the 30th week. Connective tissue, blood vessels and the tarsal plates are derived from the mesoderm of the lids, as is the orbicularis muscle.

The eyelashes are produced by the surface ectoderm, initially in the upper lid with two or three rows, some outside the others. The glands of Zeis and Molls develop from the hair follicles of the cilia. The Meibomian glands come from ectodermal cells in the region of the lids.

The lacrimal gland

This grows from ectodermal cells in the superior conjunctival fornix. The tendon of the levator divides the gland into its orbital and palpebral sections. It is only at about three months after birth that the lacrimal gland really produces tears effectively.

The *lacrimal sac* and the *nasolacrimal duct* as well as the lacrimal canal and canaliculi, emerge from surface ectoderm at the inner canthus. Firstly the tube going towards the nasal inferior meatus is formed. At its top end this channel produces the lacrimal sac and divisions extend from here to the respective canaliculi, into each eyelid.

Post natal ocular development

There is rapid growth during the initial year of life after which there is less. However, another spurt occurs around puberty. At birth, the cornea is relatively large and grows during the initial two years of life. Iris pigmentation develops during the first year of life after which time it settles to a fairly constant colour. The crystalline lens grows fast after birth, continuing to build up fibres throughout life, although the rate of growth tends to slow down with age.

Most new born eyes tend to be hyperopic, a situation which is corrected as the axial length of the globe increases during early years. Further enlargement of the eyeball may lead to myopia, but this tendency is usually annulled by compensatory flattening of the lens surfaces. The neonate is photophobic, closing the eyes when placed in a strong light. Movements of the eyes tend to be uncontrolled and it is not uncommon for a squint to be apparent. Co-ordination should become stabilized at about four months of age. The lacrimal gland is non-functional at birth, hence babies cry without shedding tears for the first two or three months.

Faulty development or disturbances of function, may be found in the visual apparatus either at birth or soon afterward. Just a few of the main possibilities are now to be described.

Strabismus

It is usual for normal binocularity to develop fairly early. Any persistence of strabismus by three or four months after birth, which does not receive professional attention, is likely to result in amblyopia. This is reduced visual acuity in the eye concerned. The probable cause is a cortical suppression of vision to overcome diplopia. There is frequently an hereditary basis for such conditions (see Chapters 9 and 11).

Cataract

In congenital cataract, the lens is opaque, possibly with some genetic connection, from an infection or even due to some malnourishment of the lens at some time within the womb. For instance, if the mother contracts the rubella virus during the initial seven weeks of pregnancy, before the capsule of the lens is formed, this frequently results in cataract. Should the infection occur later than at seven weeks' gestation, it is less likely that the lens would be adversely affected. There are many children suffering from congenital cataract whose low birth weight implies some difficulty in foetal nourishment. This can often be traced to maternal eating habits during pregnancy.

Glaucoma

Congenital glaucoma, where the intraocular pressure is abnormally high, is usually the result of faulty development of the mechanism for draining the aqueous humour from the anterior chamber. Some 80% of cases are bilateral and the condition is responsible for between 5 and 10% of blindness in children.

Persistent pupillary membrane

It is normal for the membrane covering the foetal pupil to degenerate before birth. In rare instances, part of the membrane remains in the form of some tenuous connections of tissue across part of the pupil (see Fig. 12.6 and Plate 13).

Coloboma

This condition may appear as a gap in the iris, the ciliary body, the retina or the choroid. It is caused by incomplete closure of the choroidal fissure. The condition may occur in a single structure but can be associated with anomalies in the lip or the palate (see Plate 12).

Tabulation of the main stages in ocular development during the embryonic and foetal periods (After Mann, 1957).

Stage	Resulting structures	Approximate age at end of stage
1	Primary optic vesicle produced Lens vesicle initiated	Weeks 3 to 4
2	Lens vesicle formed Optic cup formed Outer layer of optic cup pigmented	End of week 4
3	Choroidal fissure closes Lens separates from surface ectoderm Primary lens fibres appear Retinal differentiation commences Start of vascular network of lens	Week 6
4	Secondary lens fibres commence Vascular network of lens complete Rudimentary eyelid folds appear Iris ectoderm develops	Month 3

5	Posterior lens vessels degenerate
	The following appear:
	    Central retinal artery
	    Ciliary body and muscle
	    Pupil sphincter and dilatator
	    Sclera and outer layer of choroid
		Month 4

6	Pupillary membrane shrinks, from front Pars plana of ciliary body forms Myelination of optic nerve fibres starts	Month 7
7	Hyaloid artery degenerates and disappears Myelination in optic nerve reaches the lamina cribrosa	Month 9
8	Macula completely develops	4—6 months after birth

Bibliography

Andreasen, E. (1965) *Sanseorganene og huden*. Munksgaard, Copenhagen.

Bennett, A.G. & Rabbetts, R.B. (1989) *Clinical visual optics*. Butterworths, London.

Bertelsen, T. *et al.* (1988) *Nordisk laerebok i oftalmologi*. AS John Grieg, Bergen.

Brodal, P. (1990) *Sentralnervesystemet*. Per Brodal & TANO AS, Oslo.

Brodal, P., Dahl, H.A. & Fossum, S. (1990) *Menneskets anatomi & fysiologi*. Cappelens, Oslo.

Brown, F.G. & Fletcher, R. (1990) *Glaucoma in optometric practice*. Blackwell Scientific Publications, Oxford.

Brown, G.C. & Tasman, W.S. (1983) *Congenital anomalies of the optic disc*. Grune & Stratton, New York.

Ciuffreda, K.J., Levi, D.M. & Selenow, A. (1991) *Amblyopia, basic and clinical aspects*. Butterworth–Heinemann, Boston.

Davson, H. (1976) *The eye. 2A. Visual function in man*. Academic Press, New York.

Davson, H. (1984) *The eye. 1a. Vegetative physiology and biochemistry*. Academic Press, Orlando.

Davson, H. (1990) *Physiology of the eye*. Macmillan, London.

De Valois, R.L. & De Valois, K.K. (1988) *Spatial vision*. Oxford University Press, New York & Oxford.

Dowling, J.E. (1987) *The retina*. Harvard University Press, Cambridge, Mass.

Duke-Elder, W.S. (1961) *System of ophthalmology. II*. Kimpton, London.

Fatt, I. (1978) *Physiology of the eye*. Butterworths, London.

Fletcher, R. & Voke, J. (1985) *Defective colour vision*. Adam Hilger, Bristol.

Goldmann, J.N. *et al.* (1968) Structural alteration affecting transparency in swollen human corneas. *Invest. Ophthalmol.* **7**. 501–518.

Hamano, H. & Kaufman, H. (1987) *The physiology of the cornea and contact lens applications*. Churchill Livingstone, London.

Harrington, D.O. & Drake, M. (1990) *The visual fields*. Mosby, St. Louis.

Hess, A. & Pilar, G. (1963) Slow fibres in the extraocular muscles of the cat. *J. Physiol.* **169**. 780–798.

Hess, R.F. *et al.* (1990) *Night vision*. Cambridge University Press, Cambridge.

Jacob, S.W. *et al.* (1985) *Anatomi og fysiologi*. University Press, Oslo.

Kaufman, H., Barron, B.A., McDonald, M.B. & Waltman, S.R. (1988) *The cornea*. Churchill Livingstone, London.

Langham, M.E. & Rosenthal, A.R. (1966) Role of cervical and sympathetic nerves in regulating intraocular pressure and circulation. *Amer. J. Physiol.* **210**. 786–794.

Le Grand, Y. (1968) *Light colour and vision*. (English trans.) Chapman & Hall, London.

Mann, I.C. (1957) *The developmental abnormalities of the eye*. BMA, London.

Maurice, D.M. (1957) The structure and transparency of the cornea. *J. Physiol.* **136**. 263–286.

Pansky, B. & Allen, D.J. (1980) *Review of neuroscience*. Macmillan, New York.

Phillips, A.J. & Stone, J. (1989) *Contact lenses*. Butterworth, London.

Records, R.E. (1979) *Physiology of the human eye and visual system*. Harper & Row, London.

Rohen, J.W. & Rentsch. (1969) Der konstructive Bau des Zonulaapparatus beim Menschen und dessen funktionelle Bedeutung. *v. Graefes Arch. Ophthal.* **178**. 1–9.

Ruskell, G.L. (1971) Facial sympathetic innervation of the choroidal blood vessels in monkeys. *Exp. Eye res.* **12**. 166.

Ruskell, G.L. (1989) The fine structure of human EOM–spindles and their potential proprioceptive capacity. *J. Anat.* **167**. 199–214.

Salapatek, P. & Cohen, L. (1987) *Handbook of infant perception I*. Academic Press, Orlando.

Smolin, G. & Thoft, R.A. (1987) *The cornea*. Little, Brown and Co., Boston.

Snell, R.W. & Lemp, M.A. (1989) *Clinical anatomy of the eye*. Blackwell Scientific Publications, Oxford.

Solomons, H. (1978) *Binocular vision*. Heinemann Medical, London.

Spooner, J.D. (1957) *Ocular anatomy*. Hatton Press, London.

Weale, R.A. (1963) *The aging eye*. Lewis, London.

Wilson-Pauwels, L., Akesson, E. & Stewart, P. (1988) *The cranial nerves: anatomy and clinical comments*. Mosby, St Louis.

Wolff, E. (1976) *Anatomy of the eye and orbit*. Lewis, London.

Index

The Brazilian

Rain Forest

CIRCLE OF LIFE ► CIRCLE OF LIFE ► CIRCLE OF LIFE ► CIRCLE OF LIFE ► CIRCLE OF LIFE ►

8547

The Brazilian
Rain Forest

Alexandra Siy

DILLON PRESS
New York

Maxwell Macmillan Canada
Toronto

Maxwell Macmillan International
New York Oxford Singapore Sydney

For Sasha

Acknowledgments

I would like to thank the following people and organizations: Fredi Adelman (Smithsonian Institution Traveling Exhibition Service), Paul Beaver (Amazonia Expeditions), Linda Belamarich (Cultural Survival), Bill Possiel and Nanette Rutsch (Latin American Office of the Nature Conservancy), Lynne Poteau and Doug Nethercut (Rain Forest Alliance), Sandra Rode (Missouri Botanical Garden), and Frank Wadsworth (Institute of Tropical Forestry).

Also, Sheri Amsel, Berne Broudy, Nancy Cowdin, Dr. John Cunningham, Margaret Cymerys, Richard K. La Val, Marie O'Malley, Enrique G. Ortiz, Julie Roberts, and Margaret Vunck.

Photo Credits

Photographs courtesy of: Frank H. Wadsworth, Institute of Tropical Forestry: 2-3, 8; Richard Laval: 11, 23, 34, 38, 63; Berne Broudy: 14, 26, 46, 51, 56, 61; Margaret Cymerys: 17, 31, 41, 42, 49, 59; Paul Harp: 28.

Library of Congress Cataloging-in-Publication Data

Siy, Alexandra.
    The Brazilian rain forest / by Alexandra Siy.
        p. cm. — (Circle of life)
    Summary: Describes the numerous plants and animals that live in the Brazilian Rain Forest and their ecological and economic importance.
    ISBN 0-87518-470-7
    1. Rain forest ecology—Amazon River Region—Juvenile literature. 2. Rain forest ecology—Brazil—Juvenile literature. 3. Rain forests—Amazon River Region—Juvenile literature. 4. Rain forests—Brazil—Juvenile literature. 5. Rain forest conservation—Amazon River Region—Juvenile literature. 6. Rain forest conservation—Brazil—Juvenile literature. [1. Rain forests. 2. Rain forest ecology. 3. Ecology.] I. Title II. Series: Siy Alexandra. Circle of Life.
QH112.S58 1992
574.5'2642'09811—dc20   91-37640

Dillon Press
Macmillan Publishing Company
866 Third Avenue
New York, NY 10022

Maxwell Macmillan Canada, Inc.
1200 Eglinton Avenue East
Suite 200
Don Mills, Ontario M3C 3N1

Macmillan Publishing Company is part of the Maxwell Communication Group of Companies.

First edition

Printed in the United States of America

10 9 8 7 6 5 4 3 2

Contents

▼

Brazilian Rain Forest

▼

Facts

Location: One-third of the world's tropical rain forests are located in Brazil, which is the largest country on the South American continent and the fifth largest country in the world.

Geography: The Amazon River is the world's largest river and second longest. It stretches from the mountains of Peru to the Atlantic Ocean. The vast area around the river was once covered by rain forest (more than two million square miles). The Atlantic rain forests are found in the coastal mountain ranges that roll down to the ocean.

Geology: Soils are 180 million years old and lack nutrients.

Climate: Warm and wet year-round, receiving between 80 and 200 inches of rain a year.

Human History: Humans first lived in the rain forests of Brazil about 12,000 years ago. Before the Europeans came, between two and ten million Indians lived scattered in tribes throughout the forests. Today there are about 200,000 indigenous peoples, or native people, left in Brazil.

Global Importance: Rain forests support more life than any other ecosystem on earth. They cover only 6 percent of the earth but are home to 50 percent of the earth's living things. Foods, medicines, and industrial materials are important products of rain forests. Rain forests also help protect the earth from global warming.

Current Status: Rain forests around the world are being destroyed at a rate of about 50 acres per minute. If this continues, most of the remaining rain forests will be gone by the year 2000.

A Jungle Book

▼

Rain forests grow near the **equator**, where the climate is always warm and wet. This land, called the **tropics**, is a place where winter never comes, and the days and the nights are equal in length. For hundreds of millions of years, rain and sun have bathed these lands with life-giving qualities. For millions of years, plants and animals have lived in the rain forests. Today more than half of all the living things on earth make their home there.

Why are rain forests so full of life? There are many answers, some of which you could learn for yourself if you had the chance to visit a rain forest. Bring along a notebook in which to write down your observations and discoveries. You don't need complicated scientific equipment. Just use your senses. Your nose, ears, eyes, skin, and even your taste buds will help you find out how a rain forest works.

The lower Amazon near Belém

The Nutrient Cycle

Start your day near the banks of the great Amazon River. The sun is already hot. From the riverbank, the rain forest looks like a thick and mysterious jungle. Push your way through the trees, vines, and plants near the river's edge. Once inside the forest, you will discover it isn't like the imaginary jungles found in story books!

Inside the forest it's dark and there is plenty of room to walk on the open forest floor. The air is warm, damp, and fresh-smelling like the air inside a greenhouse.

Bend down and touch the ground—it is damp, too. A thin layer of rotting leaves covers the dirt below. Dig into the earth with your fingers. The earth is red and the soil, a slippery clay. From this earth grow giant trees. Some trees have roots that flare out like the spokes around a wheel.

Many rain forest trees, such as the chicle tree, which was the original source of chewing gum, have large roots that spread over the surface of the ground. Called buttress and prop roots, they give trees support and also help them take **nutrients** from the layer of **decomposing** leaves.

The canopy is like a garden of life in the sky.

Rain forests are always damp and warm. When a leaf falls off a tree in the rain forest, it does not last long on the forest floor. As soon as it touches the ground it begins to decompose, or rot. Warmth and wetness help dead plants decompose. Tiny living things called microbes break down leaves and other dead plant parts into small pieces called nutrients.

Nutrients are the parts of food or soil that help plants and animals grow. As soon as nutrients are

released from a dead plant, they are taken up again by the roots of a living plant. This is called the nutrient cycle. In rain forests, nutrients are constantly recycled, or used over and over again.

Many people are surprised to learn that most rain forest soils are infertile, or lack nutrients. These soils are ancient—some are more than 180 million years old. After so many millions of years, most of the **minerals** and nutrients have been washed away.

In the rain forest, minerals and nutrients are found in trees and plants. Therefore, if the trees are destroyed, a new rain forest cannot grow.

Photosynthesis

A large leaf falls to the ground. It is oval-shaped and has a pointed tip. It feels waxy, like the surface of a candle. Look up to see where the leaf came from. There, high above your head, is the thick and wild jungle of your imagination!

The leaves that grow on rain forest trees give life to the forest. Their shapes help trees survive in several ways. Pointed tips and waxy coatings help water drip off the surface. This prevents too many nutrients from

being washed out of the leaf. The waxy coating also keeps the leaf from losing too much water in the bright sunshine.

Rain forest leaves are usually quite large. This helps them "capture" sunlight. The chemical (called chlorophyll) in leaves that makes them look green also helps them turn the energy of the sun into the food energy found in sugar. This process is called **photosynthesis**. Photo means "light," and synthesis means "change." So, photosynthesis means "changing light energy into food energy." Plants use the food energy they make to help them grow. All other living things depend on photosynthesis for life, too. Trees and plants provide food for the animals in the forest. Rain forests are places where photosynthesis goes on all year. They turn more energy from the sun into food energy than any other place on earth. This is one of the reasons that there are so many species living in rain forests.

Succession

Now you can see why the forest seemed so dark. Over your head, like the **canopy** of a huge circus tent, are

Tropical leaves have pointed tips and waxy surfaces to help them conserve water.

thick layers of green leaves. The sun shines down to the forest floor only where there are openings in the green canopy, or roof, of the forest. In those bright spots on the ground, you can see small plants growing.

New trees grow in the rain forest when old trees die and fall down. When this happens, sunlight can reach the forest floor. There new trees will grow upward and someday will become part of the canopy. This process is called succession. It is the way the forest changes over time. Old trees die, and new trees grow in their place.

Food and Fruit

There is no need to bring along lunch while exploring the rain forest. If you know how, you can find good food in every layer of the forest. Look on the ground and you may find a piece of ripe fruit, such as a black pineapple. And every tree makes its own kind of fruit—many are edible and tasty.

Rain forest fruits are often large and soft and are easy for animals to find and eat. When a piece of fruit is eaten, seeds are carried inside the body of the animal to new places. Then they are left behind when the animal leaves its **feces**, or droppings. Sometimes birds and animals drop fruit when they are flying, swinging, or scampering through the trees. When animals scatter seeds throughout the forest it is called **seed dispersal**, and this is the key to the survival of the rain forest.

Water, Water, Everywhere . . .

After eating a meal of sweet pineapple, you fall asleep on the floor of the forest. Your dreams are interrupted by raindrops. The drops are big and splash onto your face. Sit up and see water running down tree trunks. Listen to the loud roar of the rainstorm above the

canopy. It is pouring, but you are not soaked. Where is all the rain going?

In the rain forest, it rains almost every afternoon. Even though storms are usually short, a lot of rain falls into the canopy. The layers of thick leaves in the canopy are like sponges that catch and slow down the raindrops. As the rain trickles through the leaves, it is soaked up by plants that grow in the canopy. Called **epiphytes**, or air plants, these plants do not have roots on the ground. Instead their roots twist around the branches of large trees.

By the time the rainwater reaches the forest floor, it is no longer part of a heavy downpour. The water that soaks into the ground is quickly sucked up by tree roots. Trees use some of the rain to help them grow, but almost half of the water is put back into the air. This happens by the process known as **evapotranspiration**. Transpiration is the process by which water is taken up by tree roots and "pulled" up the stem and out of the leaves. Water enters the air from the leaves by **evaporation**. When enough water evaporates into the air, it falls again as rain. In this way water is recycled, or used over and over again, in the rain forest.

Fungi help decompose rotting trees, returning nutrients to the soil where they will be used to help young trees grow—this is the nutrient cycle.

Looking Up

The rain stops after a short time, and again you hear
the distant calls of birds and animals. There is even a
faint buzz in the air that sounds like a faraway swarm of
bees. You wonder what it is like in the canopy of the
forest. You want more than anything to travel into the
sky gardens and see for yourself the amazing creatures
that live there.

Few people have traveled into the sky-garden
canopy. It is one of the last places on earth that people
have yet to explore. In the tropical forests of French
Guiana, which borders on northern Brazil, a group of
French scientists have explored the top of the canopy.
Using a giant hot-air balloon, these scientists have
placed a huge raft on the very tops of the trees. Unlike
a helicopter, the airship is quiet and doesn't disturb the
calm air below. The airship floats over the treetops and
slowly lowers the raft onto the trees.

Looking like a massive wheel with spokes, the raft
weighs one ton and can safely sit on the canopy. There,
200 feet above the ground, scientists can observe
insects, animals, flowers, fruits, and leaves. So far, the
airship and raft provide scientists with the best way

to study the rain forest.

However, most research must take place on the ground because it is so difficult to get to the canopy where most rain forest creatures live. Scientists have learned a lot about rain forests already, but there is still much to discover.

The Bee and the Nut Tree

▼

Brazil is a South American country that has one-third of the earth's rain forests—more than any other country in the world. The heart of Brazil's rain forests is the Amazon River. It is huge, holding one-fifth of all the water on earth. More than one thousand smaller rivers feed into the great Amazon.

The land around the Amazon River is called the Amazon River basin, or **Amazonia**, and includes more than two million square miles of rain forest. Brazil's largest states make up most of Amazonia. Amazonas is the biggest Brazilian state covering an area equal to Alaska and Maine put together—more than 600,000 square miles. A smaller area of rain forests also exists along the eastern coastline of Brazil. These are the Atlantic forests, which once stretched 2,000 miles along the coast of the Atlantic Ocean.

Today the Atlantic forests exist only in small pieces along Brazil's southern coastline. Much of these forests are squeezed between the cities of Rio de Janeiro and São Paulo—which is one of the largest cities in the world.

Biodiversity

Brazil's rain forests are rich in **biodiversity**. *Bio* means "life," and *diversity* means "different." Places rich in biodiversity have many different living creatures and plants in one area. For example, a person could walk for a mile through the rain forest and never find two trees of the same kind.

Another name for biodiversity is species diversity. A **species** is a group of plants or animals that are similar in several important ways. For example, members of a species look and act alike. They can breed, or mate, with each other to produce seeds, eggs, or live young.

Most of the world's species are still undiscovered. There might be up to 30 million species of plants and animals living on the earth, but we have discovered only 1.4 million of them.

Most of the species that live in the rain forests are plants and insects. In just one tree, 43 species of ants

have been counted—there aren't that many species of ants in most countries!

Habitat Is Home

Millions of species live in rain forests for several reasons: there are many places for species to live, there is a year-round supply of food because there is no winter season, and there is plenty of rain and sunshine. All these things together make up a **habitat**. Habitat is food, water, and shelter for living things.

Over many millions of years, species have **evolved**, or changed slowly. Every animal and plant has **adaptations**, which are behaviors or characteristics that help it survive in its habitat.

For example, some bats have evolved long noses and tongues to help them suck nectar out of flowers. All the species and their habitats together make up an **ecosystem**. The rain forest is a beautiful and complex ecosystem.

Green Hell and Lace

Throughout history the Amazon rain forests were called the "green hell" because they were so huge and

The long tongue and nose of this nectar-eating bat are adaptations.

awesome. Giant trees, thick vines, biting insects, screeching birds, howling monkeys, and six-foot-long snakes frightened and threatened explorers and settlers.

But now we know the forests are not places to be feared. Through scientific study, people have discovered how fragile the rain forest ecosystem really is. Like the tiny threads in delicate lace, the rain forest ecosystem is held together by thousands of connections, or relationships, between plants and animals. Tearing one thread will ruin the whole lace. And destroying just one connection in the rain forest could disrupt the entire ecosystem.

The Euglossine Bee and the Brazil Nut Tree

How are plants and animals connected like threads in a delicate lace? Here is the true story of three rain forest species. And as you learn more about the rain forests, you will find that every species has its own story to tell.

In the top of a Brazilian rain forest lives a special kind of bee. It is a beautiful insect with a shiny green body—so shiny it seems to glow, even in the bright sunshine of the sky gardens.

Scientists call it the euglossine bee. Like many

insects, birds, and bats that live in rain forests the euglossine bee gets its food from flowers.

Flowers make a sweet syrup called **nectar**. The euglossine bee feeds on the nectar found inside the white, fluffy flower of the giant Brazil nut tree.

Mysterious Messengers

When a euglossine bee lands on the Brazil nut tree blossom, a dusty powder sticks to its legs. This powder is called **pollen**, and it is made up of tiny grains that can float in windy skies. But in the thick and jumbled leaves of the rain forest, the wind barely shakes a leaf. The only way pollen gets out of Brazil nut tree flowers is on the legs of the euglossine bee.

The euglossine bee **pollinates** the flowers of the Brazil nut tree. This means it carries pollen grains from the male flower to the female flower. The bee's pollen-covered legs brush against the sticky center of the female flower. Some of the pollen sticks to the female and moves into the bottom of the blossom.

Flowers to Fruits

Deep inside the blossom, the **genes** from a male pollen

A Brazil nut tree towers in the Brazilian sky.

grain combine with the genes inside the female. When this happens there are enough genes to make a seed for a new Brazil nut tree. The flower's petals wilt and die, but the center of the flower lives and grows into a lovely fruit called a Brazil nut pod. Inside the pod are Brazil nuts—the seeds, the beginnings of life for new Brazil nut trees.

The euglossine bee needs the nectar from flowers for food. And the Brazil nut tree needs the euglossine bee in order to be pollinated and **reproduce**, or make seeds for new trees. The way plants and animals need

each other for things like food and reproduction is called species interdependence. All the species of the rain forest need one another in different ways.

Nuts for Lunch!

The euglossine bee and the Brazil nut tree are interdependent. But they both depend on another rain forest species. The agouti is a **mammal** that lives on the forest floor. It has sharp teeth that can tear open fallen Brazil nut pods. The agouti holds the pods in its claws as it feasts on the tasty Brazil nuts inside.

Sometimes agoutis leave behind or bury half-chewed and soggy nuts. These cracked and softened nuts are the seeds that may someday grow into new Brazil nut trees. Brazil nuts that haven't been chewed and softened will not grow into new trees. People have tried to copy this seed softening process, but have never been able to grow Brazil nut trees on plantations or farms. For this reason, it is illegal to cut down Brazil nut trees in Brazil.

A Tropical Triangle

The euglossine bee, the Brazil nut tree, and the agouti

The agouti is one of the most important rain forest animals.

are connected like the sides of a triangle. All three sides are needed to make a triangle complete. These three interdependent species need each other in order to survive in the rain forest. If one species is taken away the triangle will collapse.

This tropical triangle forms a solid framework for many more rain forest relationships. For example, jaguars hunt and eat agoutis, Brazil nuts are food for hundreds of animal species, and Brazil nut trees provide habitat for thousands of different rain forests species.

What seemed like a simple relationship between the euglossine bee, the Brazil nut tree, and the agouti is actually a complicated web of relationships. This is one example of the circle of life in the rain forest.

A Circle of Life

▼

How many more rain forest stories are told every day in Brazil's tropical jungles? One scientist decided to do an experiment to find out how many species could live in a small area of the rain forest. While standing on the ground he collected insects from the canopy by spraying pesticides, which are chemicals that kill insects, into the treetops. Thousands of different insects "rained" from the trees. From this experiment scientists decided that tropical rain forests could be home to 20 million to 30 million insect species.

Pretty, Plucky, and Poisonous

Heliconid butterflies are some of the most beautiful insects of the forest. Their bright colors are obvious when in flight or resting. Heliconid butterflies are also called passionflower butterflies, because as caterpillars they feed on the leaves of the passionflower.

Passionflower leaves contain chemicals that are poisonous to most leaf-eating insects. This helps protect the plant from being destroyed by insects. But the heliconids have evolved ways to digest the chemicals. Although the caterpillars are not harmed by the poisons of the passionflower, a bird that eats a full-grown heliconid butterfly may not survive. The bright colors of the heliconid butterflies are like a sign that says "Here I am, eat me if you dare!" Birds have learned that heliconids do not taste good and are sometimes deadly.

The Social Scene

Many species of bees, wasps, and ants are social insects. These fascinating animals have evolved complicated societies in which each member of the group does a certain job.

All species of termites are social, and they live in great numbers in the rain forest. Termites are wood-eating insects and are divided into three social groups. Workers are blind and follow chemical trails left by others. They can work quickly to repair a damaged nest. Soldiers are bigger than workers, and they release a

A termite nest takes over a rain forest tree.

chemical that irritates their **predators,** such as
anteaters. The queen termite is gigantic and hides deep
inside the nest. Her job is to lay eggs and do nothing
else. All her needs are taken care of by the workers.

Figs and Wasps

Fig trees are a very important plant in rain forests
because the fig fruit is food for many animals. But the
figs could never grow from flower to fruit without the
help of insects called wasps.

Tiny fig wasps live their entire life cycle inside fig

flowers. Female wasps lay their eggs inside fig flowers and then die. Male wasps hatch first and burrow into other flowers to mate with the unhatched females. Then the females are born—already pregnant! Females have only one day in which to find another fig flower and make a tunnel to the inside, where they lay their eggs and die. And then the cycle begins again.

While the wasps are reproducing and going through their life cycle, they are also pollinating the fig trees. The female carries pollen from the flower of her birth to the flower in which she lays her eggs. Without wasps, figs would not be pollinated and would not reproduce. And without figs, thousands of rain forest animals would not have enough to eat.

The Leafcutters

Wasps and figs have an amazing relationship, as do many other rain forest species. Leafcutting ants live in large colonies, or groups. Five million ants can live in one underground city. Worker ants climb into the canopy and clip the leaves off certain trees to carry back to the group's nest. But the ants do not eat the leaves. Instead, the ants chew the leaves until they are soft.

Then the leaves are placed in a pile, where they become food for a special fungus. This fungus is the ants' only food. Leafcutting ants and the fungi they grow in their underground gardens could not survive without each other.

Mammals

Trees and plants provide the basic foods in the forest in the form of leaves, nuts, seeds, and nectar. Insects are another important food source for the more complex animals, called **vertebrates**. Vertebrates have vertebrae, or backbones, and they are divided into five separate classes, or groups.

The most advanced vertebrates are mammals, which are **warm-blooded** animals that have fur or hair, give birth to live young, and feed mother's milk to their young.

Most mammals of the rain forest live in the canopy and are nocturnal, meaning they are active mostly at night. Monkeys scamper through the trees, feeding on fruit, leaves, and insects. The pygmy marmoset is only six inches long and is the smallest primate in South America. One of the largest monkey species is the howler, whose voice can be heard for over a mile in the

forest. Howlers never leave the canopy and even get their drinking water by licking wet leaves.

Monkeys belong to a group of mammals known as the **primates**. Humans are primates too. We share certain characteristics with monkeys, such as four fingers and a thumb, good eyesight, and a large brain.

The three-toed sloth is a mammal that hangs for hours, even days at a time from the branches of trees. Sloths eat leaves, and they come to the ground once a week to **urinate** and **defecate**. At the base of a tree, they dig a hole and leave behind their urine and feces. This practice helps return nutrients to the trees.

Bats are also extremely important to the rain forest because they disperse, or scatter, seeds throughout the forest. Fruit-eating bats often fly long distances and drop seeds that make the forests grow. Bats defecate while flying, dropping feces that contain seeds that may grow into new trees. Scientists have discovered that one group of 400 bats can spread 150 million seeds throughout the rain forest every year.

All bats are not blind, as many people believe. Nectar-eating bats can see the large white flowers from which they feed. They also use their sense of smell to

This baby howler monkey looks worried as he clings to his fellow primate's arm.

locate the flowers, which are open only at night. By feeding on nectar, bats help pollinate the flowers of many kinds of trees and plants, ensuring that the plants will reproduce. Without bats, many tropical plants would become **extinct**, or disappear from the earth forever.

Birds

There are more species of birds in rain forests than in any other ecosystem on earth. Birds are warm-blooded vertebrates that have feathers and lay eggs.

Rain forest birds have adapted to life in every part of the forest—from the floor all the way to the top of the canopy. And they have adaptations to help them feed off of every possible kind of food. There are fruit eaters, flower eaters, nectar eaters, leaf eaters, insect eaters, and meat eaters.

Hummingbirds are small birds that feed on the nectar of red, orange, and yellow flowers. They are important for pollinating rain forest plants. Some hummingbirds are as small as bees. Their wings can beat 80 times a second as they dip their beaks into flowers.

Toucans are colorful birds with huge, lightweight beaks adapted to snipping fruit from tree branches. They prefer very ripe fruit that is blackest in color, such as ripe figs. Once a toucan has hold of a fruit, it throws its head back and gulps the fruit down its throat.

Macaws are large parrots that usually travel in flocks. Their hooked beaks are like powerful nut-crackers, an adaptation for breaking open hard seeds and nuts. They also use their beaks to help them climb in the trees and for scooping out the soft, fleshy parts of fruit.

Hoatzins are interesting birds that live near streams and eat leaves. Young hoatzins have claws on their wings that help them climb up and down tree trunks. They often dive into a stream from a tree branch to escape danger. When it is safe, they climb out of the water and back up the tree.

Reptiles and Amphibians

Reptiles are **cold-blooded** vertebrates that have rough, waterproof skin and lay leathery eggs.

There are many beautiful species of snakes in the rain forest. Boa constrictors kill their **prey** by squeezing

them to death. Then they swallow the catch whole. Anacondas are the largest snakes in Amazonia— sometimes reaching 30 feet and weighing almost 300 pounds. They eat large mammals, birds, and other reptiles such as crocodiles, but they won't eat humans, as some people believe.

Some snakes are poisonous. Pit vipers can find warm-blooded prey using a special heat-sensing adaptation between their nostrils and eyes. Once they find their prey, they quickly make the kill by injecting a strong poison with one bite from their long fangs.

Amphibians are cold-blooded vertebrates that live part of their lives in water. Their jellylike eggs need to be kept wet until the young hatch. Rain forests have many wet places for amphibians, such as frogs and toads, to lay their eggs. Some plants are shaped like buckets and catch enough rainwater to keep the eggs wet. Some rain forest frogs and toads are poisonous to the touch. Their skin contains chemicals that will kill a predator.

Fish of the Forest

Even fish live in the rain forests of Brazil! When the

The toucan's beak is adapted for picking fruit from rain forest trees.

rainy season comes, the Amazon River floods its banks. The water level in the flooded forests can rise to cover plants and small trees for most of the year. Water levels can rise 45 feet into the branches of larger trees.

Fish, such as the tambaqui, eat seeds, leaves and fruit that fall from the canopy into the water below. Using its keen sense of smell, the tambaqui locates nuts in the water and then crushes them with its large molars.

Other fish eat large insects that cling to the bark and leaves above the water's surface. These fish have eyes that are adapted to see above the water's surface. The arowana grows to more than one yard in length and can leap a full body length out the water to grab beetles off tree branches.

The razor toothed piranha is a **carnivore**, or meat eater, and uses its sharp teeth for tearing the flesh of other fish. As is often the case in the **food web**, one predator becomes the prey of another. The black cayman, an Amazonian crocodile, eats piranhas.

The Longest-Running Show

Thousands of vertebrate species live in the tropical

The piranha's jaw and teeth are adapted for tearing flesh.

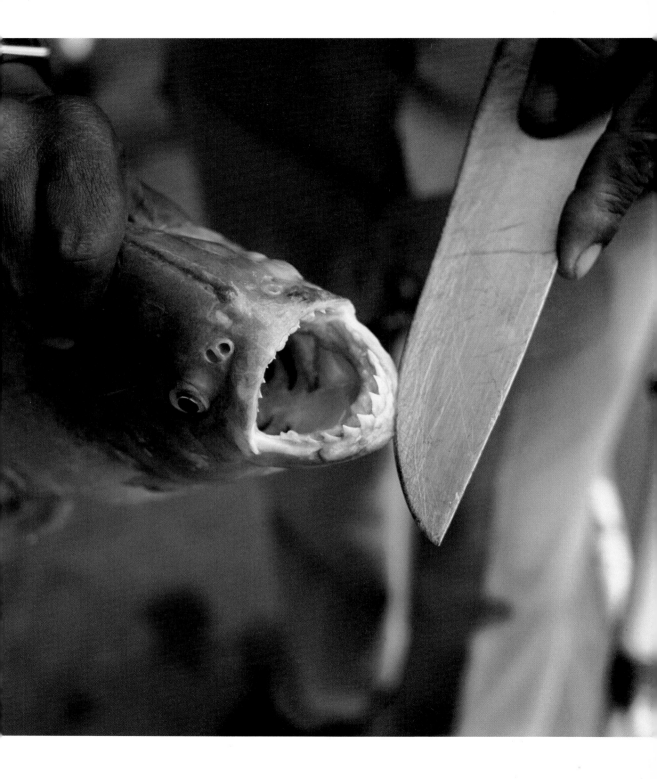

forests of Brazil. But plants and **invertebrates** account for most species in the rain forest. And the relationships that have evolved between plants and insects are among the most interesting in nature. The way two species evolve, or change over time, is called **coevolution**. Bees and nut trees, figs and wasps, and leafcutting ants and fungi are all participants in the coevolution process.

Coevolution is a process that takes place over millions of years. But the relationships that have evolved can be destroyed quickly and easily. With the destruction of habitat, many species are in danger. The spectacular evolutionary show that has been playing for millions of years in the rain forests may be about to end.

During the rainy season the Amazon River rises and floods the surrounding forests.

The Disappearing Forests

▼

Today, Brazil's rain forests, and the millions of creatures that live within them, are in danger. Scientists believe that several species become extinct every day. Extinction is taking place because the rain forests are being destroyed. About one and a half square miles of Amazon rain forest is destroyed every hour.

Most of the Atlantic forests are already gone—less than 5 percent of the original forests remains. In their place are towns and cities where 80 million people live, more than half of Brazil's population. But even though most of these forests have disappeared, those that remain still contain a unique richness of life found nowhere else on earth.

Burning for Beef

Rain forests are destroyed in many ways and for many

reasons. In Amazonia, rain forests are cut and then burned down so the land can be used to grow crops or raise cattle. Farmers can grow food and crops for about six years before all the nutrients are washed out of the infertile rain forest soil. Farmers then move to a new area of forest and start over.

Most of the people who cut and burn the forests are poor and are looking for a better way of life. But the life they find as farmers is often no better than the life they left in the slums of the cities. Farmers often leave their land and return to the cities when they can no longer grow enough food to feed their families.

The land that is left behind is taken over by large companies that raise cattle. It takes about eight acres of land to raise just one animal. Therefore ranches require large areas to raise the cattle that is sold as beef to other countries.

In the 1960s and 1970s American fast-food restaurants bought cheap beef from tropical countries. Today most American restaurants will not buy beef grown on rain forest land because many people have protested. Most rain forest beef is sold to European countries and Australia.

Roads to Destruction

Roads have opened up millions of acres in Amazonia
where the forests are being cut and burned. The
Transamazonian Highway was built in the 1970s so that
landless Brazilians could settle and clear the forests. But
crops failed to grow in the poor soil and the settlers
were forced to return to the cities. Despite these
failures, more roads were built in the 1980s, many of
them funded by the World Bank. It wasn't until the late
1980s that nations throughout the world recognized the
great waste and destruction caused by the highways.

The Amazon rain forests are being destroyed in
other ways, too. More and more trees are being cut
from the forests every year to be used for building
materials and for making things such as furniture,
pencils, chopsticks, and musical instruments. Tropical
trees are often used to make beautiful pieces of
furniture for people who live far away from the rain
forests. A logger may have to cut down hundreds of
"useless" trees to reach the one tree he wants.
Thousands of trees are destroyed and left behind in the
process of taking just a few trees that will be sold as
timber. This happens because so many species of trees

As highways penetrate into Amazonia, the forests around them
are burned and destroyed.

grow in the rain forest.

The construction of huge power plants along the Amazon River has also destroyed parts of the rain forest. When a hydroelectric plant is built, the river is dammed, and the land behind the dam is flooded with water and destroyed forever.

Brazil has large deposits of minerals, such as gold, iron, copper, nickel, and bauxite. Mining, or taking the minerals out of the earth, can destroy the forest. But a bigger problem is the way the minerals are changed into other materials, such as steel and aluminum. The minerals must be heated to high temperatures in factories called smelters. Tropical trees are cut down and burned to fire these furnaces. It takes one acre of rain forest to fuel the fires for only one hour.

Land of Poor, Land of Plenty

There are no easy ways to stop the destruction of Brazil's rain forests. Many people in Brazil are poor, and they deserve a better way of life. They do not have the choices that people in richer countries have when it comes to making a living.

But destroying the rain forests is not the answer to

The rain forests are cut, or slashed, then burned, and the land is used for cattle ranches.

helping people find jobs and grow food. For more than ten years, large parts of Brazil's forests have been cut and burned, and people have tried to farm the land. Crops do not grow on the poor soil, and farmers cannot feed their families. Destroying the forests has not helped these people.

Often it is the wealthy countries of the world, such as the United States, that are adding to the destruction of the rain forests. Americans use 40 percent of the earth's resources, such as energy, timber, and food, but make up only 6 percent of the world population.

Saving the Forests

It is becoming clear to many people that rain forests are more valuable when left standing than when they are cut down. One of the biggest and most important challenges people of the world face is to find ways to save the rain forests. And some of the ways can be found deep within the forests, from the people who know the forests best.

For 12,000 years people have lived in the rain forests of Brazil. Today they are known as the **indigenous people**, or original people of the land.

In many indigenous villages, guns and knives have replaced spears and arrows, but native people still depend on the forest for survival.

Before white settlers arrived from Europe there were more than two million indigenous people in Brazil. As their homes, the forests, were destroyed, and they came in contact with diseases from distant countries, many of these native Indians could not survive. Now there are only about 200,000 indigenous people left in Brazil.

Indigenous people know how to live in the forest without destroying it. Over thousands of years, they have developed a culture, or a way of life, that uses the resources of the forest. From the forest they take plants to use as foods and medicines. They even know how to grow crops in the forest without destroying the ancient, thin soil.

But as the rain forests are cut, burned, mined, flooded, and turned into towns and cities, the indigenous people are also destroyed. Now is the time to learn some of the secrets of the rain forest from these original people. What they know and can teach us may help save their way of life, as well as their forests.

Secrets of the Forests

▼

Among the indigenous rain forest people there are **shamans**, or medicine men. The shaman knows more about rain forest plants than anyone else does. His knowledge has been passed to him from all the shamans who lived before him. The shaman knows what plants can cure aches and pains, kill germs, protect against snakebites, and stop swelling. In his head he carries the names and uses of hundreds of different trees and plants.

Scientists think that 5 percent of all plants on earth might be useful as medicines. But less than one percent have been studied. Scientists can learn a lot from shamans about tropical plants and how they are used as medicines.

Most of the plants that are known to fight cancer come from tropical rain forests. Rain forest plants are effective as medicines because many contain poisons or

chemicals that protect them from plant-eating insects. These same chemicals can also kill germs and fight human diseases. Quinine is a drug made from the tropical cinchona tree. Over the years, it has proven to be the best medicine for malaria.

The rosy periwinkle is another rain forest plant that is made into a powerful medicine. Before this discovery, children with leukemia, a cancer of the blood, only had one chance in five of recovering from the disease. Today they have an 85 percent chance of getting well.

Much More than Medicine!

Medicines and drugs made from rain forest plants help people all over the world, every day. Rain forest plants have also provided the world with a wide variety of foods. Many of the grains and fruits we eat daily originally came from tropical rain forests. Pineapples, tapioca, cacao (for chocolate and cocoa), and Brazil nuts are a few foods that originated in Amazonia. And there are thousands of edible foods in the forests that only the indigenous people use. Someday these foods may be as common as coffee and bananas are on your breakfast table.

Because rain forests have so many different plant species living within them, they contain many different plant genes. Genes are what make each species different. Scientists have found ways to combine genes from wild plants with the genes from domesticated crops. This results in new plants that can be grown for food, but are stronger and healthier than the original domestic crops. For example, genes from wild peanuts found in Amazonia have helped domestic peanuts fight off disease. This has saved peanut farmers $500 million a year.

Rain forests have also supplied the world with valuable materials used in industry. Materials such as oils, gum, waxes, flavorings, and dyes are made from the sap or bark of tropical trees. Tropical forests may someday provide farmers with natural pesticides that do not pollute the environment. Rain forest plants and trees contain chemicals that kill insects. These natural chemicals could be used to protect crops from insect damage.

Rubber for car, bus, and airplane tires is made from the latex, or sap, found in rubber trees. Latex is tapped, or drained, from several slanted cuts made in the bark of the tree. The latex drips from the cuts and runs into a cup. Each tree produces one-half to one cup of latex a

Fish caught in the Amazon and its tributaries are an important source of food in Brazil.

day. The tree is left standing and produces latex for many years.

A Courageous Leader

The practice of draining latex from trees is called rubber tapping. The *seringueiros*, or rubber workers of Brazil, have depended on the rain forests for their way of life since the mid-1800s.

In recent years there has been conflict between the rubber workers, who want the rain forests left standing, and the ranchers, who cut down the trees. Francisco Mendes Filho (Chico Mendes), former president of the rubber workers' union, tried to stop destruction of the forests by organizing peaceful protests. In 1988 Mendes was murdered by angry cattle ranchers.

One year after the death of Chico Mendes, 1.25

million acres of rain forest were set aside as an extractive reserve, or place where rubber is tapped. Extractive reserves cannot be cut down by ranchers or loggers. Today, there are at least fourteen extractive reserves in Amazonia where seringueiros and indigenous people can harvest products from the rain forest.

Chico Mendes has become an environmental hero because he tried to prove that people can make a living from the rain forest without destroying it. Not long before he died, Chico Mendes said, "We started fighting for the rubber tree and the Brazil nut tree and the good little life we had in the forest. And then we discovered that we were defending the whole of Amazonia. And now I have come to realize that what we are fighting for is all of humanity." Today, Chico Mendes is a hero to his own people, the seringueiros, and to people all over the world who want the rain forests preserved.

The Things Money Can't Buy

Medicines, foods, industrial materials, and pesticides are all things that are bought and sold. But the rain forest also gives us things that no amount of money can buy.

Rain forests contain large amounts of fresh water—
Amazonia holds about one-third of the earth's water.
The water is continuously recycled from rain to trees
and back to rain again. When trees are taken away, the
rainwater washes into rivers and flows to the sea. This fresh
water is lost from the cycle, and the area becomes drier.

Losing fresh water causes changes in the local
climate of the rain forest. Many plants and animals will
no longer survive. If too much water is taken from the
cycle, the climate of the entire world could be affected.
Places far from the rain forests might suffer long
droughts and hotter temperatures.

Rain forests are like huge sponges that hold water
and then release it slowly. Worldwide, they provide
about one billion people—one-fifth of the human
population—with fresh water for drinking and watering
crops. They prevent soils from being washed away, which
protects fragile coastal ecosystems such as coral reefs.

The billions of trees that live in rain forests also
help keep the earth at the correct temperature for living
things. Trees use an invisible gas called **carbon
dioxide** to make sugar, the food energy made during
photosynthesis. When trees are cut down, less carbon

Many people in Brazil depend on the protein from fish.

dioxide is taken out of the atmosphere.

During the past one hundred years, people have been putting too much carbon dioxide into the atmosphere. Burning fuels, such as coal, oil, and gas, produces carbon dioxide. Almost five billion tons of carbon dioxide are pumped into the air every year. And when rain forests are cut and burned, huge amounts of carbon dioxide are released—perhaps another billion tons.

The carbon dioxide floats above the surface of the earth and makes an invisible shield. Sunlight can shine through the shield to the earth. But heat cannot escape from the earth's surface. This causes the earth to get warmer and is called **global warming**, or the **greenhouse effect**. If temperatures become too warm, many plants and animals, including crops for food, may not survive. The ice caps at the North and South poles could melt and flood shorelines all over the world. No one can be sure what other damage global warming might do to our planet.

Rain forests help protect the earth from global

warming by taking carbon dioxide out of the air.
Protecting the forests protects the earth's climate.

SOS for the Rain Forests

SOS means HELP! And that's what the rain forests
need. Today there are **conservation** groups around
the world that are working to protect the rain forests. In
Brazil some groups work to help the indigenous people
keep their cultures. Others try to teach people about the
values of the forests, set aside places that will be
protected, do scientific research in the forests, or
develop ways the forests can be used without cutting
them down. All the groups share the common goal of
saving the rain forests from destruction.

One group, called SOS Mata Atlantica (Save the
Atlantic Forest Foundation), was formed to save Brazil's
Atlantic forests. The Atlantic forests are among the
most endangered forests in the world. They are home
to 13 primate species that are in danger of becoming
extinct. Among these are the golden lion tamarin.
These beautiful and rare monkeys live in no other place
on earth. But there is hope for the future of the golden
lion tamarins and the Atlantic forests.

The Golden Lion Tamarin Conservation Program is

Workers prepare Brazil nuts for market in the Chico Mendes commemorative factory in Xapuri, Acre.

a project that takes tamarins from zoos around the world and breeds them. The new tamarin families are then released into the wild. Many of the monkeys cannot survive there, but the ones that do live will reproduce. But the golden lion tamarins will be saved only if the rain forests are preserved.

Conservation groups have a difficult job to do. Time is running out for the forests. If the destruction continues, all of the Atlantic forests, and the species within them, will be gone by the year 2005.

International Pressure Works

Conservation groups and educational programs have helped make Brazilians and people around the world more aware and concerned about the problems facing the rain forests. Many people now understand that when the rain forests are destroyed, so are Brazil's most valuable resources.

International pressure on the Brazilian government to save the rain forests has caused changes that will help the forests. Setting aside land for indigenous people and making it less profitable for ranchers and farmers to cut trees are ways the government is working to save the forests.

"Debt for nature" trades are another way in which international pressure is working to save the forests. The Brazilian government sells some of its debts to other countries or conservation groups. In return, the government must pay a portion of the debt's value into environmental projects. In 1991 the Brazilian government agreed to exchange $100 million of debt every year for environmental projects.

But the work to save the rain forests has only begun. Many leaders and businessmen in Brazil, as in countries all over the world, still favor destruction and development of the rain forests for short-term economic gain.

Hope for Tomorrow

"In the jungle, the Indian knows everything." This proverb from a Suriname tribe of South America may hold the answer for saving the rain forests. In the

Another day ends in the rain forest. As we enter the 21st century, what will be the fate of these magnificent forests?

jungles, indigenous people know how to take from the forest without destroying it. They know how to gather food, how to hunt, how to use plants for medicines, and how to raise crops in the poor forest soils. They respect the forest, knowing that it provides them with the things they need to survive. And in the Indians' culture, wealth and possessions are not very important. The forest provides enough for everyone.

Can modern people living in the developed world

learn to think and act more like the indigenous people of the rain forests? Can we regain respect and feel connected with the earth like the Indians and our ancient ancestors did?

The future of the rain forests and the entire earth is being decided today. Not just by powerful governments or huge companies, but by us, citizens of the world. Every day, we make decisions that affect the future of the earth. The energy we use, the products we buy, even the food we eat all have an effect on the environment.

Although one life may seem small and insignificant in a world of more than five billion people, together everyone has the power to save the rain forests and the earth.

Chapter 1: A Jungle Book

1. <u>Visit a botanical garden, zoo or museum and explore the tropical greenhouses or exhibits</u>. Bring along a notebook and camera. Observe what the air smells and feels like. Look closely at the shapes of leaves and flowers. Make a list of questions you could ask a scientist or horticulturist at the garden. For example:

- Are all the trees in the garden grown from seeds?
- Are insects or birds used to pollinate species grown in greenhouses?
- How much water does it take to keep the trees alive?
- What is the temperature inside the greenhouse?
- Do the trees produce fruit?
- If so, what is done with the fruit?
- How is the research going on in botanical gardens valuable to helping preserve the rain forests?

When you get home, write a short article or story about your visit. Submit the story to your school newspaper or read it aloud to your parents and friends.

2. <u>Build a rain forest</u>. You will need a fish tank, gravel and charcoal pieces, rich compost or soil, small stones, exotic plants (from a nursery or greenhouse), and plastic wrap.

a. Put a layer of charcoal and gravel on the bottom of the tank.

b. Cover with an inch or two of compost or soil.

c. Put some small stones under the soil to make an interesting landscape.

d. Water the soil and plant a variety of plants (orchids, ferns). When you buy the plants from the flower shop, ask the

owner to explain where the plants came from and how they are raised. Do not buy the plants if they are rare or were taken from the wild.

e. Cover the tank with plastic wrap and keep in a warm place, out of direct sunlight.

f. Water the plants every few days. Notice how the plants create their own rain that drips off the plastic wrap.

Chapter 2: The Bee and the Nut Tree

1. Make a map of Brazil showing Amazonia and the Atlantic forests. Be sure to include the Amazon River and the many rivers that flow into it. Use an atlas to help you. Color your map with bright colors so the rain forests and rivers can be easily seen. You should also show where the major cities are located.

2. Learn about rain forests in Central America, Africa, Asia, and Australia. Locate these places on maps and read about the rain forests in library and reference books. Use your information to make a rain forest map of the world.

3. Demonstrate the concept of biodiversity. You will need to go to the grocery store and buy three one-pound (or half-pound) bags of dried beans. One bag should be a mix of beans, containing fifteen or more different kinds (often sold as soup beans), the other two bags should each contain a different kind of bean (for example, one bag of navy, the other of lima).

a. Measure out two cups of the soup beans and one cup each of the other beans. Mix the other beans together to get two cups of two kinds of beans.

b. Take out a checker or chess board. The left side is the rain forest, the right side is a city park. On the left side, put one bean from the soup beans on each square, until each square has a bean. On the right side, put one bean on each square from

the two-bean mix, until each square has a bean.

c. Count how many squares there are on each side (they should be equal).

d. Count how many beans of each kind there are on the rain forest side. Do the same for the city park. Write down the numbers.

e. Take away one row of beans from each side and count again. Did the rain forest side lose beans that are found in no other place on the board? The city park still has two kinds of beans.

f. Take away another row and make the same observations you did above. Answer these questions:

- How do the chessboard and beans show biodiversity?
- How does this demonstrate extinction of species?
- How many species became extinct in the rain forest after one row was taken away? After two rows? Three? Did either species in the city park become extinct by the time there was one row left?
- Explain how destroying a small part of the rain forest can cause many species to become extinct.

Chapter 3: A Circle Of Life

1. <u>Make a rain forest poster showing animals and plants from the forest floor to the canopy.</u> Choose at least two invertebrates and a vertebrate from each class, or group. Your poster should show what each species does in the forest. For example, a hummingbird should be shown eating nectar out of a red flower. Use bright colors to make the different species stand out on the poster.

Chapter 4: The Disappearing Forests

1. <u>Make a pledge card that says you will try to help save the</u>

<u>rain forests</u>. On a plain piece of paper or large index card, type or write a pledge or a promise. The pledge could read something like this:

My Rain Forest Pledge

I, [*name*], promise to do everything I can to help stop destruction of the rain forests of the world.

    1. I will pay attention to the things I buy. I will not buy beef grown on rain forest land. I will not buy or use things made out of tropical woods taken from rain forests.

    2. I will try to save as much energy as I can. I will ride my bike and walk whenever possible. I will help save energy in my home by turning out lights, wearing a sweater in winter, and closing windows and doors tightly.

    3. I will recycle packaging and wastes. I will help save cans, newspaper, glass, and plastics in my home and make sure they are brought to a recycling center.

    4. I will try to learn as much as I can about the rain forests and share my knowledge with other people.

    5. I will get involved in the decision-making process by writing letters to my elected officials and to international organizations, such as the United Nations and the World Bank, which affect the futures of rain forest countries.

signed _____

witness _____

date _____

You may add more to your pledge card if you like. Make a card for every member of your family. Put the cards on the refrigerator or bulletin board where family members will see them every day.

2. <u>Learn more about the indigenous people of the rain forests</u>. Borrow books from the library about the people of rain forests and write a story about a day in the life of a rain forest child. Try to imagine that you are that child. Explain how you get your food, where you live, and where you play.

Chapter 5: Secrets of the Forests

1. <u>Create a rain forest T-shirt, sweatshirt, backpack, or tote bag</u>. Buy a plain shirt, pack, or bag and some fabric paints and marker (available in craft or fabric stores). On a blank piece of paper, plan out what you will write or draw on your shirt or bag. You could draw a picture of a rain forest scene or write a message or slogan about the rain forest. When you have decided what you will write or draw, carefully put the design or letters on the shirt or bag with the marker. Add color with the paints. Be creative and have fun. Wear your shirt, or carry your bag for people to see.

2. <u>Make a list of items you use daily that come from rain forests</u>. Divide the list into things that can be taken from the forest without destroying it, and things that are contributing to the destruction of the forests.

3. <u>Make a collage showing products taken from the rain forest</u>. Cut pictures out of magazines of things that come from rain forests. Glue the pictures onto a large piece of paper or poster board. You may even glue actual items onto the collage if they are small and light enough. For example, a piece of chewing gum, a chopstick, and a latex surgical glove are all made from parts of rain forest trees.

Environmental Organizations

▼

Here is a list of some of the groups that are working to help save rain forests around the world. Write to them to learn more about what they do. If you join one or more of the groups, you will be helping to preserve the world's rain forests.

Bat Conservation International, Inc.
P.O. Box 162603
Austin, TX 78716-2603

The Children's Rain Forest
P.O. Box 936
Lewiston, ME 04240

Conservation International
1015 18th St., NW, Suite 1000
Washington, DC 20036

Cultural Survival, Inc.
53-A Church Street
Cambridge, MA 02138

Greenpeace
1436 U St., NW
Washington, DC 20009

Missouri Botanical Garden
P.O. Box 299
St. Louis, MO 63166

National Audubon Society
700 Broadway
New York, NY 10010

National Museum of Natural History/Smithsonian
Institution
Washington, DC 20008

National Wildlife Federation
1400 16th St., NW
Washington, DC 20036

National Zoological Park/Smithsonian Institution
Washington, DC 20008

Natural Resources Defense Council
P.O. Box 1400
Church Hill, MD 21690

The Nature Conservancy
1815 North Lynn St.
Arlington, VA 22209

Rainforest Action Network
301 Broadway, Suite A
San Francisco, CA 94133

Rainforest Alliance
270 Lafayette Street, Suite 512
New York, NY 10012

Sierra Club
730 Polk Street
San Francisco, CA 94109

World Wildlife Fund/Conservation Foundation
1250 24th St., NW
Washington, DC 20037

Glossary

adaptations—traits or characteristics of an animal or plant (including the way it looks and behaves) that helps it survive in its environment.

Amazonia—the Amazon River basin in South America, which includes the Amazon River, its tributaries, and two million square miles of land in the region.

amphibians—a class of vertebrates that have moist skin, lay jelly-like eggs, and spend part of their life cycle in the water.

biodiversity—many different kinds of plants and animals living in one area.

canopy—the tops of the trees in a forest that form a kind of roof; in the rain forest, most species live in the canopy.

carbon dioxide—an invisible gas that is given off when fuels are burned and living things breathe.

carnivore—an animal that eats flesh.

coevolution—the process by which two species slowly, over millions of years, adapt to each other in ways that help them both survive.

cold-blooded—animals, such as reptiles, fish, and amphibians whose body temperature doesn't remain the same but changes with the surroundings.

conservation—the practice of saving resources for the future.

decompose—the process by which tiny living things, called microbes, break down dead plants and animals into nutrients that can be used again by living things.

defecation—the process by which an animal releases solid waste from its body.

ecosystem—a place where certain animals and plants live and depend on each other for life.

epiphytes—plants that grow on other plants without taking

nourishment from them; also called air plants.

equator—the imaginary line around the center of the earth, which divides it into two equal halves called the Northern and Southern hemispheres.

evaporation—the process by which liquid water changes its form and enters the air as water vapor; this change takes place using energy from the sun.

evapotranspiration—the total water loss from soil including transpiration from leaves and evaporation.

evolve—the way living things change, or adapt, over time in order to survive in their environment.

extinction—the disappearance of a species from the earth forever.

feces—an animal's solid waste material.

food web—the way all living things in an ecosystem need each other for food; all species are connected to one another.

genes—the units in every living cell that determine the characteristics or traits each individual will have; equal numbers of genes are passed from each parent to its offspring.

global warming—the warming of the earth's climate due to the greenhouse effect.

greenhouse effect—the warming of the earth due to the increased production of carbon dioxide and other invisible gases, which act like a blanket and trap heat close to the earth's surface.

habitat—the home of any animal or plant, which includes its food, water, shelter and protection from danger.

indigenous peoples—the original or native people of a land or region.

invertebrates—animals that lack backbones, including insects, worms, and spiders.

mammal—the class of vertebrates that have fur or hair on their bodies, give birth to live young, feed mother's milk to their young, and are warm-blooded.

minerals—the parts of soil or food that are found in the earth and are necessary for growth.

nectar—a sweet syrup made by flowers.

nutrients—the parts of soil or food that help plants and animals grow.

photosynthesis—the way plants change energy from the sun into energy used for food (sugar).

pollen—powderlike male sex cells containing the genes of the male plant or flower.

pollinate—the process where pollen grains are transferred from a male flower to a female flower so that seeds can grow and the plant can reproduce.

predators—animals that hunt and kill others animals for food.

prey—animals that are hunted and killed for food by other animals.

primates—the order, or group, of mammals including humans, apes, and monkeys, which share certain characteristics such as hands with five fingers and feet with five toes.

reproduction—the way living things make seeds, eggs, young, or babies.

reptiles—the class of vertebrates that have dry, rough skin, lay leathery eggs, and are cold-blooded.

seed dispersal—the scattering of seeds throughout the rain forest by animals.

shaman—a medicine man.

species—a group of animals or plants that is alike in many ways and can breed or mate to produce seeds, eggs, or live young.

tropics—the regions north and south of the equator where the climate is warm all year.

urination—the release of urine, or liquid waste, from an animal's body.

vertebrates—animals that have backbones.

warm-blooded—animals such as mammals and birds that maintain a constant body temperature, regardless of the surrounding temperature.

Appendix

▼

Here are ten ways in which you can help save Brazil's and other rain forests of the world.

1. Help the United States set a world example by protecting our own ancient forests. (See *Ancient Forests* for ideas.) People from the United States and other countries cannot expect tropical countries to protect their rain forests if we do not protect our own biologically diverse forests.

2. Write letters to your representatives, the president, and cabinet members and ask them to support laws that will help protect the rain forests. Ask them to support laws that will protect forests in the United States too, because this will help set examples for protection in other countries.

> The Honorable Senator [*name*]
> U.S. Senate
> Washington, DC 20510
>
> The Honorable Representative [*name*]
> U.S. House of Representatives
> Washington, DC 20515
>
> The Honorable President [*name*]
> The White House
> 1600 Pennsylvania Ave. NW
> Washington, DC 20500
>
> Secretary of State [*name*]
> U.S. State Department
> 2201 C St., NW
> Washington, DC 20520

Secretary of Treasury [*name*]
U.S. Treasury Department
1500 Pennsylvania Ave., NW
Washington, DC 20250

Secretary of Agriculture [*name*]
U.S. Department of Agriculture
14th Street and Independence, SW
Washington, DC 20250

3. Write letters to international organizations that are involved in making decisions about the rain forest.

President, The World Bank, 1818 H St., NW, Washington, DC 20433 (The World Bank has lent money to tropical countries to help them fund large projects that are destroying the forests. Ask them to fund small projects that help the people and do not destroy the forests.)

Secretary-General, The United Nations, New York, NY 10017 (Ask the Secretary-General to hold a special meeting of the UN that concerns tropical rain forests around the world.)

4. Write to companies that are contributing to the destruction of the rain forests. You can get a list of these companies from Rainforest Action Network, 301 Broadway, Suite A, San Francisco, CA 94133.

5. Don't buy products that harm the rain forests. Don't buy hamburgers from fast-food restaurants, unless the restaurants can guarantee that the beef is grown in the United States. Don't buy pets that come from tropical countries, such as parrots, macaws, monkeys, snakes, lizards, and fish, unless the pet-store

owner can guarantee that the animals were bred in captivity and were not taken from the wild.

6. Ask your parents and their friends not to buy furniture and other things made from tropical woods, such as apitong, banak, bocote, bubinga, cocobolo, cordia, ebony, goncalo avles, greenheart, iroko, jelutang, koa, lauan, mahogany, meranti, padauk, purpleheart, ramin, rosewood, satinwood, teak, virola, wenge, or zebrawood. Ask your local furniture stores not to sell furniture made from newly cut tropical woods.

7. Recycle packaging materials such as aluminum and tin cans, glass bottles, newspapers, and plastics. Avoid buying things that are packaged in materials that are not easily recycled. The raw materials used to make many materials come from trees and mines found in the forests. If there is a baby in your family, ask your parents to use cloth diapers instead of disposable ones, which add to the destruction of forests.

8. Save energy by riding your bike, walking, or taking the bus or train whenever possible. Learn about ways to make your house more energy efficient. Eat less meat, because it takes more energy to raise livestock than it takes to grow grains for human consumption. Energy conservation will reduce the demand for oil exploration around the world and the need for huge hydroelectric factories and dams.

9. Buy rain forest products that are taken from the forest without destroying it. For example, nuts and fruit grown in rain forests and other foods like candy and ice cream containing Brazil nuts and cashews are sold in many stores. Soaps, lotions, and other cosmetics are also being developed that are made of

ingredients that are grown in rain forests. (To learn more, write to Cultural Survival, 53-A Church St., Cambridge, MA 02138.)

10. Join a conservation group that is working to save the rain forests. (See list on pages 70-71.) You can also help "buy" rain forest land. Write to The Nature Conservancy, Adopt-an-Acre Program, 1815 N. Lynn St., Arlington, VA 22209, or World Wildlife Fund, 60 St. Clair Ave., Suite 201, Toronto, Ontario, M4T 1N5, or The Children's Rain Forest, P.O. Box 936, Lewiston, ME 04240.

Index

▼